Omar-Qais Noorshams

Modeling and Prediction of I/O Performance in Virtualized Environments

The Karlsruhe Series on Software Design and Quality
Volume 18

Chair Software Design and Quality
Faculty of Computer Science
Karlsruhe Institute of Technology

and

Software Engineering Division
Research Center for Information Technology (FZI), Karlsruhe

Editor: Prof. Dr. Ralf Reussner

Modeling and Prediction of I/O Performance in Virtualized Environments

by
Omar-Qais Noorshams

KIT Scientific Publishing

Dissertation, Karlsruher Institut für Technologie (KIT)
Fakultät für Informatik
Tag der mündlichen Prüfung: 12. Februar 2015
Referenten: Prof. Dr. Ralf Reussner, Prof. Dr. Samuel Kounev

Impressum

KIT Scientific Publishing

Karlsruher Institut für Technologie (KIT)
KIT Scientific Publishing
Straße am Forum 2
D-76131 Karlsruhe

KIT Scientific Publishing is a registered trademark of Karlsruhe Institute of Technology. Reprint using the book cover is not allowed.

www.ksp.kit.edu

Print on Demand 2017

ISSN 1867-0067
ISBN 978-3-7315-0359-0
DOI: 10.5445/KSP/1000046300

Modeling and Prediction of I/O Performance in Virtualized Environments

zur Erlangung des akademischen Grades eines

Doktors der Ingenieurwissenschaften

der Fakultät für Informatik
des Karlsruher Instituts für Technologie

genehmigte

Dissertation

von

Omar-Qais Noorshams

aus Kabul, Afghanistan

Tag der mündlichen Prüfung: 12. Februar 2015
Erster Gutachter: Prof. Dr. Ralf Reussner
Zweiter Gutachter: Prof. Dr. Samuel Kounev

Für meine Mutter

Abstract

Modern, future-oriented data centers increasingly rely on virtualization technology to host their services and applications efficiently and flexibly by sharing the resources and allocating them on-demand. The dramatically increasing amount of data generated and stored by today's applications, however, poses significant challenges for the data center operators to respect Service-Level Agreements (SLAs) and guarantee adequate performance for their users. To cope with such challenges, storage resources in today's data centers have evolved from simple disk-based arrays to sophisticated tiered systems with complex caching and optimization strategies. Still, the storage resources are usually highly underutilized and overprovisioned to avoid bottlenecks along the infrastructure's data I/O path, thus leaving highly expensive resources lie waste. Performance modeling techniques in the area of performance engineering can usually support to anticipate I/O performance bottlenecks and employ the storage resources more reasonably. For a practical applicability, however, these techniques need to be refined and tailored to capture the I/O performance in modern virtualized environments. The increasing complexity of the I/O infrastructure is a major challenge for practical performance engineering approaches. Existing approaches usually address this issue at a low modeling abstraction level and with specific focus on certain application scenarios such that important capacity planning questions frequently remain unanswered.

In this thesis, we present a novel performance modeling approach tailored to I/O performance prediction in virtualized environments. The main idea is to identify important performance-influencing factors and model them at a practical abstraction level. Capturing these factors, we develop tailored storage-level I/O performance models using complementary modeling formalisms based on statistical regression analysis and queueing theory. To increase the practical applicability of these models, we combine the low-level

I/O performance models with high-level software architecture models bridging the gap between the two abstraction levels. In summary, the contribution of this thesis is a novel, systematic I/O performance modeling approach using multiple complementary formalisms for practical performance predictions in virtualized environments. Our approach is validated in a variety of case studies in state-of-the-art, real-world environments based on IBM System z and Sun Fire hardware. Throughout the case studies, we successfully predict the performance of I/O-intensive applications within the required accuracy of less than 30 % mean prediction error. In general, our approach is designed for different application scenarios, such as answering capacity planning and system sizing questions, evaluating the effect of system configuration and hardware design decisions, and analyzing the scalability and the impact of workload consolidation on shared resources in virtualized environments. Hereby, our approach is targeted at an efficient resource usage and the continuous SLA compliance with respect to I/O performance.

Kurzfassung

Moderne Rechenzentren setzen zunehmend Virtualisierungstechnologien ein, um die verfügbaren Ressourcen zu teilen und sie gezielt bei Bedarf zuzuweisen. Die immens steigende Menge an Daten, die von den heutigen Anwendungen erzeugt und gespeichert werden, stellen die Betreiber der Rechenzentren jedoch vor große Herausforderungen, die Dienstgütevereinbarungen und die Performanzanforderungen der Anwendungen zu gewährleisten. Um diesen hohen Anforderungen gerecht zu werden, haben sich die heutigen Speicherressourcen von einfachen Festplattensammlungen hin zu komplexen, vielschichtigen Systemen mit ausgeklügelten Zwischenspeicher- und Optimierungsstrategien entwickelt. Dennoch verbleiben die Speicherressourcen für gewöhnlich hochgradig unausgelastet und überdimensioniert, um Performanz-Flaschenhälse entlang des Daten-I/O-Pfades zu vermeiden, wodurch wertvolle Ressourcen verschwendet werden. Allgemein helfen die Modellierungs- und Vorhersage-Techniken aus dem Bereich des Performance Engineering, Performanz-Probleme vorauszusehen bevor sie auftreten, um die Speicherressourcen effizient einzusetzen. Für die praktische Anwendbarkeit müssen diese Techniken allerdings zur Bestimmung der I/O-Performanz in modernen virtualisierten Umgebungen aufgrund der Komplexität der Systemumgebung und der Virtualisierungsschichten erweitert und verfeinert werden. In der Forschung gibt es lediglich vereinzelte Ansätze, die die I/O-Performanz in virtualisierten Umgebungen vorhersagen. Diese sind allerdings bei der Modellierung häufig auf einem niedrigen Abstraktionsniveau und beschränken sich auf die Betrachtung ausgewählter Szenarien, so dass wichtige Fragen zur Kapazitätsplanung unbeantwortet bleiben.

Diese Arbeit präsentiert einen neuen und speziell entwickelten Ansatz zur Modellierung von I/O-Performanz in virtualisierten Umgebungen. The Kernidee ist hierbei, die wichtigsten Einflussfaktoren zu identifizieren und diese zur Performanzvorhersage auf einem angemessenen Abstraktionsniveau zu modellieren. Zu diesem Zweck entwickelt diese Arbeit maßgeschneiderte, speicherorientierte I/O-Performanzmodelle mit Hilfe komplementärer Formalismen aus den Bereichen der statistischen Regressionsanalyse sowie der Warteschlangentheorie. Um die Anwendbarkeit dieser Modelle zu erhöhen, werden diese speichorientierten Modelle in anwendungsorientierte Modelle von Software-Architekturen eingebettet, indem die Lücke der Abstraktionsniveaus dieser Modelle überbrückt wird. Zusammengefasst ist der Beitrag dieser Arbeit ein neuer, systematischer Ansatz zur Modellierung von I/O-Performanz mit Hilfe komplementärer Formalismen zur praktikablen Performanzvorhersage in virtualisierten Umgebungen. Der Ansatz wird im Rahmen von mehreren Fallstudien in repräsentativen, realen Systemumgebungen basierend auf IBM System z sowie Sun Fire Servern validiert. Hierbei wird die Performanz von datenintensiven Anwendungen erfolgreich innerhalb der erforderlichen Genauigkeit von bis zu 30 % durchschnittlicher Abweichung vorhergesagt. Im Allgemeinen verspricht der Ansatz mehrere Einsatzmöglichkeiten, wie Fragen zur Kapazitätsplanung und Systemdimensionierung zu beantworten, verschiedene Systemkonfigurationen und Hardware-Entscheidungen zu bewerten, sowie die Skalierbarkeit und den Einfluss bei der Konsolidierung von Arbeitslasten in virtualisierten Umgebungen zu untersuchen. Das Ziel des Ansatzes ist einen effizienten Ressourceneinsatz sowie die durchgängige Gewährleistung von Dienstgütevereinbarungen hinsichtlich I/O-Performanz zu ermöglichen.

Danksagung

Diese Arbeit ist das Ergebnis, was erst durch die Unterstützung vieler Menschen möglich gemacht wurde.

Ein großer Dank gilt meinen Betreuern Ralf Reussner und Samuel Kounev. Ralf hat mich bereits in meiner Zeit als Student mit seiner einzigartigen Art fasziniert und war einer der Hauptgründe für meinen Verbleib in Karlsruhe, als ich nach dem Studium schon fast auf dem Weg in die weite Welt war. Für die einzigartige Unterstützung während der Promotion möchte ich mich sehr bedanken. Samuel hat mich in den unzähligen Treffen und Diskussionen während den vergangenen Jahren sehr inspiriert und bei jeglichen Fragen stets unterstützt. Für die intensive Zusammenarbeit und Hilfe, wie ich es selbst nie erwartet hätte, bin ich sehr dankbar.

Weiterhin möchte ich mich bei allen Kollegen am SDQ und der Descartes-Gruppe bedanken, mit denen ich zusammenarbeiten durfte. Einige möchte ich an dieser Stelle für die Zusammenarbeiten, Diskussionen und die Unterstützung besonders erwähnen. Den ersten Schritt in die Gruppe habe ich dank Anne Koziolek geschafft, die mich während der Diplomarbeit super betreut hat. Ich möchte mich auch bei Andreas Rentschler bedanken, der es mit mir während der Promotion in einem Büro aushalten musste und mir bei Projekten und Zusammenarbeiten ein toller Kollege war. Ebenso möchte ich mich bei Robert Vaupel für die Zusammenarbeit bei verschiedensten Projekten und den Blick aus der Industrie bedanken. Dank Philipp Merkle habe ich es geschafft, verschiedene „architekturelle“ Probleme zu lösen und auch so manch Diskussion am Abend in einer sportlichen Atmosphäre fortzuführen. Vielen Dank insbesondere auch an Alexander Wert für das Gegenlesen der Ausarbeitung.

Darüberhinaus möchte ich mich auch bei den von mir betreuten Abschlussarbeitern und Studenten für die spannende Zusammenarbeit und Hilfe bei

Publikationen bedanken: Axel Busch, Dominik Bruhn, Kiana Rostami, Roland Reeb, Safa Omri. Es freut mich auch zu sehen, dass sich Axel und Kiana auch für eine Promotion in unserer Gruppe entschieden haben.

Schließlich gilt ein ganz besonderer Dank meiner Mutter, ohne die diese Arbeit nicht entstanden wäre und der ich diese Arbeit widme.

Karlsruhe, im Februar 2015 Qais Noorshams

Contents

List of Figures

List of Tables

1. Introduction

1.1. Motivation

Today's data centers are at the core of any IT-related activities as they host a large number of both public and private enterprise software applications. The data centers provide the four IT resource types comprised of processing, memory, communication, and storage resources in form of CPU, RAM, network, and disk hardware, respectively. As the application of IT in business processes increases, for example because of higher process automation or more extensive data analysis, the demand for data center capacity is expected to grow steadily. This growth consequently results in higher IT operating costs that have been estimated in 2008 to already account for approximately 25 % of the total corporate IT budget (Kaplan et al., 2008). With all the demand in capacity, analysts have estimated that the global Information and Communications Technology (ICT) systems currently consume roughly as much electricity as was used for global illumination in 1985 (Mills, 2013).

In recent years, virtualization technology has emerged to face and mitigate the trend in increasing IT costs and energy consumption in data centers. By enabling to pool physical resources and share them among multiple, consolidated applications running in virtual machines (VMs), virtualization technology is a key factor for decreasing management overhead as well as increasing resource efficiency. Virtualization technology has meanwhile become a central part of today's data centers and keeps gaining in importance as the server virtualization market is expected to grow annually by more than 31 % in the next years (TechNavio, 2013). In parallel to these developments, latest trends, such as Big Data and Cloud Computing, as well as the ever-increasing amount of data generated and processed in today's applications are contributing to the exponential growth of demand in modern environments for storage resources (Oliveira et al., 2012). Overall from 2005 to 2020, the amount of digital data is expected to grow by a factor of 300 (Gantz et al., 2012). Furthermore, virtualization introduces I/O workload patterns for which traditional storage systems were not designed (InformationAge, 2011) and as a consequence, storage resources have evolved from simple disk collections to sophisticated tiered systems with complex scheduling and optimization algorithms.

Overall, the escalating amount of data as well as the increasing complexity of modern IT infrastructures pose significant concerns for data center operators. A central challenge is to manage the available resources efficiently while at the same time guaranteeing Service-Level Agreements (SLAs) and performance requirements. This is especially due to the complex performance effects between the multiple, consolidated application workloads along the infrastructure's data I/O path. The many performance-influencing factors as well as the shared storage resources struggling to provide a robust performance isolation among different workloads lead to complex I/O performance and interference effects for the applications disturbing the overall system performance in a non-trivial manner. In general, performance evaluation and modeling techniques can help to cope with such challenges to anticipate and mitigate the relevant performance effects before SLA violations occur. For their applicability and practical parameterization in virtualized environments, however, these techniques need to be refined and tailored to the I/O performance issue at hand. This is not only due to the complexity in the virtualized system infrastructure, but also due to the many logical layers and physical tiers from the application to the physical storage resources that need to be captured effectively.

Major obstacles of typical performance modeling approaches for software applications are that they are either too fine-grained or too coarse-grained, thus struggling to provide a practical balance between abstraction level and prediction accuracy. On the one hand, fine-grained performance modeling approaches may require an in-depth instrumentation and analysis of the system environment to create and calibrate the performance models, which is in general technically and practically infeasible. For example, low-level queueing theory-based models are well-established because of their expressiveness and modeling power, however, classical I/O queueing model approaches require detailed system information and monitoring data inside the physical tiers and logical layers along the data I/O path. On the other hand, too coarse-grained performance modeling approaches may not be able to capture the

I/O performance of an application with sufficient accuracy. For instance, predictive modeling approaches at the software architecture level are popular approaches allowing to model applications at a high abstraction level. However, such approaches usually abstract from many system details introducing performance-relevant gaps between the modeled system and its real behavior. This results not only in lacking to reflect the influence of specific performance-relevant factors, but also in causing potential for critical prediction inaccuracies. As a consequence of such observations, developing practical performance modeling approaches is the main goal of this thesis and addressed with multiple techniques throughout the main parts of this work.

1.2. Thesis Goal and Research Questions

The system infrastructures in virtualized environments are becoming increasingly complex in order to cope with the high requirements to serve many applications simultaneously and efficiently. In our work, we develop approaches for extracting performance models supporting to employ resources in virtualized environment efficiently while respecting SLA requirements. In general, predictive performance models are created with the goal to abstract from specific details and to be applicable in realistic setups. To address the I/O performance issues in virtualized environments, we formulate the goal of this thesis as follows:

The goal of this thesis is to develop practical performance engineering approaches tailored to model and predict the I/O performance of software applications in virtualized environments.

We employ two steps in this thesis to realize this goal. We first develop reproducible I/O performance modeling approaches at a reasonable abstraction level that balances practicability and prediction accuracy. Second, we use the I/O performance models and develop techniques for performance prediction at the software architecture level to increase the applicability of our approach. To this end, we formulate the two high-level research questions addressed in this thesis as follows:

1. *What is an appropriate approach to practically model and predict the I/O performance in virtualized environments?*

   An important challenge is to first identify the required input parameters for a performance modeling approach at an appropriate abstraction level such that the parameters can be reasonably specified and included in I/O performance modeling approaches. Furthermore, an appropriate formalism with reasonable abstraction level is then required for the performance models to hide the complexity of the system environment while still predicting the I/O performance with sufficient accuracy. For the practical applicability, a modeling approach should be automated to a high extent and provide reproducible concepts and processes.

2. *How can the I/O performance models be employed in software architecture-level modeling approaches?*

   Performance prediction approaches at the software architecture level are a powerful and practical mechanism because of the high modeling abstraction level and largely intuitive modeling constructs. To increase the applicability of the I/O performance models, they need to be constructed ideally in a way that they can be used in software architecture-level modeling approaches. A central challenge to achieve this is to bridge the gap between the abstraction levels of the two modeling approaches. While software architecture models describe the high-level structure of a software application, I/O performance models typically provide a low-level representation of the I/O performance along the infrastructure's data I/O path from the application through to the physical storage resources.

1.3. Existing Approaches

There are multiple existing approaches related to the approach presented in this thesis. In summary, however, the major distinguishing factor is that we are, to the best of our knowledge, the first work to model the performance of I/O-intensive applications in virtualized environments at the software architecture level. Furthermore, we create practical performance modeling abstractions and provide highly automated and reproducible processes to reasonably abstract real-world system environments and capture their I/O performance, which is addressed rudimentarily by existing approaches.

The existing approaches closely related to the approach of this thesis can be grouped into five general areas:

- The first area is focused on I/O performance analysis and modeling in virtualized environments. The existing approaches in this area (Kraft et al., 2012; Ahmad et al., 2003; Kundu et al., 2012; Gulati et al., 2009) model the I/O performance at a low abstraction level and it is unclear if the models can be used in software architecture models, since the required information and parameterization between the two modeling abstractions need to be synchronized. This synchronization is required to allow for a combined modeling and model solving approach. Furthermore, the approaches are usually focused on certain scenarios, for instance, the consolidation of VMs (Kraft et al., 2012), leaving important capacity planning questions unanswered as, for example, the impact of an increasing number of users on the application performance remains unclear.
- Analyzing I/O performance interference, approaches in the second area model the effects of multiple I/O-intensive applications competing for the shared resources in virtualized environments and causing mutual performance deteriorations. Similar to the previous area, the approaches in this area (Chiang et al., 2011; Koh et al., 2007; Groot et al., 2013; Yang et al., 2012; Pu et al., 2010) are addressing the analysis at a low abstraction level without considering the performance at the architecture level. Furthermore, some approaches use system-specific monitoring tools to obtain a global view of the system environment (e.g., Chiang et al., 2011), which is not necessarily always possible.
- Approaches in the third area address I/O performance modeling at the architecture level (Becker et al., 2009; Huber et al., 2010) and using low-level models in architecture-level models (Wert et al., 2012; Woodside et al., 2001; Shanthikumar et al., 1983). Among these works is a case study for modeling I/O performance in virtualized environments (Huber et al., 2010), however, the goal of this case study is to evaluate the expressiveness of the modeling approach to answer system design decisions. In general, modeling I/O performance in virtualized environments for capacity planning, i.e., defining a representative workload for

modeling I/O-intensive applications and predicting their performance impacts, is not addressed by existing approaches.

- In the final two areas, approaches for I/O performance prediction in native, disk-based environments (Bucy et al., 2008; Harrison et al., 2007; Lebrecht et al., 2011; Lee et al., 1993; Varki et al., 2000) as well as general performance evaluation and modeling approaches not specifically focusing on I/O performance (Balsamo et al., 2004; Koziolek, 2010; Huber et al., 2012; Hauck et al., 2013; Barham et al., 2003; Iyer et al., 2009) are more distantly related to our approach and not specific to the I/O performance modeling challenges in virtualized environments addressed in this work.

At a later point in this thesis, the approaches highlighted in this section are presented and discussed in Chapter 10 in more detail.

1.4. Evaluation Criteria

In this thesis, we present a novel approach to model I/O performance capturing its influencing factors in virtualized environments. The goal is to enable practical performance predictions as well as to include the models into software architecture-level modeling approaches. The main technical challenge is the increasing complexity of today's system environments. Furthermore, the main conceptual challenge is to find an appropriate abstraction level for the models that allows a reasonable parameterization and provides accurate predictions. Despite these challenges, our approach aims to fulfill the following evaluation criteria that are considered essential for the success of a modeling and prediction approach (cf. Rathfelder, 2012; Brosig, 2014):

1. Abstraction: The modeling approach and I/O performance models should be able to hide the complexity of the IT infrastructure and allow for a practical use and parameterization.
2. Accuracy: The I/O performance models should provide accurate predictions close to measurements on the real system to allow for performance analysis and capacity planning. For the models, we are primarily focused on response time as the performance metric, where a prediction error of up to 30 % is generally acceptable (cf. Menascé et al., 2000).

3. Efficiency: The modeling approach should increase the overall model building efficiency without introducing a higher modeling overhead compared to other approaches.
4. Scalability: It should be possible to model and predict the I/O performance of realistic and non-trivial system environments.
5. Automation: To increase the applicability and reduce the risk of manual errors, the approach should have a high degree of automation and be tool-supported whenever possible. This also enables non-performance engineering experts to apply the approach.

1.5. Approach and Contributions

We will address the goal of this thesis and propose a novel, versatile performance modeling approach to capture the influencing factors of I/O performance in virtualized environments. To this end, we develop tailored modeling approaches using complementary formalisms based on statistical regression analysis and queueing theory. To increase the applicability of the models, the I/O performance models are created at an appropriate abstraction level to allow for their combination with software architecture-level modeling approaches. The approach of this thesis is summarized in Figure 1.1. To capture the I/O performance, we analyze I/O-intensive applications deployed in virtualized environments and identify the performance-influencing factors. The factors are modeled in I/O performance models, for which we employ both statistical regression analysis and queueing theory, to predict the I/O performance of the application. Finally, the I/O performance models are integrated into software architecture models that consider the performance-influencing factors and that model the application at a higher level of abstraction to hide the complexity. This process is realized by extending the model-based performance prediction process (Becker, 2008), a concept employed to allow for performance evaluations of software architecture models, as detailed in the main part of this thesis in Chapter 4. Overall, the process is supported by providing a high degree of automation to increase the applicability and reproducibility of our work.

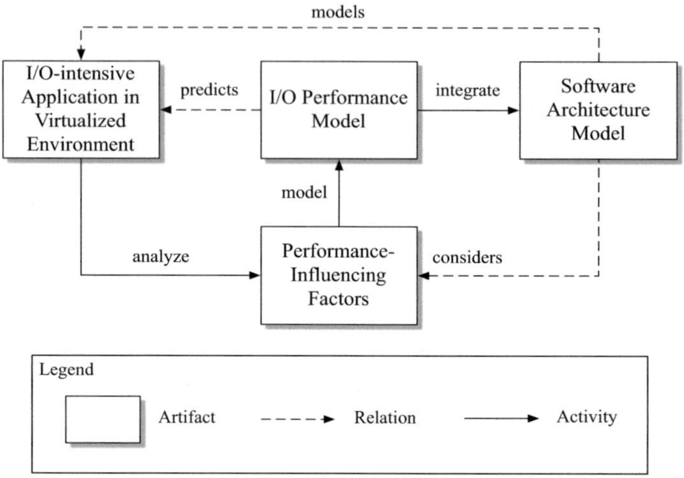

Figure 1.1.: Thesis Approach at a Glance

The main practical benefits of our approach can be summarized as follows. First, we enable accurate I/O performance predictions in non-trivial, complex virtualized environments. Second, we employ multiple, complementary formalisms beneficial in different situations and conditions, i.e., depending on the available expertise and time, to increase the applicability and efficiency of our work. Finally, the high degree of automation throughout our approach as well as the abstraction level hiding the complexity of the infrastructure reduce the effort and expertise required to analyze and understand the system environment and modeling concepts, thereby allowing also non-experts to effectively and productively apply our approach.

In brief, the scientific contribution of this thesis is a systematic approach for modeling and predicting the I/O performance in virtualized environments using multiple, complementary formalisms at an appropriate abstraction level to allow for a practical parameterization and a combination with software architecture-level modeling approaches. Moreover, our approach is validated in representative, state-of-the-art system environments in a variety of case studies demonstrating the effectiveness of our approach. More specifically, the core contributions of this thesis are summarized in the following four items:

1. *Identification and Analysis of I/O Performance-influencing Factors in Virtualized Environments*

   We systematically identify and classify the major performance-influencing factors. The factors are determined at a reasonable abstraction level to derive an appropriate workload characterization that is the basis for the I/O performance modeling approaches. Furthermore, we develop an automated approach for quantitative evaluation of the factors enabling an efficient I/O performance analysis and modeling.

   Scientifically, the main insight is that we identify major I/O performance-influencing factors such that they can be specified and derived without requiring system-specific or possibly invasive monitoring mechanisms. Furthermore, based on these factors we derive a workload characterization that can be extracted from running applications in an automated process and that captures the I/O behavior of I/O-intensive applications.

   The respective parts of this contribution were highlighted and published in Noorshams et al. (2013b), Noorshams et al. (2015), and Busch et al. (2015).

2. *Efficient Optimal Parameterization of Statistical Regression Techniques for I/O Performance Modeling*

   Statistical regression techniques are a practical formalism for performance modeling, since they are able to statistically derive the relationship between the influencing factors and the performance from observations. Since regression techniques often have tuning and configuration parameters that affect the prediction accuracy for a given scenario, we develop a deterministic search algorithm with bounded runtime complexity for the efficient parameterization of statistical regression techniques. We tailor and fully automate the approach for creating and selecting regression models for I/O performance prediction. Nonetheless, the approach is general and not limited to the target domain per se.

   Here, the scientific insights can be summarized as follows. We develop a novel, efficient regression technique parameterization approach that significantly increases the prediction accuracy of regression models. Furthermore, we create regression analysis-based models while neither needing to assume specific relationships between the modeled factors and the I/O performance nor requiring to manually analyze the regression techniques and their characteristics.

The optimization approach and its automation were published in Noorshams et al. (2013a) and Noorshams et al. (2014a).

3. *Tailored Systematic Approach based on Queueing Theory for Modeling the I/O Performance in Virtualized Environments*

   To gain a deeper knowledge and understanding of the modeled environment, we develop a systematic approach to create queueing theory-based models tailored to I/O performance prediction in virtualized environments. The approach does not require possibly invasive monitoring tools and is calibrated with end-to-end response time measurements only. In comparison to the automated regression analysis-based modeling approach, the queueing theory-based models require a higher degree of expertise and manual effort for their creation initially. However, the queueing theory-based models simplify reuse and adaptability, since only their calibration parameters need be adjusted if the system environment changes or a similar system is to be modeled.

   In short, the main scientific novelty is a tailored, iterative queueing theory-based modeling approach for virtualized environments relying on end-to-end response time measurements only.

   The overall modeling approach was published in Noorshams et al. (2013d) and Noorshams et al. (2014c)

4. *Combination of Low-level I/O Performance Models with High-level Software Architecture Models for Performance Prediction*

   To increase the applicability and usability of the I/O performance models, we extend the model-based performance prediction process to combine low-level I/O performance models with high-level software architecture-level modeling approaches. To bridge the gap between the two abstraction levels, we analyze and identify the required parameters at the software architecture level. The parameters are used during a simulation-based analysis and mapped on the required parameters of the I/O performance models. The latter in turn are solved during the simulation to estimate the contention at the storage resource and to obtain the delays of the I/O requests.

The main scientific insight of this novel approach for software architecture-level I/O performance prediction is twofold. First, we embed the storage-level I/O performance models into a software architecture-level modeling approach using a well-defined encapsulation concept. Second, we analyze the combined modeling approach in a simulation-based model solution, thereby successfully coupling low-level I/O performance models and high-level software architecture models to obtain performance predictions.

The general process and the concrete realization were the focus of our publications in Noorshams et al. (2013c) and Noorshams et al. (2014b).

The contributions of this thesis are validated in multiple case studies using real-world, representative system environments based on IBM System z and Sun Fire server hardware. We present a variety of case studies to demonstrate the effectiveness of our approach, where we specifically analyze our workload characterization, our storage-level models, and our software architecture-level models. With the case studies, we address our evaluation criteria and demonstrate that i) we are able to abstract sufficiently complex system infrastructures with reasonably parameterizable models, ii) we are able to successfully predict the performance of I/O-intensive applications with an average prediction error in response time of less than 30 %, iii) we provide efficient approaches for performance modeling without increasing the model building effort, iv) we are able to model and predict the performance of state-of-the-art system environments that are not straightforward to capture in traditional modeling approaches, and v) we provide a high degree of automation throughout our approach for an increased applicability and reproducibility of our work.

1.6. Application Scenarios

The modeling approach in this thesis has multiple practical application scenarios to enable I/O performance predictions for different requirements. The application scenarios are grouped into the following three areas:

1. *Capacity Planning and System Sizing.*

   To run the IT infrastructure efficiently, the I/O performance models can be used for capacity planning of the required storage resources and for sizing the storage systems accordingly. Typical questions that can be answered are:

- Is the storage environment sufficient for the applications to meet the SLAs?
- Is it required to balance increasing load onto multiple storage systems?
- Should the storage systems be upgraded to a newer model?

2. *System Configuration and Hardware Design Decisions.*

   Usually, there are many configuration possibilities that can be considered to optimize the overall performance. However, disturbing the applications and evaluating the options in the production system is not possible. On a model basis, it is usually much easier to answer configuration questions, such as:

   - What operating system and storage system configurations are best for the applications? Does changing the setup improve or deteriorate the performance?
   - Does upgrading the storage resources to faster disks provide a reasonable speed-up in performance?
   - Is it worth introducing an additional caching tier to speed-up performance? How much cache is required?

3. *Scalability and Impact Analysis of Workload Consolidation.*

   In virtualized environments, consolidating applications has non-trivial implications on all the workloads that share the resources. Not only does this increase the workload intensity on the storage resources, it also introduces performance interference effects among the co-located applications. Multiple question arise when applications are consolidated, for example:

   - Are the applications that are consolidated still able to conform to the SLAs?
   - Does an application disturb the performance of co-located applications?

- On which system should an application be deployed to optimize overall performance?

1.7. Outline

To address the overall goal and application scenarios introduced in the previous sections, this thesis is organized into three parts. The next two chapters in Part I present the foundations of this thesis. First, Chapter 2 introduces the technical foundations discussing both server virtualization and storage virtualization to define the context of this work. Then, Chapter 3 introduces the theoretical foundations of the thesis. The chapter presents the performance modeling formalisms used in this thesis, in particular, statistical regression analysis and queueing theory. Furthermore, we introduce our target software architecture-level modeling approach. To this end, the Palladio Component Model (PCM) and its concepts are presented, which concludes the chapter.

As the largest part containing Chapters 4 – 9, Part II constitutes the core of this thesis. To introduce the big picture of our work, Chapter 4 gives an overview of the approach and the general methodology on which the main chapters are built. Furthermore, this chapter introduces our reference system environment to elaborate on the specific challenges when addressing I/O performance modeling in virtualized environments. Chapter 5 is the initial part and the basis for I/O performance evaluation and modeling. We analyze I/O performance-influencing factors and develop a workload characterization as a basis for the I/O performance models. Furthermore, we introduce our automation approach for measuring the I/O performance, monitoring the system environment, and employing statistical analysis of the results. In Chapter 6, we introduce our modeling approach based on statistical regression analysis. We address the problem how to create optimally parameterized regression models and we develop a search algorithm to find optimal parameterization candidates efficiently. Furthermore, we analyze a representative set of statistical regression techniques to select from multiple models created with the techniques. This selection approach is used to identify our I/O performance modeling process. In Chapter 7, we identify our I/O performance modeling process based on queueing theory and tailored to virtualized environments. We elaborately demonstrate how to use this process and create queueing Petri net (QPN) models of the I/O performance in our reference system environment. The QPN models capture both tiered hardware aspects and scheduling aspects across heterogeneous virtual machines. Then, Chapter 8 shows how to integrate the I/O performance models into software architecture-level modeling approaches. To realize this, we extend the model-based performance prediction process and demonstrate our approach using the PCM as example. We will present the modeling concepts as well as the required design of the I/O performance models such that they can be integrated into the PCM and solved using a simulation-based approach. To conclude the main part, Chapter 9 validates our approach along multiple dimensions in a variety of case studies. We present case studies on our workload characterization as well as on the storage-level and software architecture-level performance models. Furthermore, we discuss the scope and applicability of our approach including its assumptions and limitations.

In the final part, we systematically highlight related work and conclude the thesis in Part III. First, Chapter 10 surveys the approaches related to the concepts presented in this thesis. The approaches are grouped into five areas. We first highlight I/O performance analysis and modeling approaches. Second, we specifically review approaches focusing on analyzing and modeling of I/O performance interference effects observed in virtualized environments. Then, we discuss I/O performance modeling approaches at the software architecture level. Furthermore, we highlight approaches for modeling I/O performance for disk-based systems in native environments. Finally, we present performance evaluation and modeling approaches not specifically focusing on I/O performance. As the final chapter of this thesis, Chapter 11 summarizes the thesis by highlighting the main aspects and results of our work. Furthermore, we address open issues and directions for future research.

Part I.

Foundations

2. Virtualization Technology

The basic technology for many new concepts and emerging trends is virtualization. It is generally a broad field and the terminology is at times ambiguously used. In this first foundations chapter, we present the technical concepts and terminology in the area of virtualization technology on which this work is based. The goal is to introduce the context of our work highlighting its links to related fields. To keep this chapter compact, we refer to foundational work for more information where appropriate. This chapter is divided into two parts. First in Section 2.1, we introduce general terms and information on virtualization technology. Then, Section 2.2 focuses on storage virtualization concepts highlighting the relevant aspects for analyzing storage I/O performance as presented in this thesis.

2.1. Server Virtualization

The concepts for *virtualization technology* reach multiple decades back with the beginning of mainframe computing systems in the 1960/70ies (cf. Vaupel, 2013) and has already then been academically relevant (cf. Goldberg, 1974). In general, virtualization abstracts physical resources by creating an additional abstraction layer and providing virtual (logical) resources to use by an application (Wolf et al., 2005). This abstraction layer is called *hypervisor* or *virtual machine monitor (VMM)* and is responsible for decoupling the physical and logical resources as well as for managing the mapping between them. The server system running in such a virtualized environment is called *virtual machine (VM)*.

A hypervisor is typically classified as *type-1* or a *type-2* hypervisor (cf. Hauck, 2013; Baun et al., 2011). In a native environment, a server is run directly on dedicated hardware, cf. Figure 2.1. In a virtualized environment employing a type-1 hypervisor as illustrated in Figure 2.2a, the hypervisor is run on the hardware and manages one or more VMs. By contrast, the type-2 hypervisor is hosted by an operating system running on the hardware, where the hypervisor can manage the VMs, cf. Figure 2.2b. The virtualization type that is typically employed in server environments is the type-1 hypervisor (such as the hypervisor in our reference environment, which is introduced later in Section 4.2).

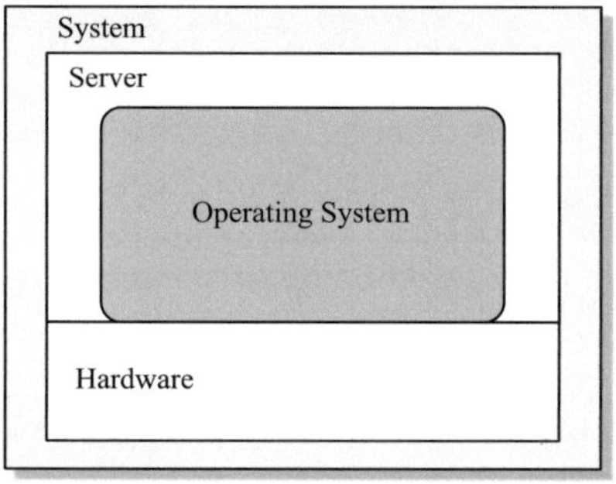

Figure 2.1.: Native System Environment

Virtualization is a key technology for service-oriented and modern Cloud-based IT environments and provides multiple benefits for both the service provider and consumer (cf. Baun et al., 2011), such as, for instance:

- Management: The IT landscape can be managed more easily through a collective administration interface. For instance, VMs can be migrated, replicated, and saved on demand within a short period of time, since such VM operations can be handled in software.
- Consolidation: Applications can be consolidated and share physical resources, thus reducing the required number of physical systems and hardware. This in turn saves data center space and hardware administration overhead.
- Resource efficiency: By sharing the physical resources, operating the IT landscape at a higher utilization results in a more efficient resource usage leading to reduced energy and data center cooling costs.

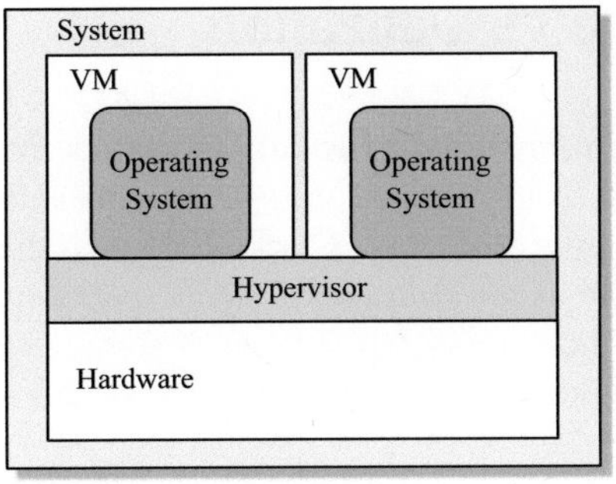

(a) Type-1

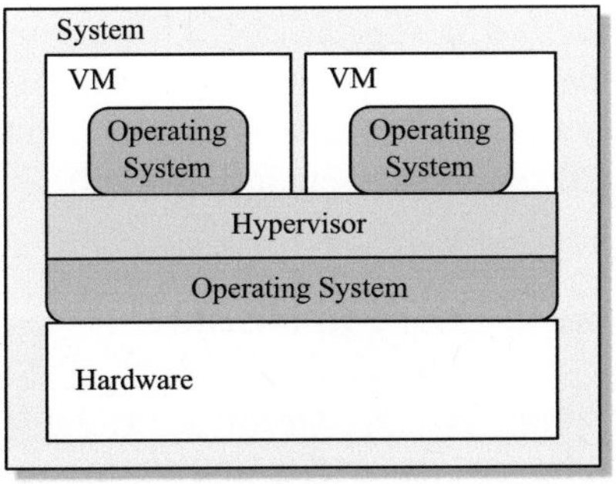

(b) Type-2

Figure 2.2.: Types of Virtualization Hypervisors

While these benefits provide the basis for a substantial amount of cost savings, virtualization usually comes at the price of performance if the performance considerations in the system environments affected by the increased complexity and workload intensity are not addressed and carefully studied. This is because the applications are no longer run on dedicated hardware as they share the physical resources and the resource consumptions need to be managed by the hypervisor in a non-trivial manner. As the focus of our work is I/O performance, we will dedicate special attention to storage virtualization concepts in the next section.

2.2. Storage Virtualization

The term *storage virtualization* is usually loosely defined and generally denotes the abstraction from physical storage systems and storage networks to logical storage resources (cf., e.g., Clark, 2005). In this thesis, we refer to *storage virtualization* as the *storage infrastructures employed in virtualized environments*. Still, there are different types of storage virtualization with different concepts for data access. In the following of this section, we highlight storage paradigms and scalable, networked storage infrastructures used in virtualized environments, specifically *block-based*, *file-based*, and *object-based storage*, to discuss the focus of this thesis. To lay the foundation, we first introduce the *SNIA Shared Storage Model (n.d.)*, a standardized descriptive model developed by the *Storage Networking Industry Association (SNIA)*. For further information on storage virtualization, we refer to the work of Troppens et al. (2009), Clark (2005), and Massiglia et al. (2003).

2.2.1. SNIA Shared Storage Model

The SNIA is a non-profit association for advancing IT technologies and standards in the storage domain. The SNIA proposed the SNIA Shared Storage Model (n.d.), which can be compared to the seven-tier Open System Interconnection (OSI) model for computer networks, in order to unify the terminology used for storage environments. The second version of the model is illustrated in Figure 2.3. The model has been published some years before the time of this writing and is briefly summarized in the following. For more information, please refer to the web representation of the SNIA Shared Storage Model (n.d.) and Troppens et al. (2009), on which this section is based.

The SNIA Shared Storage Model is in parts straightforward and basically consists of an application layer and four layers in the storage domain, which can be grouped into a file layer and a block layer comprised of two layers each (cf. Figure 2.3):

1. *Block subsystem*

   The first layer consists of the physical, low-level storage devices.

2. *Block virtualization*

   The physical storage is *virtualized* into logical block storage. This abstraction can be realized in the device, the network, or the host, for example, using a RAID controller, specialized servers in the network, or a logical volume manager (LVM), respectively.

3. *File/record subsystem*

   The first file layer uses the block-level storage and contains a database, a file system, or a database using a file system.

4. *File/record/namespace virtualization*

   The second file layer may employ another virtualization in form of logical abstraction.

5. *Application*

   Finally, the application layer uses the storage to save data.

2.2.2. Storage Paradigms in Virtualized Environments

The storage paradigms employed in virtualized environments can be classified into the categories *block-based*, *file-based*, and *object-based storage*, which also have an implication on the storage infrastructure. In traditional environments, disks or disk arrays are used by one system exclusively. In complex environments, the storage resources are pooled usually using a dedicated storage network to process the increased storage requirements (cf. Troppens et al., 2009). Furthermore, the storage systems themselves are increasingly complex, tiered systems. In the following, we introduce the typical storage paradigms and the infrastructures associated with them.

Block-based Storage and Storage Area Networks (SAN) In traditional systems, an operating system addresses its storage in logical blocks instead of, for instance, the physical addressing scheme of a disk device that is comprised of cylinder, head, and sector information (cf. Massiglia et al., 2003). An operating system uses a logical block storage at the block layer (cf. first example in Figure 2.4) and typically allows the applications to use the storage using a database or a file system. The translation from the file layer to the block layer is then realized in the operating system.

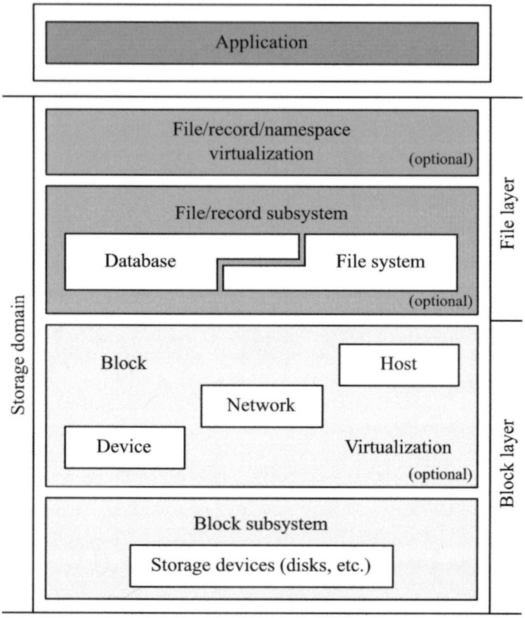

Figure 2.3.: SNIA Shared Storage Model (simplified)

Regarding the infrastructure, a logical block storage may be created from hard disks, whose firmware is responsible for the translation of logical to physical addresses. Modern systems also use RAID arrays (cf., e.g., Troppens et al., 2009), which group a number of storage devices to pool the storage space and possibly implement redundancy mechanisms to increase the reliability of the storage in case of disk failures. In a more sophisticated environment, the pooling of storage devices can be realized in a typically dedicated *storage area network (SAN)*. A SAN can be physically based on Fibre Channel or Ethernet, for example, and employ the Fibre Channel Protocol (FCP) or TCP/IP to issue SCSI commands for data access. For an operating system using a SAN, the storage access is block-based and appears as a traditional logical block storage. While the overall physical storage is shared for multiple applications, the logical block storage is exclusive for a system and the data access is not shared. Example realizations of block-based storage are illustrated in

Figure 2.4 (first and second example). The realization can also be stacked, e.g., a SAN environment may also contain RAID arrays.

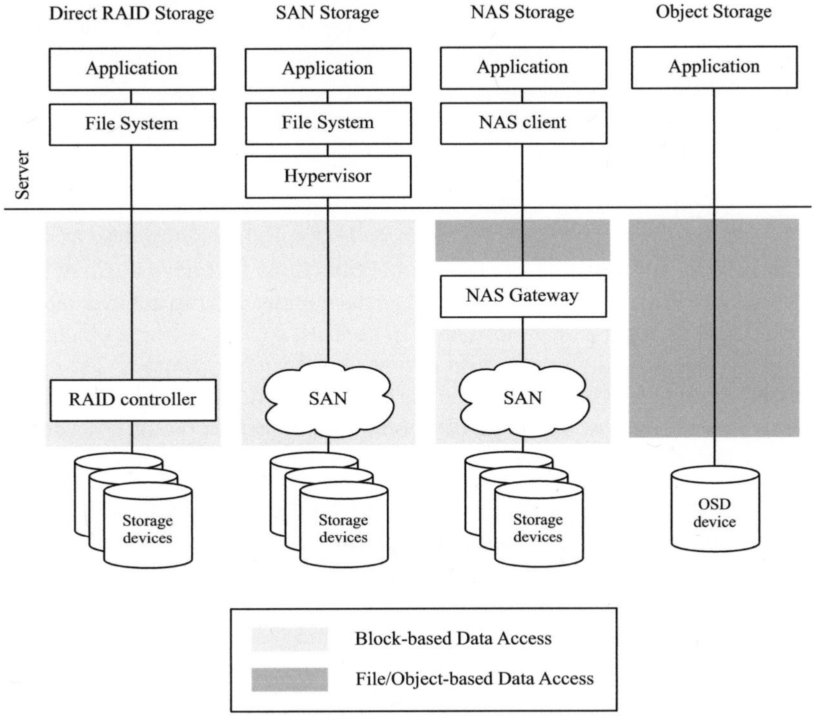

Figure 2.4.: Example Realizations of the Storage Paradigms (derived from Troppens et al. (2009) and the SNIA Shared Storage Model (n.d.))

File-based Storage and Network Attached Storage (NAS) File-based storage runs on top of block-based storage at the file layer and an operating system accesses the data with file system operations. A traditional example for file-based access is using a file server with the File Transfer Protocol (FTP). In virtualized environments, the typical file-based storage is *network attached storage (NAS)* (cf., e.g., Troppens et al., 2009). A NAS server or NAS gateway runs a file system on top of block-based storage and provides file-based data access over TCP/IP Ethernet using, for example, the NFS (network file system) protocol. In general, there are dedicated NAS systems, but also traditional servers can be configured as NAS gateways and expose the file-based storage to other systems. In contrast to block-based storage, the access at the file layer can be shared, i.e., multiple systems can access the same data. An example of a NAS-based storage structure is shown in Figure 2.4 (third example).

Object-based Storage and Cloud Computing While there is also block-based storage concepts in Cloud Computing, a paradigm frequently employed in Cloud environments is *object storage*. In general as defined by Mesnier et al. (2003), storage objects are logical collections that have attributes and are variable in size. They can be used to store entire data structures, such as files, database tables, or multimedia. In contrast to files, storage objects are units of storage and a concept on a lower level such as blocks. The SNIA Shared Storage Model also defines the Object-based Storage Device (OSD), which is described as a storage device that incorporates the object concept and whose access is on the file layer, cf. Figure 2.4 (fourth example).

The object storage concept is popular in Cloud environments and used to implement a scalable and reliable storage infrastructure. Clouds are designed to run on traditional hardware and, e.g., the popular Open Stack Object Storage (Swift) (n.d.) is realized by an object server saving the objects as binary files on the file system. The Cloud management replicates the data and stores them redundantly in the background to account for hardware failures. The object storage is focused on serving static data, such as backups and archives, and OpenStack uses block-based storage for performance-sensitive applications (cf. Open Stack Object Storage (Swift) n.d.).

2.2.3. Discussion

Similar to Cloud storage, there are new technologies and trends emerging. Trends, such as Big Data, for example, introduce new programming models and storage usage scenarios. The common MapReduce programming model (Dean et al., 2008) for Big Data applications uses a cluster of nodes and a distributed file system to analyze large amounts of data. It is not unusual that the nodes are deployed in a virtualized environment. Another storage usage scenario is based on in-memory databases that use the memory of a system as a storage resource to increase performance.

To put our work into context, the focus of this thesis is I/O performance of storage resources in virtualized environments. More specifically regarding the storage paradigm, we analyze block-based storage employed in virtualized environments, which is illustrated in the second example in Figure 2.4. The main distinguishing factor to, e.g., the new paradigms mentioned above is that there can be domain-specific application logic and further resources that affect the I/O performance. In other words, our work can be used and extended to account for such scenarios at a higher level, but we will not elaborate on these trends in the following.

3. Performance Engineering

In this chapter, we present the theoretical foundations of this thesis as well as the terminology and concepts used in this context in the remainder of this work. The general foundations are in the area of performance engineering and, in particular, concerned with performance modeling for predictive analysis. For the sake of understandability, we refrain from presenting complete formal definitions and refer to well-established work where applicable. Overall, this chapter is structured as follows. We begin in Section 3.1 with a brief introduction to performance modeling. In Section 3.2, we introduce the main concepts and terminology on regression analysis as well as on the evaluation of regression models. Then, Section 3.3 presents the foundations on queueing theory-based modeling. Finally, important concepts for software architecture-level modeling is explained in Section 3.4 taking the Palladio Component Model (PCM) as example.

3.1. Performance Modeling

The term *Software Performance Engineering (SPE)*, also referred to as *Performance Engineering (PE)*, has been coined by some frequently cited authors, such as Smith (1990) and Woodside et al. (2007), for instance, and can be defined as follows:

> *Software Performance Engineering (SPE)* represents the entire collection of software engineering activities and related analyses used throughout the software development cycle, which are directed to meeting performance requirements. (Woodside et al., 2007)

In the SPE methodology (Smith, 1990), creating and evaluating performance models is a central concept to quantitatively evaluate the performance of a system design and predict the performance of design alternatives. A performance model captures the performance-relevant behavior of a system to identify the effect of workload or configuration changes on the overall performance. It allows to predict the effect of such changes without physically implementing and deploying the system stack, which can be not only costly, but also wasteful if the acquired hardware environment proves to be insufficient to support a required workload intensity.

The form of a performance model can be diverse comprising mathematical functions, structural modeling formalisms, and simulation models, for example. These models vary in their key characteristics, e.g., modeling assumptions of the formalisms, required modeling effort, and abstraction level. In the following sections, we introduce the modeling formalisms employed in this thesis. At this point, we merely present the main concepts of the formalisms and in the main part of this work, we will show why and how the approaches are used for I/O performance modeling.

3.2. Regression Analysis-based Modeling

Regression analysis is a statistical approach to model the effect of one or more *independent variables* (as input) on a *dependent variable* (as output), e.g., the effect of an I/O request size and a request type on the request response time at a storage system. In general, there are many *regression techniques* to create a specific *regression model* for given training data. Creating a regression model is a *supervised learning problem*, where the correct outcome of the training data is known in advance. By contrast, *unsupervised learning techniques* aim to find relationships without knowledge of the correct outcome, e.g., clustering techniques for classification of data sets.

3.2.1. Regression Model Creation

Regression techniques aim to learn and model the underlying structure of the training data and the more information and domain knowledge is employed to choose the appropriate regression technique, the closer can the model represent and generalize to predict the outcome of previously unseen data. For example, if a given variable is known to have a quadratic effect on another variable, it is most reasonable to represent the effect with a quadratic model and not, for example, with a logarithmic one. Usually, however, the actual relationship between given variables is not known in advance. Consequently, there are many techniques to regression modeling that address the learning problem reaching up into the area of *machine learning*, such as artificial neural networks, for example. Furthermore, the regression techniques usually have *configuration parameters* that effect the resulting regression model that a given technique creates for a given set of training data. For example, the number of hidden units in an artificial neural network can be a configurable parameter (cf., e.g., Kuhn et al., 2013).

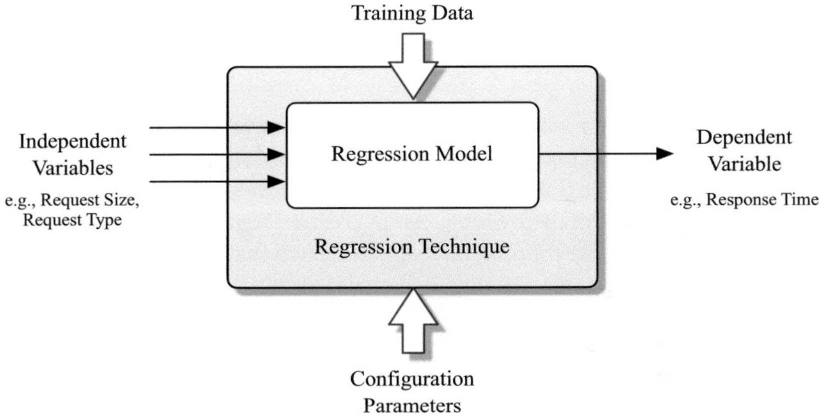

Figure 3.1.: Illustration of Regression Modeling

The concept of regression modeling is illustrated in Figure 3.1. Formally, a regression model is a function f that maps values for the independent variables $\vec{x}$ on a value for a dependent variable y and is parameterized with a vector of configuration parameters $\vec{p}$, i.e.,

$$y = f^{\vec{p}}(\vec{x}). \tag{3.1}$$

The regression model f is created from training data $\{(\vec{x}_i, y_i)\}_i$. This is usually realized in a form that minimizes a metric of error, such as the squared difference between the model and the training data, for example.

Obviously, different configuration parameters $\vec{p}$ and $\vec{q}$ may lead to different regression models, i.e.,

$$\exists \vec{p}, \vec{q} : \vec{p} \neq \vec{q} \wedge f^{\vec{p}} \neq f^{\vec{q}} \tag{3.2}$$

In general, the best choice for a regression technique and its configuration parameters is not straightforward and the prediction accuracy differs for different domains and the training data at hand.

For formal definitions and more information on regression analysis, the reader can refer to the works of Kuhn et al. (2013), Izenman (2009), Hastie et al. (2008), and Walpole et al. (2007).

3.2.2. Regression Model Evaluation

In general, regression models can be more or less complex depending on their configuration, i.e., the parameterization of a regression technique affects the resulting model. While this is not an issue per se, an overly complex regression model may suffer from *over-fitting*. An over-fitted regression model may be excessively fitted to the training data at hand, such that the model resembles the training data perfectly, but does not represent the underlying structure of the data. Thereby, the regression model is not able to generalize and accurately predict unseen data. By contrast, a regression model that is too simple may not be able to even represent the training data sufficiently, let alone capture the underlying structure of the data.

Based on the established work of Hastie et al. (2008), Izenman (2009), and Kuhn et al. (2013), this section compares and discusses main concepts for evaluating the prediction quality of regression models by estimating their generalization error. Typical metrics for the generalization error of a regression model are based on *resampling* techniques. Here, multiple subsets of the training data, which are often overlapping, are used to create multiple regression models. Then, the remaining data of the respective subset is used to predict the outcome using the respective regression model, hereby estimating the prediction error for unseen data. The prediction errors of all subsets are finally aggregated to obtain the quality estimation of the regression technique and its parameterization. The metrics can be usually categorized into two groups, *cross-validation* and *bootstrapping*. The two groups are introduced next and briefly discussed afterwards.

Cross-Validation The basic idea of cross-validation is to divide the available training data into two disjoint sets, a *learning set* and an *evaluation set*. A regression model is created using the learning set first, then the evaluation set is predicted, and finally the difference between the outcomes of the evaluation set and the actual values is determined. The main question of cross-validation is how to define the learning and the evaluation set?

There are generally different variants and special forms for certain regression techniques (e.g., for linear regression models, cf. Kuhn et al., 2013), however, they are not discussed at this point. The most typical form of cross-validation is *k-fold cross-validation*. Here, the training data is split randomly into k partitions of approximately equal size. Each of the partitions is used once as evaluation set, while the rest of the data is used as learning set, cf. Figure 3.2. The prediction errors of all partitions are aggregated to evaluate the regression model. A special case for k equal to the size of the training data is called *leave-one-out cross-validation*. In the process of a k-fold cross-validation evaluation, k regression models are created to obtain the evaluation of a certain regression technique and its parameterization. Once the training data is partitioned into the folds, the k regression model creations are independent, i.e., from a practical point of view, the models can be created in parallel. In general, k is set to 5 or 10 (Hastie et al., 2008; Kuhn et al., 2013), which appears to be a better choice than leave-one-out cross-validation (Izenman, 2009).

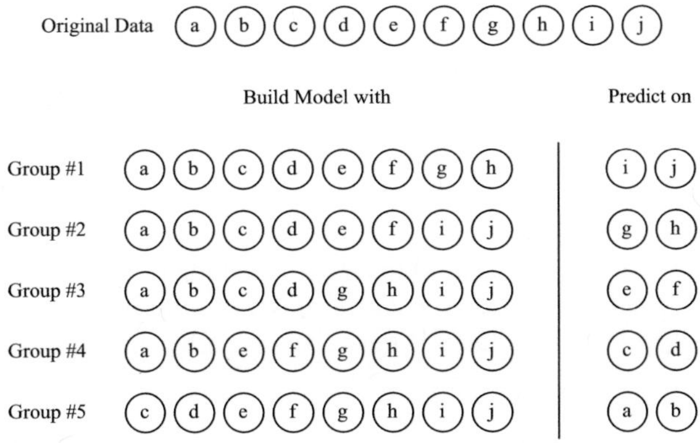

Figure 3.2.: Illustration of 5-fold Cross-Validation (based on Kuhn et al., 2013)

Bootstrap Bootstrapping employs a similar idea as cross-validation in a slightly different approach. A *bootstrap sample* is a random sample with replacement of the training data. The bootstrap sample is of the same size as the training data, but may contain duplicates, whereas the training data may contain elements that are not in the bootstrap sample. Hereby, the partition of the training data into the learning set and the evaluation set is defined implicitly. The bootstrap sample is the learning set, the remaining training data that is not contained in the bootstrap sample is the evaluation set, cf. Figure 3.3. Overall, the process is repeated by creating b bootstrap samples, where it is not unusual that $b = 100$ or $b = 1000$ (cf., e.g., Hastie et al., 2008; Izenman, 2009), and the prediction errors of the samples are aggregated. Thus, in the bootstrap process, b regression models are created to evaluate a certain regression technique and its parameterization. Again, the b model creations are independent.

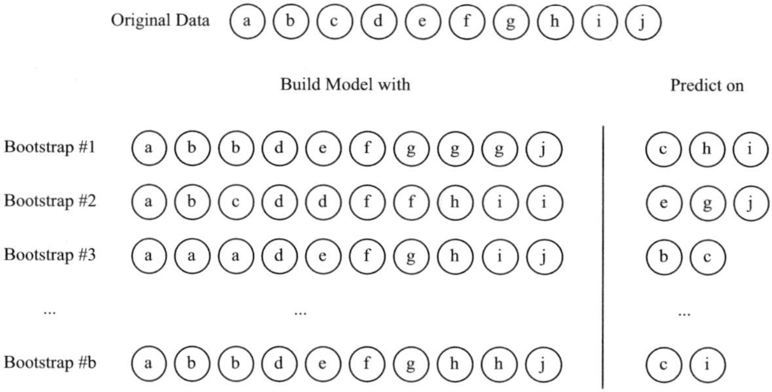

Figure 3.3.: Illustration of Bootstrapping (based on Kuhn et al., 2013)

Discussion Based on Hastie et al. (2008), Izenman (2009), and Kuhn et al. (2013), important aspects of a resampling technique are *bias* and *variance*. Here, bias refers to the difference between the estimated and the true prediction error of a given regression technique and its parameterization, whereas variance is the difference in estimated prediction error when the evaluation process is repeated. For k-fold cross-validation, for example, a larger value of k results in a smaller difference in size between the training data and the learning set, thereby the bias of the technique becomes smaller if k gets larger. In comparison, k-fold cross-validation tends to have a higher variance than other methods (Kuhn et al., 2013). For a large set of training data, however, the considerations of variance and bias become negligible (Kuhn et al., 2013).

It can be said that, in general, no resampling method is universally better than another (Kuhn et al., 2013). Depending on the regression technique, creating a regression model for a given set of data can be computationally expensive. Since the focus in our work is to create practical models and, thus, to evaluate the regression models efficiently, our goal is to limit the number of regression model creations. As noted by Kuhn et al. (2013), 10-fold cross-validation provides acceptable variance, low bias, and is comparably efficient to compute. Therefore, later in our work we will focus on using k-fold cross-validation as a quality criterion for regression models, where we keep in mind that k is set to 10 in general.

3.3. Queueing Theory-based Modeling

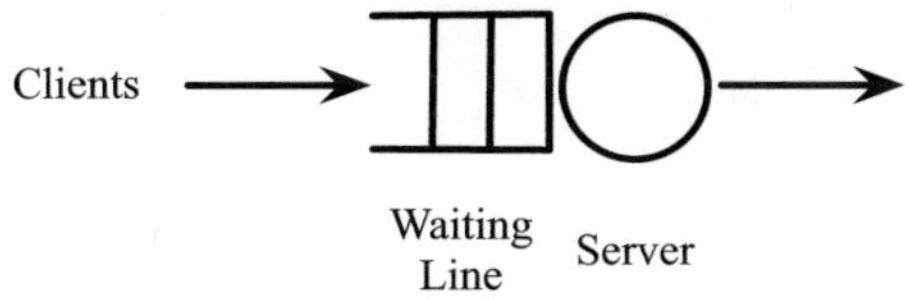

Figure 3.4.: A Queue comprised of a Waiting Line and a Server

Queueing theory is a broad field with different specializations and extensions, in all their core is the concept of a *queue* (cf., e.g., Menascé et al., 2004; Bolch et al., 2006). As illustrated in Figure 3.4, a queue consists of a *waiting line*, where arriving clients are held until they are handled by a *server* according to its *scheduling strategy*, e.g., *First-Come-First-Served (FCFS)*, where the clients are served in arriving order, or *Infinite Server (IS)*, where a client is served immediately after arriving at the queue. A *queueing network (QN)* is a graph, where different clients travel through a set of interconnected queues. A queueing model can be *open*, where clients arrive at the model with a given *interarrival time* and leave the model after they have been served, or *closed*, where there is a fixed number of clients that need to be served by the model and, after a client has been processed, the client waits for a given *think time* before it needs to be served again.

The main queueing theory-based modeling approach used in this work is an extension of basic queueing networks and their combination with the Petri net formalism resulting in *queueing Petri nets (QPNs)*. *Petri nets (PN)* are bipartite directed graphs and are comprised of *places* containing *tokens* (clients) that use *transitions*, whose behavior is defined in *incidence functions*, to travel through the net, which describes a certain behavior. As illustrated in Figure 3.5, the places are connected over the transitions that *fire* and execute their incident functions when they are enabled, i.e., when the required tokens are available. In the example in Figure 3.5, the transition uses one token from two places each to produce one new token when it fires.

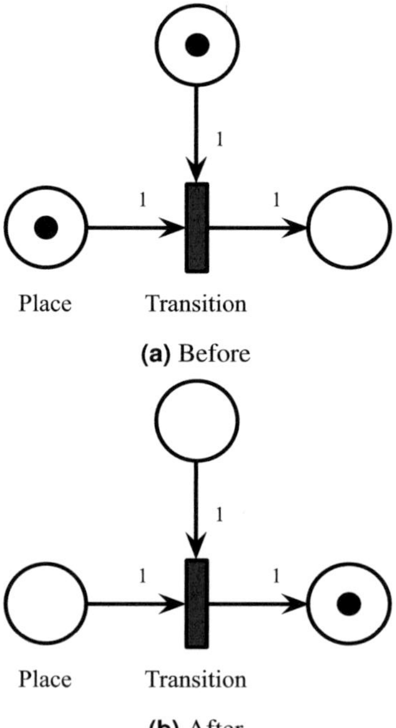

Figure 3.5.: A Petri Net before and after Transition Firing

PNs have been extended with concepts such as *colored tokens* in *Colored PNs (CPNs)* introduced by Jensen (1981), which also play a role in QPNs. CPNs use typed tokens whose colors define different types or classes. In addition to introducing token colors, CPNs can also contain transitions that fire in different *modes* (transition colors).

Further extensions to PNs introduce temporal (timing) aspects to the net model in addition to the behavioral description. Here, *Stochastic PNs (SPNs)* (Bause et al., 2002) contain transitions that have an exponentially distributed *firing delay*, which specifies the time the transition is delayed after being enabled before it fires. *Generalized Stochastic PNs (GSPNs)* use both types of transitions, i.e., immediate and timed transitions. Immediate transitions fire as soon as they are enabled. The immediate transitions can have *firing weights* that decide which transition fires if multiple immediate transitions are enabled at the same time in the GSPN. The timed transitions fire after an exponentially distributed delay and the firing of immediate transitions is prioritized over the firing of timed transitions.

The *Queueing PNs (QPNs)* extend the *Colored GSPNs (CGSPNs)* by means to represent queueing strategies and introduce *queueing places*. A queueing place represents an intuitive form of contention for a server (or resource) and consists of two parts as illustrated in Figure 3.6, a *queue* and a *depository* for tokens that were served by the queue. If a token is fired into a queueing place by any of the queueing place's input transitions, the token is inserted into the queue, where the token is processed according to the queue's scheduling strategy. After the token has been served, it is put in the depository. In contrast to tokens in the queue, only the tokens in the depository can be used by the output transitions. If the servers have a service time, the place is called a *timed* queueing place. If the place only represents scheduling aspects it is called an *immediate* queueing place. To obtain timing results, a QPN model is typically solved in a simulation-based approach (cf. Kounev et al., 2010b).

Further information on queueing theory is given by Bolch et al. (2006) and Menascé et al. (2004). The introduction of QPNs in this section is based on Kounev (2006), more information and formal definitions of QPNs is provided by Bause (1993).

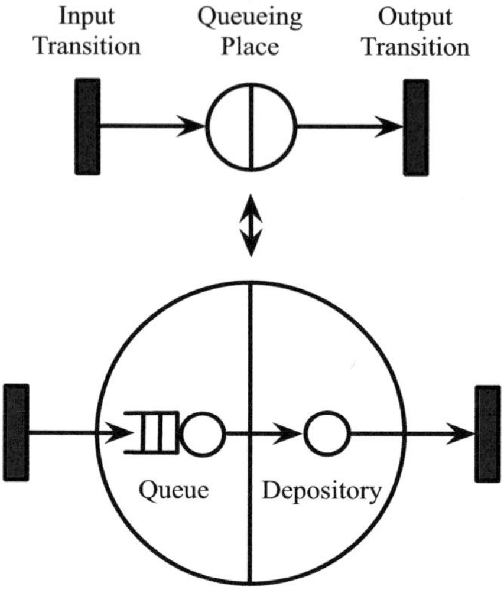

Figure 3.6.: A Queueing Place and its Notation (Source: Kounev et al., 2010b).

3.4. Software Architecture Modeling with the Palladio Component Model (PCM)

The *Palladio Component Model (PCM)* (Reussner et al., 2011; Becker et al., 2009) is a modeling approach for component-based software architectures allowing a model-based performance prediction. The PCM supports the component-based software engineering (CBSE) development process and provides modeling concepts to describe the i) software components, ii) software architecture, iii) component deployment, and iv) usage profile of a component-based software system in different sub-models, cf. Figure 3.7:

- *Component specifications* are an abstract, parametric description of software components at a type level. In the component specifications, an abstract description of the internal behavior of a component as well as its resource demands are provided in *RDSEFFs* (*Resource Demanding Service EFFect specifications*) in a UML (Object Management Group (OMG), n.d.) activity diagram-like syntax.

- An *assembly model* specifies which component types are used at an instance level in the modeled application and if the component instances are replicated. Furthermore, it defines how the component instances are connected representing the software architecture.
- The execution environment and resources as well as the deployment of component instances to such resource containers are defined in an *allocation model.*
- The *usage model* specifies the interaction of users with the system also in a UML activity diagram-like syntax providing an abstract description of the sequence and frequency of users triggering the system operations that are available.

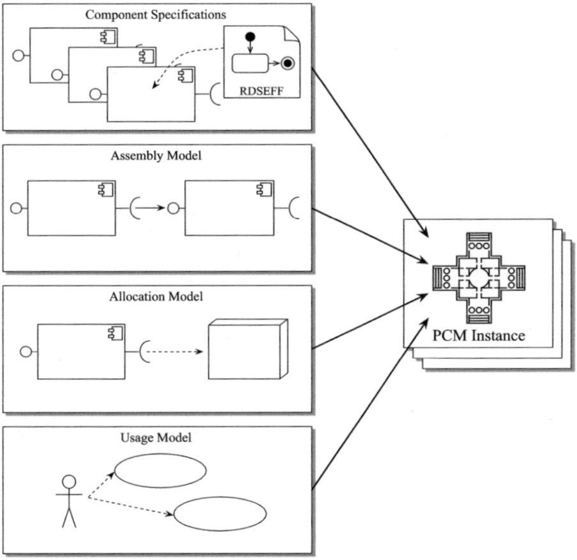

Figure 3.7.: PCM Model Instance (Source: Becker, 2008)

A PCM model abstracts a software system at the architecture level and it is annotated with measured or estimated resource consumptions. The model can then be used in model-to-model or model-to-text transformations to a required analysis model (e.g., to queueing networks or to simulation code) that can be analytically solved or simulated to obtain performance results and predictions of the modeled system. The performance results and predictions can be used as feedback to evaluate and improve the initial design, thus allowing a quality assessment of software systems on a model basis. The general *model-based performance prediction process* employed in the PCM is shown in Figure 3.8.

More analysis of the PCM in the context of our work is provided at a later point in Chapter 8 and is also available in our work (Noorshams et al., 2014b), on which this section is based. Further information on the PCM in general is available by Reussner et al. (2011) and Becker et al. (2009).

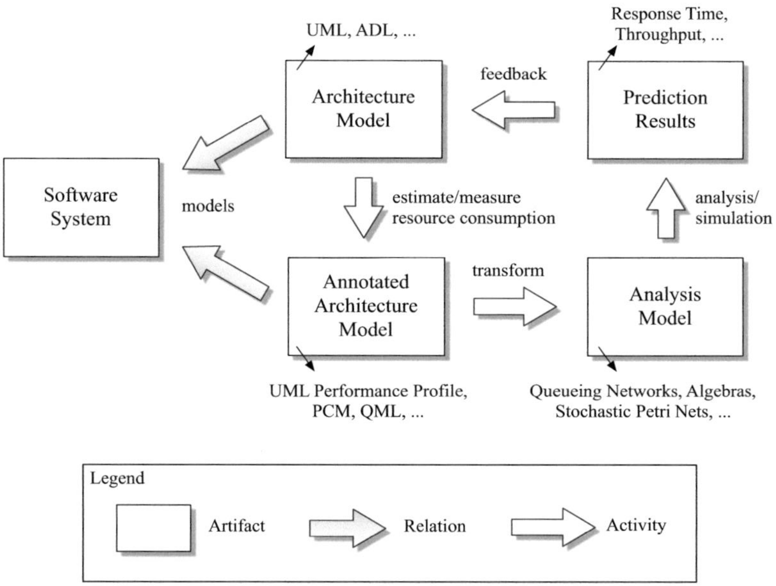

Figure 3.8.: Model-based Performance Prediction (Source: Becker, 2008)

Part II.

Versatile I/O Performance Analysis in Virtualized Environments

4. Methodology

Typically, performance considerations concerning storage I/O in virtualized environments have a multitude of implications on the overall applications' performance, the hardware costs, and beyond. These considerations usually require an in-depth analysis of the infrastructure environment as well as the impact of software and hardware design decisions on the I/O performance of all the applications that share the storage resources.

The goal of this thesis is to develop practical performance modeling and prediction techniques tailored to support I/O performance considerations in virtualized environments. By developing a portfolio of approaches, we allow for a versatile I/O performance analysis using storage-level as well as software architecture-level performance models tailored to the target domain, i.e., for virtualized environments. This chapter provides an overview of this thesis' I/O performance modeling approaches. Aligned with the model-based performance prediction process, we develop implicit and explicit I/O analysis models based on statistical regression analysis and queueing theory, respectively. Furthermore, we show how these I/O analysis models can be integrated into software architecture-level performance modeling approaches to increase the applicability of our approach.

Before going into details on the I/O performance modeling approaches, in the following in Section 4.1 we present an overview of the approach we pursue in this thesis. Then, we introduce our reference system environment in Section 4.2 to illustrate the storage infrastructure challenges arising in virtualized environments. Furthermore, we briefly introduce the infrastructure aspects that are to be considered in performance modeling approaches. Finally in Section 4.3, we give an outlook on the structure of the thesis and its main parts, where the I/O performance models are developed and validated in multiple case studies.

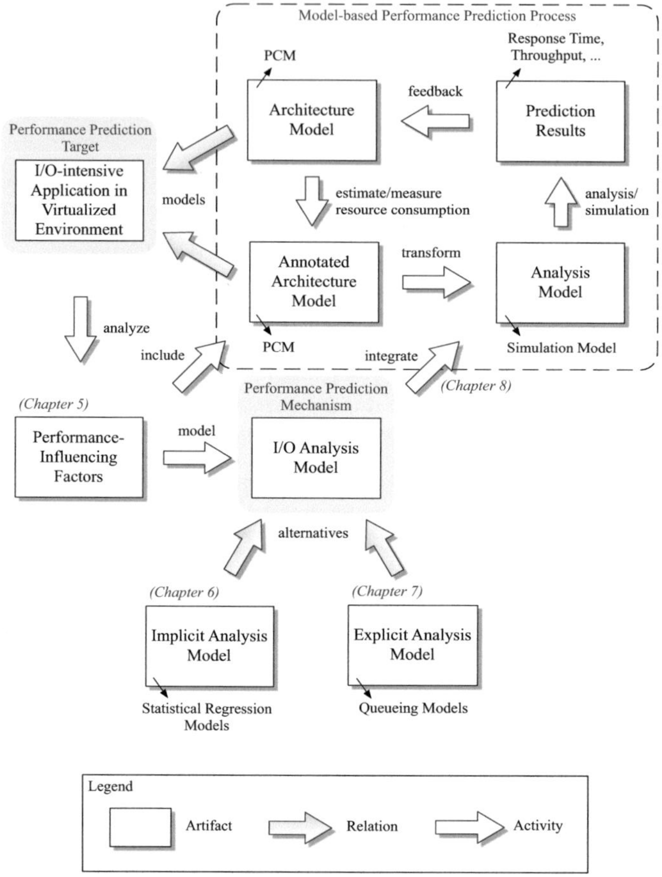

Figure 4.1.: General Overview of the Thesis Approach and Structure

4.1. Approach Overview

The high-level overview of this thesis for our I/O performance modeling approach is given in Figure 4.1 (cf. Noorshams et al., 2013c; Noorshams et al., 2014b), which is the realization of the approach summary shown in Figure 1.1. The *performance prediction target* is an I/O-intensive application deployed in a virtualized environment producing I/O workload on the storage resource. The background of our approach is the model-based performance prediction process (cf. Becker, 2008 and Section 3.4), indicated by the dashed box in Figure 4.1. Starting point is an *architecture model* of the performance prediction target comprised of a static and dynamic representation of the application and a description of the target environment. For this architecture model, we employ the Palladio Component Model (PCM) designed for component-based software architectures (cf. Section 3.4), since it is a mature approach with a large amount of validation case studies, e.g., Becker (2008), Becker et al. (2009), Hauck et al. (2009), Huber et al. (2010), Krogmann (2010), and Kuperberg et al. (2008). The PCM incorporates the model-based performance prediction process to obtain performance prediction results from application models at the software architecture level. The architecture model is *annotated* with estimated or measured resource consumptions. The annotated architecture model is transformed into an *analysis model*, for which we use a simulation model. In general, the analysis model can be any formalism and it can be solved analytically or using simulation-based approaches to obtain performance *prediction results*, e.g., for response time, throughput, and resource utilization. The prediction results serve as feedback for the architecture model to evaluate design and deployment alternatives.

To refine this process focusing on the I/O performance, which constitutes the prediction target of this thesis, we first identify the *performance-influencing factors* of I/O-intensive applications in virtualized environments. We analyze the workload of the application as well as the system environment providing and managing the storage resources. To develop the *performance prediction mechanism*, we model the performance-influencing factors in *I/O analysis models* with different alternative formalisms. We use *implicit analysis models* based on statistical regression analysis that are able to learn the behavior from measurements implicitly without correlating the observed performance effects to a specific cause in the system environment. Furthermore, we use *explicit analysis models* based on queueing theory that need to be created by an expert such that they explicitly capture the observed and expected system behavior. The two analysis model formalisms can be seen as complementary approaches: On the one hand, regression analysis-based models can be created in an automated process, however, the required amount of measurements grows exponentially with the number of factors that should be included in the model. On the other hand, queueing theory-based models need to be created manually and require knowledge of the environment and performance modeling expertise, but once created, they can be applied and reused with a small number of calibration measurements.

Since the I/O analysis models created with the two formalisms capture the I/O performance at a low abstraction level, we integrate the I/O analysis models into the higher-level architecture models aiming to increase the applicability of our modeling and prediction approach. To this end, we include the performance-influencing factors into the architecture model, in particular the PCM, such that the required information can be specified during architecture model building. Then, we combine the analysis model of the architecture model, in particular the simulation model, with the I/O analysis model. After a PCM model is transformed to the simulation model, the I/O analysis model is used during simulation to evaluate and predict the I/O performance, whereas the simulation model captures the general behavior of the application and the contention of other resources such as CPUs, for example. The combined analysis model is used to obtain performance predictions that can be used to evaluate the application and system design.

4.2. Reference System Environment

To describe a typical virtualized environment including the inherently emerging complexity and challenges, in this section we present our reference system environment as a representative basis for our analysis, cf. Noorshams et al. (2013b). However, while we demonstrate our approach in a representative, sufficiently complex environment, the approach and concepts of this thesis are of general nature and not dependent on a specific environment.

In today's modern data centers, a typical virtualized environment is comprised of servers providing computational resources connected to a set of storage systems. Such storage systems typically differ significantly from traditional hard disks and RAID-based arrays to address the challenges virtualization technology entails, for instance, the increased workload intensity due to workload consolidation, which aims for a high resource utilization to run the infrastructure more efficiently. Purely disk-based storage is rapidly overburdened with the competing requests because of its mechanical nature constantly seeking to the required disk sectors such that the requests magnify the storage latency.

In this thesis, we analyze a representative virtualized environment based on the IBM *System z* server and the *DS8700* storage system. These are state-of-the-art high-performance virtualized systems with redundant and hot swappable resources for high availability. The System z combined with the DS8700 represent a typical virtualized environment that is used as a building block of a data center in large companies. The environment supports on-demand scale-up and scale-out of pooled resources. The structure of this environment is illustrated in Figure 4.2.

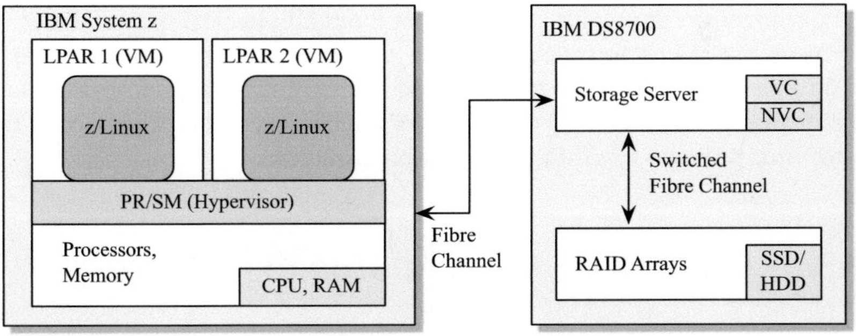

Figure 4.2.: Reference System Environment comprised of IBM System z and IBM DS8700

The System z provides processors and memory and is connected via fibre channel to the DS8700 providing storage space. The environment is virtualized by the *Processor Resource and System Manager (PR/SM)* hypervisor, which manages the logical partitions (*LPARs*), i.e., virtual machines (VMs), of the system. The System z supports the classical mainframe operating system *z/OS* and special Linux ports for System z commonly denoted as *z/Linux*.

In the DS8700, storage requests are handled by a storage server having a volatile cache (VC) and a non-volatile cache (NVC). The storage server is connected via switched fibre channel with SSD-based or HDD-based RAID arrays. As explained by Dufrasne et al. (2010), the storage server combines several pre-fetching and destaging algorithms for optimal performance, such as Sequential Adaptive Replacement Cache (SARC), Adaptive Multi-stream Prefetching (AMP), and Intelligent Write Caching (IWC). Summarizing these algorithms, read-requests are served from the volatile cache if possible, otherwise they are served from the RAID arrays and stored in the volatile cache for future requests. Write-requests are written to the volatile as well as the non-volatile cache, but they are destaged to the RAID arrays asynchronously.

In conclusion, modeling the I/O performance in such an environment is not straightforward. The I/O workloads may be merged and are subject to scheduling and optimization policies on multiple tiers and layers starting from the operating system through to the physical storage. At the same time, it is not practically and technically feasible to observe and monitor the complete environment to capture all aspects throughout all physical tiers and logical layers in the I/O performance models. A central challenge of this thesis is to be able to model the I/O performance in such complex environments at a reasonable abstraction level that allows a practical model creation and at the same time provides a sufficient prediction accuracy.

4.3. Outlook on Core Approach

The main part of this thesis is aligned with the extending steps of the model-based performance prediction process as shown in the overview in Figure 4.1. Next in Chapter 5, we analyze the performance-influencing factors of I/O-intensive applications. At this point, we keep in mind that the performance factors are eventually integrated into a software architecture-level modeling approach. Thus, the factors need to be identified at a level of abstraction such that they can be reasonably specified and determined, still allowing for accurate performance predictions. We use the factors as a basis to derive a workload characterization to be included and used as input for the I/O analysis models. In Chapter 6, we present an automated I/O performance modeling approach with statistical regression techniques. The chapter addresses the regression modeling question more generally by presenting a regression optimization approach for regression technique parameterization. We survey a representative set of techniques ranging from linear regression to machine learning and show how to select and parameterize a regression model. To create I/O queueing models, Chapter 7 describes a general process for queueing theory-based modeling of I/O performance. The process is tailored to virtualized environments by two main ideas, i) we use end-to-end measurements instead of monitoring and instrumentation data for model parameterization to avoid possibly unreliable or system-specific monitoring tools and ii) we start from a simple model that is extended step-by-step to cope with the complexity of the system environment. Using the I/O analysis models within the model-based performance prediction process is detailed in Chapter 8. We combine the I/O analysis models with the software architecture-level modeling approach realized in the PCM and show how the transformation process is extended to integrate the I/O analysis model into the analysis model transformed from the software architecture model. Finally, Chapter 9 presents a variety of validation case studies along multiple aspects. We first evaluate the workload characterization used for our approach to show that it can reasonably capture the workload of an I/O-intensive application. We then evaluate the prediction accuracy of the I/O performance modeling approach in different scenarios considering the I/O analysis model in isolation as well as combined with the software architecture-level modeling approach. To conclude the validation, we discuss the applicability of our work. The overall, high-level evaluation goal is to show that we can obtain practical performance models with sufficient prediction accuracy.

5. Systematic Analysis of I/O Performance-influencing Factors

After introducing the big picture of our approach in the previous chapter, this chapter is the first part of our approach for I/O performance modeling in virtualized environments. We lay the foundation for I/O performance evaluation by identifying the major factors that need to be considered when creating I/O performance models. More specifically, in this chapter we identify the important influencing factors of I/O performance in virtualized environments. Here, we consider both workload-relevant and system-relevant factors. The main challenge is to identify the factors at an appropriate abstraction level, such that they can be reasonably determined and included in I/O performance modeling approaches and yet allow the models to capture the I/O performance at a sufficient level of accuracy. We use the workload-relevant factors as a basis to establish a workload characterization for the I/O performance models, i.e., the workload information that describes an I/O-intensive application and is used as input for the models to obtain a prediction for the given requests. Since obtaining such workload information of an existing application may require detailed knowledge of the application, we develop an automated characterization approach for running applications by monitoring the workload of the application and calculating the required information.

This chapter is structured along these steps indicated above: Next in Section 5.1, we first emphasize the scientific challenges of this chapter. As a basis of our work, in Section 5.2 we identify and classify important influencing factors of I/O performance in virtualized environments. Using the workload-relevant performance-influencing factors, we derive a unified workload characterization in Section 5.3, which is later used for our I/O performance models as workload information. Section 5.4 shows how to obtain the workload characterization automatically to map a given application to the required modeling parameters. Finally, Section 5.5 summarizes the chapter.

5.1. Scientific Challenges

This chapter deals with the following challenges, where the results of this chapter have appeared in our publications (Noorshams et al., 2013b; Noorshams et al., 2015; Busch et al., 2015) and the thesis we supervised (Busch, 2013):

Challenge 1 — *What are major influencing factors of I/O performance in virtualized environments?*

An important prerequisite for performance evaluation is the identification of performance influences. The systematic identification of I/O performance influences in virtualized environments lays the foundation for both performance analysis and performance modeling.

Challenge 2 — *What is an appropriate abstraction level for the influencing factors?*

Generally, many factors may affect the performance of an I/O intensive application to a certain extent. Identifying an appropriate abstraction level for the factors is key to develop performance analysis approaches that allow both a practical characterization of the factors and accurate performance evaluations.

Challenge 3 — *What is an appropriate workload characterization to adequately capture I/O-intensive applications in virtualized environments?*

Derivable from the performance-influencing factors, the workload characterization of I/O-intensive applications describes the application's I/O behavior. Furthermore, the workload characterization is the direct input for performance analysis approaches defining the required information for performance modeling. An adequate workload characterization with respect to the considered characteristics and their abstraction level is needed. This is to be able to obtain the characterization with appropriate effort as well as to avoid introducing to much overhead in form of both amount of manual work and technical monitoring overhead during the characterization process.

Challenge 4 — *How can the workload of a running application be characterized automatically?*

In general, a manual workload characterization of an existing application is cumbersome and error-prone. Thus to increase applicability and reproducibility, an automated and system-independent characterization approach is desirable. This facilitates to apply the performance evaluation approaches to existing I/O-intensive applications.

Based on these challenges, we derive the following four hypotheses that are demonstrated in the course of this chapter:

H1: We can categorize the performance-influencing factors hierarchically and group them along workload-relevant and system-relevant factors.

H2: We can identify the performance-influencing factors in a way that allows to specify and derive the factors with standard monitoring mechanisms.

H3: Similar to the performance-influencing factors, we can define the workload characterization in a way that allows to derive it with standard monitoring mechanisms.

H4: We can extract the workload characterization for running applications in an automated process.

5.2. Classification of I/O Performance-influencing Factors

In a virtualized environment, there are a wide variety of heterogeneous performance-influencing factors. By systematically and hierarchically analyzing our reference system as a representative virtualized environment, we identify and classify significant performance-influencing factors (cf. Noorshams et al., 2013b). In multiple cases, the factors have a different effect in virtualized environments than in traditional, disk-based storage devices because of the many complex abstraction layers and optimization algorithms employed in multi-tiered storage systems typically used in virtualized environments. Figure 5.1 illustrates our hierarchical classification of the major I/O performance-influencing factors in form of feature trees, which are a graphical representation of hierarchical configurations or properties and their relationships (cf. Czarnecki, 1998). The factors we present are of general nature and not limited to a specific system. Overall, we distinguish *workload-relevant* and *system-relevant* factors, which are explained in more detail in the following.

5.2.1. Workload-relevant Factors

Workload factors are classified into three groups, i) *workload intensity*, ii) *request information*, and iii) *workload locality*, cf. Figure 5.1a. The former two are generally affecting I/O performance. The latter affects the storage cache effectiveness and caching optimization algorithms. The factors are elaborated in the following:

- *Workload Intensity*: The intensity can be represented in form of *closed* or *open* workload. In a closed workload, the requests are created by a certain number of clients (physical or logical users, e.g., threads or processes). After the completion of a request, a client may have a certain *think time* (e.g., to process the requested data) before issuing another request. Open workload is characterized by the interarrival time between consecutive users arriving at the system and issuing a request. The workload intensity affects the performance by the number of concurrent requests that require scheduling and introduce resource contention.

- *Request Size*: Most I/O optimization strategies in the various layers of the infrastructure's I/O path aim at maximizing throughput by merging subsequent requests if possible. Serving many small requests results in a lower throughput than serving fewer large requests. Thus, small requests may be held back at times by the scheduling policies hoping for a mergeable request to follow.

- *Request Mix*: While *read requests* are usually synchronous, *write requests* may be served asynchronously without blocking the application. This leads to complex optimization strategies, such as request reordering, when having mixed requests. Still, the optimizations must preserve the integrity of an application and prevent, e.g., read accesses to already overwritten data.

- *Request Access Pattern*: The access pattern affects performance because of the physical access of the data as well as the optimization strategies in the various layers from the application to the physical storage. Typical request access patterns are *random* or *sequential* requests. Because of the mechanical nature of traditional storage devices, requests can only speed up performance of such devices if the requests are *strictly sequential*, i.e., all requests are immediately subsequent. By contrast, many sophisticated storage systems are able to recognize *interleaved sequential* requests, e.g., caused by multiple users each with strictly sequential requests, thereby anticipating and prefetching data to caches in order to increase the I/O performance.

- *Workload Locality*: The locality of the workload and of the requests has an impact on the effectiveness of caching algorithms and data placement strategies. The locality can be estimated using the *file set size*, i.e., the size of the files from which the applications read and into which the applications write, as well as the *access distribution*, e.g., uniform (if all files are accessed equally of randomly) or Gaussian or similar distributions (if there are hot spots).

5.2.2. System-relevant Factors

System factors are also classified into three groups comprising i) *operating system (OS)*, ii) *virtualization architecture*, and iii) *hardware* configurations, cf. Figure 5.1b. Among the factors, especially the virtualization architecture and hardware caching factors are distinctive for virtualized environments. In the following, the factors are explained in more detail:

- *Operating System*: The major I/O configuration factors of a host OS are the file system and the I/O scheduler. The factors are discussed for Linux distributions here, but other operating systems have comparable factors.
  - *File System*: Modern file systems, e.g., *EXT4* as the de facto standard for Linux or *XFS*, exhibit performance differences under the same workload as they are implemented and optimized differently. Furthermore, the recordings of journaling file systems usually introduce additional overhead compared to non-journaling file systems.
  - *I/O Scheduler*[1]: Aiming to optimize throughput, the current Linux standard *CFQ (Completely Fair Queueing)* scheduler performs several optimizations (e.g., splitting/merging and request reordering) to minimize disk seek times, which account for a major part of I/O service times in disk-based storage systems. The *Deadline* scheduler imposes a deadline on requests to prevent request starvation with read requests having a significantly shorter deadline than write requests. The *NOOP (NO OPeration)* scheduler only merges and splits I/O requests and has been increasingly used as the standard scheduler in virtualized environments to defer I/O scheduling to the hypervisor and storage systems (cf. Ling et al., 2013).
- *Virtualization Architecture*: There are different hypervisors with individual virtualization concepts and architectures. For instance, Xen-based hypervisors translate disk devices to the VMs (cf. Barham et al., 2003),

[1] Note: The *Anticipatory* scheduler was removed from recent Linux distributions and is highly discouraged in virtualized environments.

whereas DS8700 volumes undergo multiple layers of logical abstraction (cf. Dufrasne et al., 2010). Understanding the architecture is important for performance evaluation and modeling to identify the involved I/O scheduling aspects in the hypervisor and the storage systems for the environment.

- *Hardware*: Considerations on a hardware level are generally not only focused on maximizing performance, but are rather a trade-off between multiple dimensions, e.g., performance and costs, and the detailed setup is usually specific to the implemented environment. The most typical hardware factors include the disk type, RAID configuration, caching and scheduling, and storage connection and network.
  - *Disk Type*: A volume used in a VM can be created with disks of a specific type advantageous for different usages: Fast, but more expensive *SSDs* for higher performance requirements or regular *HDDs* (usually between 7.2k r/min and 15k r/min) for lower cost per storage space. In contrast to HDDs, SSDs have no mechanical arms, thus reducing the seek time to a negligible minimum. Tape storage is intentionally left out of scope at this point as it is usually used for, e.g., data archiving and backups rather than active application data.
  - *RAID*: The different RAID types offer a trade-off between performance, reliability and resource efficiency. Typical RAID configurations are RAID 5 (or RAID 6) and RAID 10 (a combination of RAID 1 and RAID 0), either using parity information or mirroring for data redundancy.
  - *Caching/Scheduling*: Modern storage systems that are designed for virtualized environments include a tiered caching architecture as well as sophisticated, adaptive management and request scheduling to handle intensive, parallel workloads. Usually, read caches are used to buffer frequently requested and anticipated data, write caches are used to buffer write requests with asynchronous destaging to physical storage.
  - *Storage Network*: The connection between servers and storage systems as well as the storage network topology is an important factor and is usually dedicated and designed to not become the bot-

tleneck. Still, there can be significant differences in performance, e.g., between iSCSI over Ethernet and Fibre Channel-based connections.

5.3. I/O Workload Characterization for Performance Modeling

In this section, we derive an I/O workload characterization from the workload-relevant performance-influencing factors presented in Section 5.2. Furthermore, we formalize workload characteristics and derive representations that can be used in automation using monitoring mechanisms to obtain the workload characterization from existing applications. The following workload characteristics will be extracted from the applications, cf. Figure 5.1a:

- *Workload intensity*: Number of clients issuing requests or requests arriving per unit of time.
- *Request size*: Average size of issued requests.
- *Request mix*: Proportion of read and write requests.
- *Request access pattern*: Proportion of (interleaved) sequential requests.
- *Workload locality*: The file set size comprised of the average file size and number of files.

While we explicitly account for fluctuations of the workload along these dimensions, we assume the workload to be steady without, e.g., variable or bursty elements, and calculate mean values for each workload characteristic.

5.3.1. Workload Intensity

In a typical workload, the workload intensity may vary over time. For closed workload, we capture the number of clients accessing the system over time and average the value over the observation period. For open workload, we estimate the mean interarrival time of the clients using the mean number of requests per time averaged over the observation period.

Formally, let $[0,T]$, where $T \in \mathbb{R}_{>0}$, be the observation period. The workload intensity for closed workload is estimated by

$$workloadIntensity_{closed}^{avg} := \int_0^T \frac{\chi(t)}{T} dt \tag{5.1}$$

$$= \lim_{\tau \to \infty} \sum_{k=1}^{\tau} \frac{\chi(x_k)}{T} \cdot \Delta t_k \tag{5.2}$$

$$= \lim_{\phi \to \infty} \sum_{t=0}^{T-1} \sum_{\rho=1}^{\phi} \frac{\chi(t + \frac{\rho}{\phi})}{T\phi} \tag{5.3}$$

$$\approx \frac{1}{T\phi} \sum_{t=0}^{T-1} \sum_{\rho=1}^{\phi} \chi(t + \frac{\rho}{\phi}), \tag{5.4}$$

where $\chi(t)$ is the number of active clients at time t, $\dot{\mathscr{P}} := \{([t_{k-1}, t_k], x_k), 1 \leq k \leq \tau\}$ is a tagged partition of the interval $[0,T]$, i.e., $0 =: t_0 \leq x_1 \leq t_1 \leq x_2 \leq \ldots \leq x_\tau \leq t_\tau := T$, and $\Delta t_k := t_k - t_{k-1}$. In Equation (5.1) to Equation (5.4), the integral is transformed to the Riemann sum using $\dot{\mathscr{P}}$ and approximated using equidistant points in time with sampling frequency ϕ. This transformation is required, since practical monitoring mechanisms merely provide discrete observation points in general. Consequently, $T\phi$ is the number of actual observation points in the observation period.

The workload intensity for open workload is characterized by the average arrival rate of requests using the average number of requests per time. Assuming a sampling frequency ϕ, we obtain

$$workloadIntensity_{open}^{avg} := \int_0^T \frac{\chi^*(t)}{T} dt \tag{5.5}$$

$$\approx \frac{1}{T} \sum_{t=0}^{T-1} \sum_{\rho=1}^{\phi} \eta^{\phi}(t + \frac{\rho}{\phi}), \tag{5.6}$$

where $\chi^*(t)$ is the interarrival rate of clients at time t that is approximated using the number of requests arriving $\eta^{\phi}(t)$ in the last $\frac{1}{\phi}$ time units at time t.

5.3.2. Request Size

To calculate the average request size, we calculate the average size per request type over the observation period. Let Γ_r and Γ_w be the non-empty sets of observed read and write request sizes, respectively. The average request size for read and write requests is determined as follows:

$$requestSize_{read}^{avg} := \frac{\sum_{j=1}^{|\Gamma_r|} \Gamma_{r,j}}{|\Gamma_r|} \tag{5.7}$$

$$requestSize_{write}^{avg} := \frac{\sum_{j=1}^{|\Gamma_w|} \Gamma_{w,j}}{|\Gamma_w|} \tag{5.8}$$

5.3.3. Request Mix

The request mix is determined as the read and write proportion

$$prop_{read} := \frac{|\Gamma_r|}{|\Gamma_r| + |\Gamma_w|} \text{ and } prop_{write} := \frac{|\Gamma_w|}{|\Gamma_r| + |\Gamma_w|}. \tag{5.9}$$

By definition, $prop_{read} + prop_{write} = 1$.

5.3.4. Request Access Pattern

Classical algorithms for the recognition of request access patterns classify every disk seek, i.e., any address difference in subsequent requests, as a random access event (cf., e.g., Gregg, 2005). To account for the ability of modern storage systems to anticipate parallel, strictly sequential requests by multiple users, we propose a heuristic algorithm for request pattern recognition shown in Algorithm 1 to identify interleaved sequential workload (cf. Busch et al., 2015). Our algorithm determines the percentage of requests that are accessed sequentially regardless of interrupting requests or time delays. The result is used to estimate the ratio of sequential requests, which can be used to classify the access pattern of the workload as (interleaved) sequential or random. To do so, we compare the requested block addresses and search for requests with matching start and end addresses representing subsequent requests. To distinguish between the access pattern of read and write requests, the request space can be divided into separate read and write request lists.

Algorithm 1 `getAccPat(S)` – Access Pattern Recognition Algorithm (Busch et al., 2015)

`Configuration:`
$S \leftarrow$ Sequence of request pairs

`Init:`
$req \leftarrow |S|$ *// Number of requests*
$req\_seq \leftarrow 0$

`Algorithm:`
for $(i \leftarrow 0,\ i < req,\ i{+}{+})$ **do**
  $block\_end = S_{i,2}$ *// End block of request S_i*
  for $(j \leftarrow i+1,\ j \in (i, req),\ j{+}{+})$ **do**
    $block\_start = S_{j,1}$ *// Start block of request S_j*
    if $block\_end = block\_start$ **then**
      $req\_seq \leftarrow req\_seq + 2$ *// Count both S_i and S_j*
      $S \leftarrow S \setminus \{S_i, S_j\}$
       // Correct outer loop counters:
      $req \leftarrow req - 2$
      i--
      break;
    end if
  end for
end for

`Return:`
$\frac{req\_seq}{req}$

More formally, the algorithm's input parameter is a list S of n block address pairs, i.e., $S := \{R_i\}_{i=0,\dots,n-1}$, each pair R_i representing a request. The pairs are defined as

$$R_i := (block\_start_i, block\_end_i), \tag{5.10}$$

where $\forall i:\ 0 \leq block\_start_i \leq block\_end_i$, and $block\_start_i$ and $block\_end_i$ represent the start and end block number of the i-th request, respectively.

The algorithm compares the end block numbers of one request with the start block numbers of the following requests to search for sequential accesses and returns the proportion of sequential requests in the list S.

To avoid overestimation of sequential requests that are too far apart, we enhance the algorithm to analyze specific windows by dividing the observation space into ω subsets S_ι, i.e.,

$$S_\iota := \begin{cases} \{R_{\iota \cdot \lceil \frac{n}{\omega} \rceil}, \ldots, R_{(\iota+1)\cdot \lceil \frac{n}{\omega} \rceil - 1}\}, & (\iota+1)\lceil \frac{n}{\omega} \rceil \leq n \\ \{R_{\iota \cdot \lceil \frac{n}{\omega} \rceil}, \ldots, R_{n-1}\}, & else \end{cases}, \tag{5.11}$$

where $\iota \in \{0, \ldots, \omega - 1\}$.

Finally, we use the average of the request pattern recognition algorithm for each subset to obtain the proportion of (interleaved) sequential requests, which we can use as a metric to classify a workload as (interleaved) sequential or random:

$$accPatternRatio(S) := \frac{\sum_\iota getAccPat(S_\iota)}{\omega} \tag{5.12}$$

$$accPattern(S) := \begin{cases} sequential, & accPatternRatio(S) \geq 0.5 \\ random, & accPatternRatio(S) < 0.5 \end{cases} \tag{5.13}$$

As we iterate through the subsequences in two nested loops to find matching pairs, the complexity of the request pattern recognition approach in Algorithm 1 w.r.t. the length n of the sequence S is $\Omega(n)$ and $\mathcal{O}(\omega \lceil \frac{n}{\omega} \rceil^2)$, which is the best and worst case complexity, respectively.

5.3.5. Workload Locality

For the workload locality, we usually assume to have a uniform distribution over all files representing random file accesses, since we do not expect specific access patterns among the files. In case there are certain hot spots expected in the file set, a certain distribution may be assumed, e.g., a Gaussian distribution. The distribution can then be compared with or estimated from monitored data of the requested I/O block addresses for evaluation. Then, the significant subset of the files can be used to adjust the workload locality estimation. Since we estimate the locality of requests using the file set size comprised of the number of files and their respective file size, we formalize the average key estimates over the observation period taking into account typical file system operations, such as file creation and deletion, which modify the file set during application run. Thus, we have

$$fileSize^{avg} := \int_0^T \frac{\sum_{\iota=1}^{n(t)} \psi^\iota(t)}{T \cdot n(t)} dt \tag{5.14}$$

$$= \lim_{\tau \to \infty} \sum_{k=1}^{\tau} \frac{\sum_{\iota=1}^{n(x_k)} \psi^\iota(x_k)}{T \cdot n(x_k)} \cdot \Delta t_k \tag{5.15}$$

$$= \lim_{\phi \to \infty} \sum_{t=0}^{T-1} \sum_{\rho=1}^{\phi} \frac{\sum_{\iota=1}^{n(t+\frac{\rho}{\phi})} \psi^\iota(t+\frac{\rho}{\phi})}{T\phi \cdot n(t+\frac{\rho}{\phi})} \tag{5.16}$$

$$\approx \frac{1}{T\phi} \sum_{t=0}^{T-1} \sum_{\rho=1}^{\phi} \sum_{\iota=1}^{n(t+\frac{\rho}{\phi})} \frac{\psi^\iota(t+\frac{\rho}{\phi})}{n(t+\frac{\rho}{\phi})}, \tag{5.17}$$

and

$$fileSetSize^{avg} := \int_0^T \frac{\sum_{\iota=1}^{n(t)} \psi^\iota(t)}{T} dt \tag{5.18}$$

$$= \lim_{\tau \to \infty} \sum_{k=1}^{\tau} \frac{\sum_{\iota=1}^{n(x_k)} \psi^\iota(x_k)}{T} \cdot \Delta t_k \tag{5.19}$$

$$= \lim_{\phi \to \infty} \sum_{t=0}^{T-1} \sum_{\rho=1}^{\phi} \frac{\sum_{\iota=1}^{n(t+\frac{\rho}{\phi})} \psi^\iota(t+\frac{\rho}{\phi})}{T\phi} \tag{5.20}$$

$$\approx \frac{1}{T\phi} \sum_{t=0}^{T-1} \sum_{\rho=1}^{\phi} \sum_{\iota=1}^{n(t+\frac{\rho}{\phi})} \psi^\iota(t+\frac{\rho}{\phi}), \tag{5.21}$$

where $\psi^\iota(t)$ is the size of the ι-th file at time t and $n(t)$ is the number of files at time t. The integral in the equations is transformed similar to the Equations (5.1) – (5.4) above.

5.4. Automation of I/O Performance Evaluation and Workload Characterization

To increase the applicability and reproducibility of our approach, we automated our I/O performance evaluation and workload characterization as part of our *Storage Performance Analyzer (SPA)* framework (cf. Noorshams et al., 2015). In this section, we first introduce the static view and the architecture of SPA, then we present the process of the experiments for performance evaluation and workload characterization.

5.4.1. Architectural View

As illustrated in Figure 5.2, our framework basically consists of a benchmark harness that coordinates and controls the execution of I/O benchmarks for performance measurements as well as monitors and a tailored analysis library used to process and evaluate the collected data.

The *benchmark harness component*, which is realized in Java, contains a *benchmark controller* that automatically explores the configuration space and coordinates the benchmark runs accordingly. The benchmark controller is connected to the *benchmark driver*, which is used to configure and execute the integrated and attached benchmarks. The experimental evaluations in this thesis are based on benchmarks integrated in SPA. In addition to the benchmarks, the measurement process can be monitored using a given *monitor driver* to analyze the system environment during measurements and extract the workload characterization presented in Section 5.3. A dummy benchmark can be used, for example, if a running application should be monitored without producing additional load. The actual monitors are provided by the operating system as well as tailored scripts that have a maximum sampling frequency of 1 Hz. The benchmark controller and the drivers are deployed on a controller machine managing the measurement process. The drivers use a *remote execution* mechanism to communicate with the actual benchmarks and monitors, which are deployed on the targets, for example multiple VMs on a physical host. In our realization, the remote execution is achieved using SSH connections, but it could be easily modified to use another connection type.

The benchmark controller saves the results using the persistence component, which is realized with a lightweight database. The *analysis library* can then load and prepare the measurement data, e.g., by filtering and aggregating the data, to evaluate the results. Thereby, the measurements can be post-processed for further evaluation and statistical analysis as employed in this thesis for our performance modeling approaches.

5.4.2. Dynamic Sequence View

The measurement and workload characterization process is illustrated in Figure 5.3. The starting point is the benchmark controller, which is configured with the experiment setup and the configurations that should be executed. The process is repeated for every configuration. The persistent data store, i.e., the database in our realization, is prepared by initializing the setup. Then, the experiment is prepared using the benchmark driver by configuring the target and starting a warm-up phase of the actual, physically deployed benchmark. Since there can be multiple targets, the calls to a specific driver at any given phase are in parallel for all enabled drivers, which is indicated by the covered drivers and the parallel blocks in Figure 5.3. Before the measurements begin, the monitors are started on all targets to collect data. After the monitors are active, the experiments are started on all targets and return a set of measurement results after they are finished. The monitors can then be stopped and the required metrics and results are calculated from the monitoring data. The results are stored and, finally, all experiments and monitors are concluded, e.g., by cleaning up temporary data, and the data store can be closed. After the process has been completed, the results in the data store can be evaluated to analyze the system environment.

5.5. Summary

In this chapter, we have established the basis for creating I/O performance models in virtualized environments. We first identified and classified the major performance-influencing factors of I/O performance in virtualized environments in a systematic analysis and grouped them hierarchically into workload-relevant and system-relevant factors. Based on the workload-relevant factors, we defined a workload characterization along five dimensions: workload intensity, request size, request mix, request access pattern, and workload locality. We defined average estimates for these dimensions and showed how the estimates can be calculated from observations obtained with standard monitoring mechanisms. Finally, to increase the applicability of our approach we presented an automated process for I/O performance evaluation and extraction of the workload characterization for running applications. The main part of our automation is a benchmark harness coordinating the experiment executions and the monitoring mechanisms automatically. The benchmark harness is enhanced with a tailored analysis library to evaluate the collected data.

Building upon this chapter in the following chapters of this thesis, we use the performance-influencing factors and the workload characterization for I/O performance modeling. In the next two chapters, we will use separate formalisms to capture the I/O performance. We first show how we can learn and derive regression analysis-based performance models from measurement data. Using our automation presented in this chapter, we have automated the process of regression analysis-based performance modeling. This process, however, may require a potentially large amount of training data. We therefore afterwards show how we can systematically create queueing theory-based performance models. Once created, such models can be reused in similar environments by recalibrating with a much smaller number of calibration measurements in contrast to the regression analysis-based models. After the creation of these two types of I/O performance models, we will show how to integrate the performance-influencing factors into software architecture-level performance modeling approaches and demonstrate the combination with the I/O performance models to obtain performance results. The key question along these chapters is how to effectively capture the I/O performance in virtualized environments while respecting the performance factors presented here.

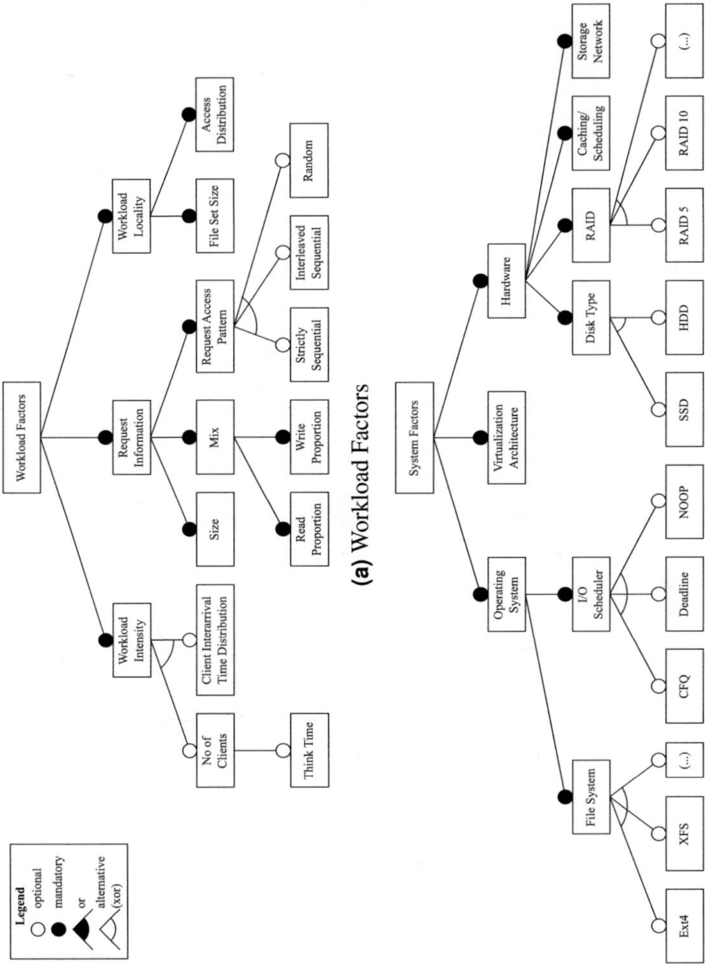

(a) Workload Factors

(b) System Factors

Figure 5.1.: Performance Influences (derived from Noorshams et al., 2013b)

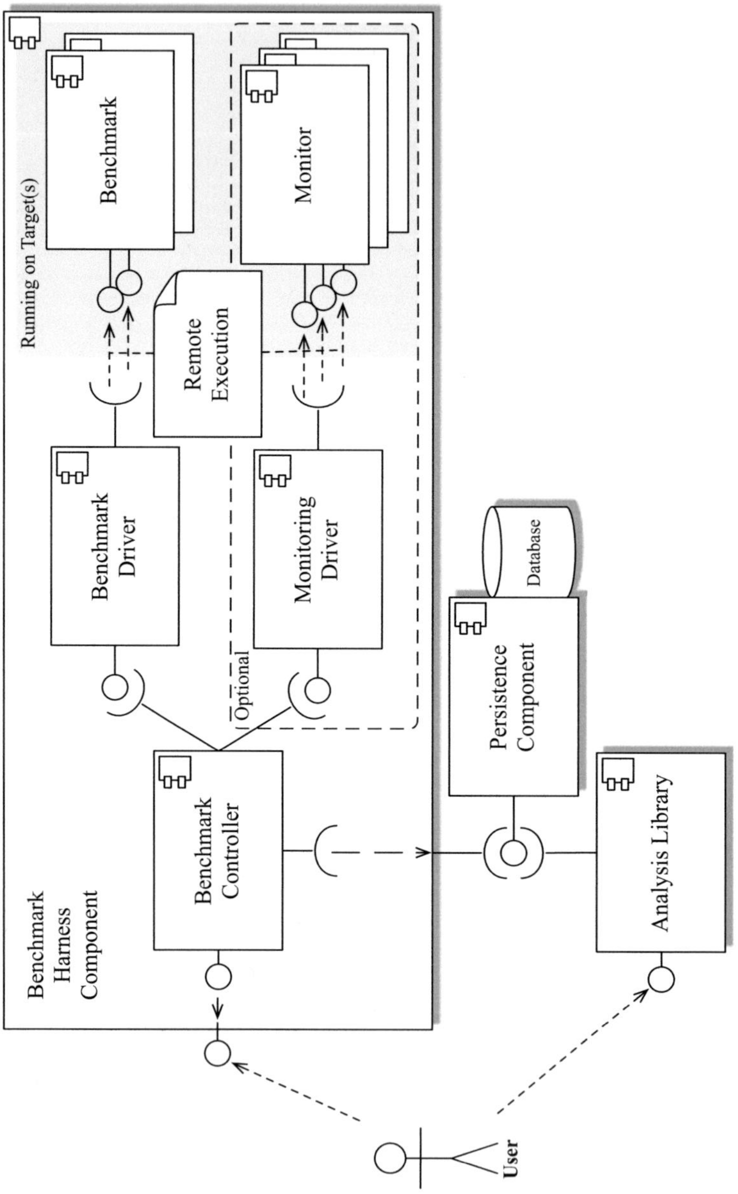

Figure 5.2.: Automation Components

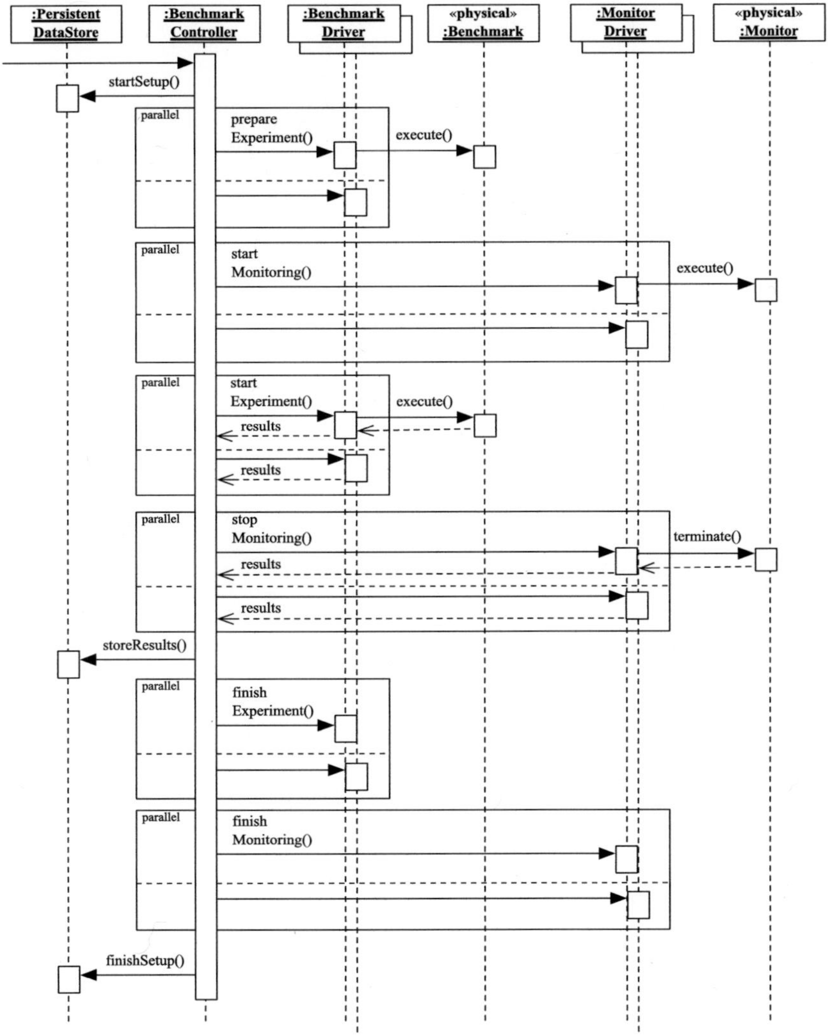

Figure 5.3.: Experiment and Workload Characterization Sequence

6. Creating Regression Analysis-based Models with Optimal Parameterization

I/O performance prediction requires models that are able to capture the relationship between the I/O performance-influencing factors, as input variables, and the I/O performance, as output variable. One approach is to employ statistical regression analysis-based models (or short, regression models) that can be created from a wide range of regression techniques. In general, most techniques have a variety of parameters with tuning opportunities that significantly affect the models' ability to predict unseen data. Finding an appropriate regression technique and parameterization, however, is not straightforward and is dependent on the actual data that should be modeled. When certain regression techniques are chosen, common practice is to leave their parameters at the standard values (e.g., Elish et al., 2009), which however might result in underperforming models. Some approaches may use an educated guess (e.g., Guo et al., 2013), which requires expert knowledge, or apply an exhaustive search to find good parameters (e.g., Yigitbasi et al., 2013), which is usually computationally expensive. The question is whether regression techniques can be parameterized and selected efficiently to increase the prediction quality with decreased computational overhead?

To address this question, in this chapter we develop a regression technique parameterization and model selection approach that is generally not limited to a certain domain and has been used and fully automated for I/O performance modeling in virtualized environments. The specific goal we pursue is to efficiently create high quality models, i.e., to create regression models with high predictive power within a limited amount of time. To achieve this goal, we formulate it as an optimization problem and develop a search algorithm that is able to find a good parameterization for regression techniques. Furthermore, we survey and evaluate a representative set of regression techniques for their computational overhead and complexity. Based on these results we develop a general regression model selection process. Finally, the model selection approach is then embedded into the I/O performance modeling process to obtain performance models in the target domain.

This chapter is aligned with the steps presented above and structured as follows: We next in Section 6.1 elaborate on the scientific challenges of this chapter. In Section 6.2, we formulate the parameterization of regression techniques as an optimization problem and introduce our Stepwise Sampling Search (S3) algorithm to efficiently solve the problem. Section 6.3 surveys and evaluates a selected set of regression techniques to identify a regression model selection process. The model selection approach of that section is embedded in Section 6.4 in an I/O performance modeling process. Finally, this chapter is concluded in Section 6.5 with a summary.

6.1. Scientific Challenges

This chapter is based on our publications (Noorshams et al., 2013a; Noorshams et al., 2014a) and the thesis we supervised (Bruhn, 2012) and addresses the following challenges:

Challenge 1 — *How can regression techniques be parameterized to obtain I/O performance models with high prediction accuracy?*

Regression techniques typically have multiple configuration parameters for various purposes and goals. Choosing the appropriate parameters is not straightforward, since the best choice is usually both problem-specific and data-specific. The parameters are usually just left to their standard values or either chosen based on an educated guess or an exhaustive search. We aim to find appropriate parameters automatically and efficiently to increase the prediction accuracy of the regression models without requiring expertise and knowledge of a given regression technique and the parameters' effects in the algorithm of the technique.

Challenge 2 — *What is the process to create a regression analysis-based I/O performance model in a virtualized environment?*

In general, regression analysis-based models are applied in various domains, however, what performs well in one domain does not necessarily suit other domains. For example, linear regression models are popular because of their simplicity and efficient calculation, yet it is unclear if linear regression models are able to capture both workload-relevant and system-relevant factors influencing the I/O performance in virtualized environments. Therefore, we define a process creating performance models with different regression techniques and parameterization options, which consequently leads to the next challenge.

Challenge 3 — *How can an appropriate I/O performance model be selected from a range of models and their parameterization?*

From a set of regression techniques and their parameterization options, choosing the appropriate regression model depends on multiple objectives and constraints. The traditional model selection problem addresses linear regression models and the choice of their coefficients. In contrast to the typical problem formulation, we address the problem to select a model across multiple regression techniques and to find their parameterization.

This chapter addresses these challenges and demonstrates the following three hypotheses:

H1: We can efficiently optimize the parameterization of regression techniques, hereby significantly increasing the prediction accuracy of the resulting models.

H2: We can create regression models of I/O performance without assuming any specific relationships between the modeled factors and the I/O performance.

H3: We can choose from a set of regression techniques and their parameterization without requiring to manually analyze the resulting regression models.

6.2. Regression Parameterization as an Optimization Problem

The configuration parameters of a regression technique have an important impact on the eventually created regression model. Most notably, an appropriate parameterization varies for different data. In this section, we will treat this regression technique parameterization as an optimization problem and first state the problem formulation based on an appropriate quality criterion for regression models. We will then show how to solve the problem using an efficient search algorithm.

6.2.1. Problem Formulation

As our goal is to build a model with high prediction accuracy for unseen configurations, we define the *regression optimization problem* as a single-objective optimization problem to minimize the generalization error of the regression model. More specifically, as a metric for the generalization error, we average the root mean squared error of a model with its parameterization over a k-fold cross-validation, where k is set to 10 (cf. Section 3.2.2). The k-fold cross-validation has the practical benefit that the calculation can be parallelized (at least) k-times. Formally, the problem is defined as follows (cf. Izenman, 2009):

Definition 1. *Let $\mathscr{P}$ be a random partition of the training data D, $D := \{(\vec{x}_j, y_j)\}_{k \leq j < \infty}$, with k disjoint elements of approximately equal size, i.e., $\mathscr{P} := \{S_i\}_{1 \leq i \leq k}$ and $S_i \subset D$, $\bigcup_i S_i = D$, $\forall i, j : i \neq j \Rightarrow S_i \cap S_j = \emptyset$, and $\forall i, j : |S_i| \leq |S_j| + 1$. Let $f^{\vec{P}}_{-\xi} : \mathscr{S} \to \mathscr{T}$ be the regression model parameterized with* *the vector of l parameters $\vec{p} := (p_1, p_2, \ldots, p_l)$ and created with the learning data $\bigcup_{i \neq \xi} S_i$. The* regression optimization problem *is*

$$\min_{\vec{p}} \frac{1}{k} \sum_{\xi=1}^{k} \sqrt{\sum_{(\vec{x}_j, y_j) \in S_\xi} \left(y_j - f^{\vec{p}}_{-\xi}(\vec{x}_j)\right)^2} \qquad (6.1)$$

subject to

$$p_i \in P_i, \forall i \qquad (6.2)$$

where P_i is the domain of the i-th parameter p_i, $\mathscr{S}$ is the source space of the training data, i.e., $\vec{x}_j \in \mathscr{S}$, and $\mathscr{T}$ is the target space of the training data, i.e., $y_j \in \mathscr{T}$, with $\mathscr{T} \subseteq \mathbb{R}$.

6.2.2. Stepwise Sampling Search (S3)

As there is no closed form for the optimization problem, it is therefore not differentiable and typical solution approaches, such as classical *steepest descent* (cf. Snyman, 2005), cannot be applied. Other approaches, such as genetic algorithms or tailored searches (cf. Kuhn et al., 2013) are either too computationally expensive or problem-specific. Therefore, we have designed a general metaheuristic search algorithm called *Stepwise Sampling Search (S3)*. The S3 algorithm was designed with the following four objectives:

- *Deterministic search*

  If the search is deterministic, it does not have to be repeated to obtain stable results, which reduces the runtime and computational cost of the search. As long as the evaluation of the regression optimization problem is deterministic, which is the case for a deterministic regression technique and fixed training data partition $\mathscr{P}$, the search is not supposed to exhibit a stochastic behavior.

- *Assessable runtime complexity*

  If the complexity of the algorithm is known, an upper bound for the search time can be estimated before actually running the algorithm.

- *Global search*

  A global search reduces the risk that the search is trapped in a locally optimal region. Consequently, it does not require actions to mitigate such a risk, e.g., using random restarts, which would again increase the computational cost of the search.

- *Guaranteed local optimum*

  As the properties of the objective function are unknown, globally optimal solutions cannot be easily discovered. Still, a locally optimal solution is desirable from a theoretical point of view.

The former two objectives allow to estimate the computational cost of the search in order to find a solution efficiently. This makes the search also interesting for runtime sensitive scenarios, such as online approaches, for instance, where a solution needs to be found in a given period of time. The algorithm does not have to be repeated as it provides the same solution for a given data. The latter two objectives allow to evaluate the quality of a solution, such that the search is global and given a long enough search, at least a locally optimal solution is found. Although the search time is limited in practice, the property is interesting theoretically.

The design of the S3 algorithm is shown in Algorithm 2 and illustrated in Figure 6.1. The core idea is to split the search space into multiple subspaces and then stepwise refine the search in the most promising regions. The algorithm has two configuration parameters to regulate the search and its computational complexity, the *number of splits* (i.e., splitting points) ζ and the *number of subspace explorations* η in each iteration. The number of splits configures the sampling frequency of the search space and the subspaces. It can be set to a high value if multiple narrow optima can be assumed, such that the potential optima can be detected early to explore the subspaces around the optima. The number of explorations determines how many potential solutions are analyzed in their adjacent area. It can be set to a high value if many local optima can be assumed, such that not only the best, but also suboptimal solutions are explored. The algorithm can be configured with any stopping criterion, e.g., when the improvement between iterations falls below a certain threshold or when a certain maximum number of iterations is reached. The algorithm operates on a bounded search space, such that for each of the given parameters p_i, a reasonable range $p_i \in [a_i, b_i]$ needs to be defined to limit the search space. The lower bound usually exists for most

Algorithm 2 Stepwise Sampling Search (S3)

`Configuration:`
$\zeta \leftarrow$ Number of splits
$\eta \leftarrow$ Number of explorations
$\mathscr{C}$ *// Stopping criterion*
`Definitions:`
$\vec{p} := (p_1, \ldots, p_l)$, $L := \{1, \ldots, l\}$ *// l parameters*
$p_i \in [a_i, b_i]$, $a_i, b_i \in P_i$, $\forall i \in L$ *// Ranges of parameters*
$\phi(\vec{p}) :=$ Objective function, cf. Equation (6.3)
`Init:`
$E \leftarrow \{(\vec{a} := (a_1, \ldots, a_l), \phi(\vec{a}))\}$ *// Evaluate first border parameters*
$M \leftarrow E$ *// M: Set of best parameters*
`Algorithm:`
for $j \leftarrow 1, \neg\mathscr{C}, j{+}{+}$ **do**
  for all $(\vec{v}^{\,j}_{(h)}, \cdot) \in M$ **do** *// h-th pivot*
    for all $i \in L$ **do**
      $A_i \leftarrow \{p_i \mid (p_i, \cdot) \in E \wedge p_i < v^{\,j}_{(h)i}\}$
      if $A_i \neq \emptyset$ **then** $a_i^* \leftarrow \max A_i$
        else $a_i^* \leftarrow a_i$
      $B_i \leftarrow \{p_i \mid (p_i, \cdot) \in E \wedge p_i > v^{\,j}_{(h)i}\}$
      if $B_i \neq \emptyset$ **then** $b_i^* \leftarrow \min B_i$
        else $b_i^* \leftarrow b_i$
      $s_i^* \leftarrow \frac{b_i^* - a_i^*}{\zeta + 1}, \forall i \in L$ *// Step width*
      $S_i^* \leftarrow \{a_i^*, a_i^* + s_i^*, \ldots, a_i^* + \zeta\, s_i^*, b_i^*\}$
      for all $s \in S_i^*$ **do**
        if s invalid **then** round s to next valid value
      end for
    end for
    // Evaluate parameters if not evaluated yet:
    $E^j_{(h)} \leftarrow \{(\vec{x}, \phi(\vec{x})) \mid \vec{x} \in S_1^* \times \ldots \times S_l^*\}$
  end for
  $E \leftarrow E \cup \bigcup_h E^j_{(h)}$ *// Set of all evaluated parameters*
  $M \leftarrow \eta$ best tuples in E (w.r.t. ϕ)
end for

parameters and the upper bound can be derived based on the used training data. The objective function $\phi : \times_i P_i \rightarrow \mathbb{R}$ is the regression optimization problem defined in Equation (6.1), i.e.,

$$\phi(\vec{p}) := \frac{1}{k} \sum_{\xi=1}^{k} \sqrt{\sum_{(\vec{x}_j, y_j) \in S_\xi} \left(y_j - f^{\vec{p}}_{-\xi}(\vec{x}_j) \right)^2}. \tag{6.3}$$

The search first evaluates one initial point in the search space. As this is the only evaluated point in the initial step, it is the only candidate in the set M of intended exploration points in the next iteration. During the exploration phase in each iteration, every point $\vec{x}$ in the set M containing the η best candidates is explored by splitting the unevaluated space around $\vec{x}$ bounded by the search space $\times_i [a_i, b_i]$ into $(\zeta + 1)^l$ subspaces. Initially, the whole search space is explored. The objective function is then evaluated for each corner point of the subspaces and the best η candidates found so far are held in M to be explored in the next iteration. During the search, a set E of all evaluated candidates is maintained. The algorithm repeats the exploration and evaluation until the stopping criterion applies.

Figure 6.1 illustrates the first iterations of the search configured with $\zeta = 3$ and $\eta = 2$ in a 2-dimensional search space, i.e., $l = 2$. The search starts evaluating one corner point. This pivot $\vec{v}^{1}_{(1)}$, marked with a dark gray circle, is explored in the first iteration. Since the initial pivot is not bounded by other evaluated points, the whole parameter space is subdivided with $\zeta = 3$ splits for each parameter as indicated by the grid lines. Each of the grid intersection points is evaluated indicated as small light gray points at the Iteration 2 level. Then the best $\eta = 2$ evaluated points are held in M and become the pivots $\vec{v}^{2}_{(1)}$ and $\vec{v}^{2}_{(2)}$ being explored successively in the second iteration. First, when $\vec{v}^{2}_{(1)}$ is explored, the unevaluated space around the pivot limited by the neighboring points evaluated in the previous iterations is explored, cf. dashed lines between Iteration 2 and Iteration 3. Then, the same is done for the second pivot $\vec{v}^{2}_{(2)}$ unaffected by the newly evaluated points in the current iteration. This exploration and evaluation process is repeated in the next iterations and the best parameters found during the search are used for model building. In the iterations, the algorithm is designed to split the unevaluated subspaces as determined by the configuration parameter ζ, such that the space does not necessarily have to be split equidistantly across all parameters, cf. $\vec{v}^{\,3}_{(1)}$ in Figure 6.1.

Evaluating a point in the search space requires to build k regression models, which is the most computationally expensive part of the algorithm. The complexity of the S3 algorithm is therefore specified in the required number of evaluated points.

Theorem 1. *Let θ be the maximum number of iterations of the S3 algorithm, i.e., $\theta := \max j$. The complexity of the S3 algorithm is*

$$\mathcal{O}(\theta\,\eta\,\zeta^l). \tag{6.4}$$

Proof. In every iteration, the S3 algorithm evaluates for every pivot at most every set of parameter values except the initial corner one in the first iteration and the 2^l corner ones in every other iteration. This leads to at most $(\zeta+2)^l - c_j$ evaluated points for every pivot in every iteration j in the worst case, where $c_1 = 1$ and $c_j = 2^l$ for $j > 1$. Thus, for the complexity of the algorithm in terms of the total number of evaluated points χ, it holds that

$$\chi \leq 1 + \left((\zeta+2)^l - 1\right) + (\theta-1)\cdot\eta\,\left((\zeta+2)^l - 2^l\right),$$

which establishes the theorem. □

Consequently, by configuring ζ, η, and θ, the overhead of the algorithm can be controlled and kept within required bounds. In terms of model creations, from Theorem 1 follows:

Corollary 1. *Let θ be the maximum number of iterations of the S3 algorithm, i.e., $\theta := \max j$. The overall number of regression model creations is in*

$$\mathcal{O}(k\,\theta\,\eta\,\zeta^l). \tag{6.5}$$

The search is generally designed to find reasonable solutions in a limited amount of time. Theoretically, if the algorithm is allowed to search long enough, the search converges to a locally optimal solution. To show this, we first require the following lemma:

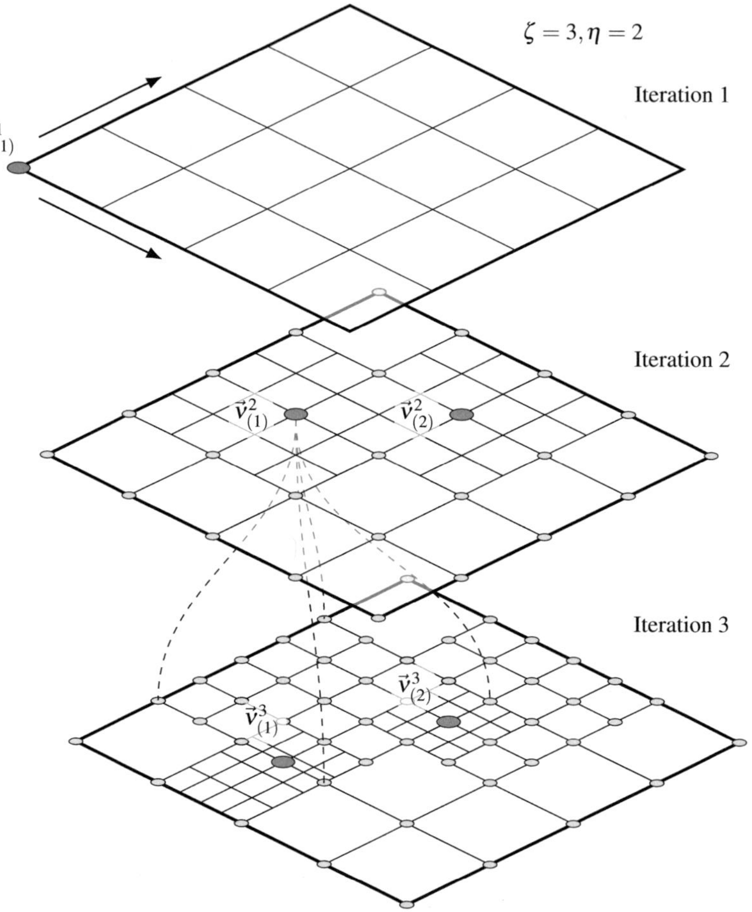

Figure 6.1.: Illustration of the S3 Algorithm

Lemma 1. *Let* $\zeta > 1$ *and* $\eta > 0$. *It holds that*

$$\lim_{j \to \infty} s_i^* = 0, \; \forall i \in \{1, \ldots, l\}. \tag{6.6}$$

Proof. The proof is straightforward for $l = 1$. Without loss of generality, let $[a_1, b_1] = [0, 1] \subset \mathbb{R}$. Furthermore, we require a consistent ranking of evaluated points in case of equal quality, i.e., a point cannot become a pivot if it did not become one before because of a point with equal quality. At iteration j it holds for the first pivot $h = 1$ as well as for all pivots $h \geq 1$ if the number of pivots does not increase that

$$s_1^* \leq \frac{1}{2} \left(\frac{2}{\zeta + 1} \right)^j. \tag{6.7}$$

We will proof the worst case $s_1^* = \frac{1}{2} \left(\frac{2}{\zeta+1} \right)^j$ by induction.
Initial step: For $j = 1$, $s_1^* = \frac{1}{\zeta+1}$ by definition.
Induction step: For $j = n + 1$, $b_1^* - a_1^*$ is at most twice the step width of the previous iteration, i.e.,

$$b_1^* - a_1^* = 2 \cdot \frac{1}{2} \left(\frac{2}{\zeta + 1} \right)^n. \tag{6.8}$$

By definition,

$$s_1^* = 2 \cdot \frac{1}{2} \left(\frac{2}{\zeta + 1} \right)^n \cdot \frac{1}{\zeta + 1} = \frac{1}{2} \left(\frac{2}{\zeta + 1} \right)^{n+1}. \tag{6.9}$$

Having established the worst case for s_1^*, it holds that

$$\lim_{j \to \infty} \frac{1}{2} \left(\frac{2}{\zeta + 1} \right)^j = 0. \tag{6.10}$$

For $l > 1$, the pivots can, theoretically, travel through the search space if they are a newly evaluated point at the borders of the subspaces. For $l = 1$, this cannot occur as otherwise the border point would have been a pivot in the previous iteration. Still, the Lemma also holds for $l > 1$ and for all the pivots as the search space is bounded and there is a finite number of times the step width can increase. □

Theorem 2. *Let $\zeta > 1$ and $\eta > 0$. The S3 algorithm finds at least one locally optimal solution.*

Proof. Without loss of generality, let $l = 1$. The proof follows a similar pattern for $l > 1$. Using Lemma 1, we distinguish two cases:

1. Let P_1 be discrete. Without loss of generality, let $P_1 = [n_1, n_2] \cap \mathbb{N}, n_i \in \mathbb{N}, n_1 < n_2$.
   $\lim_{j \to \infty} s_1^* < 1 \implies \exists h' \exists j' : \phi(v_{h'}^{j'}) \leq \phi(\overline{v_{h'}^{j'}}) \wedge \phi(v_{h'}^{j'}) \leq \phi(\underline{v_{h'}^{j'}}) \wedge (v_{h'}^{j'}, \cdot),$ $(\overline{v_{h'}^{j'}}, \cdot), (\underline{v_{h'}^{j'}}, \cdot) \in E$, where $\overline{v_{h'}^{j'}} := \min\{v_{h'}^{j'} + 1, b_1\}$ and $\underline{v_{h'}^{j'}} := \max\{v_{h'}^{j'} - 1, a_1\}$.
2. Let P_1 be continuous. Assume $\forall j \forall (e_1, \cdot) \in E \backslash \{(b_1, \cdot)\} \forall (e_2, \cdot) \in E \backslash \{(a_1, \cdot)\} \exists \varepsilon' > 0 \forall \varepsilon \in (0, \varepsilon'] : \phi(e_1) > \phi(e_1 + \varepsilon) \vee \phi(e_2) > \phi(e_2 - \varepsilon)$.
   $\lim_{j \to \infty} s_1^* = 0 \implies \exists j^* \exists h' \forall h'' : s_1^* \in (0, \varepsilon'] \wedge \phi(v_{(h')}^{j^*}) \leq \phi(v_{(h'')}^{j^*}) \wedge$ $(v_{(h')}^{j^*}, \cdot), (v_{(h')}^{j^*(+)}, \cdot), (v_{(h')}^{j^*(-)}, \cdot) \in E_{(h')}^{j^*-1}$, where $v_{(h')}^{j^*(+)} := \min\{v_{h'}^{j^*} + s_1^*, b_1\}$ and $v_{(h')}^{j^*(+)} := \max\{v_{h'}^{j^*} - s_1^*, a_1\}$, in contradiction to the assumption.

□

Consequently, since for convex problems a locally optimal solution is also globally optimal, our approach guarantees globally optimal solutions if the search space is convex.

6.3. Regression Model Selection

To select from a set of regression models, it is important to understand the regression techniques used to create the models. In this section, we establish a regression selection process by first analyzing and surveying a representative set of regression techniques. Afterwards, the techniques are evaluated with regard to their computational overhead and complexity. Finally, we use the computational overhead, the complexity, and the model quality as criteria to define the selection process.

6.3.1. Survey of Popular Regression Techniques

In this section, we analyze and survey a selected set of regression techniques that can be used in the model selection process. We selected regression techniques that are popular and frequently used, however, this section is neither intended as a comprehensive knowledge base nor is our approach limited to the given set of techniques. The intention of this section is to present a methodology how to evaluate the different techniques and the resulting models that is a basis for our regression model selection process.

6.3.1.1. Linear Regression Model (LRM)

A simple and popular approach is creating a *linear regression model (LRM)* (Hastie et al., 2008). LRM assumes a linear relationship between the independent variables and the dependent variable, i.e., the dependent variable is modeled as a linear combination of the independent variables with an additive constant. Formally, for a vector of independent variables $\vec{x} := (x_1, \ldots, x_n)$ a model f with coefficients $\beta_0, \ldots, \beta_n$ is created of the form

$$f(\vec{x}) = \beta_0 + \sum_{i=1}^{n} \beta_i x_i. \tag{6.11}$$

The model f is linear in the independent variables, however, it does not necessarily have to be a first degree function. The representation of the independent variables can be derived, e.g., $x_2 = x_1^2$ or $x_3 = x_1 x_2$. For the sake of clarity, we explicitly consider two forms: The *linear regression models* are first degree functions. The *linear regression models with interactions (IA)* can include terms expressing the interaction between independent variables, e.g., $x_1 x_2$. Such models have a maximum degree n, but the effects of the independent variables x_i remain linear in the model. In general, higher degree polynomials and other terms, such as e^{x_i} and $\ln(x_i)$, are possible, however, denoting the resulting models as *linear regression models* might be confusing and they are disregarded at this point.

To create a model based on given training data, the coefficients of the model are determined to minimize the difference between the model and the training data. A typical approach is to minimize the squared difference creating a model using the *method of least squares*. Formally, for a set of training data $\{(\vec{x}_1, y_1), \ldots, (\vec{x}_N, y_N)\}$, where $\forall j$: $\vec{x}_j := (x_{j,1}, \ldots, x_{j,n})$, this method finds the coefficients $\vec{\beta} := (\beta_0, \ldots, \beta_n)$ such that the *residual sum of squares (RSS)* defined as

$$RSS(\vec{\beta}) := \sum_{j=1}^{N} (y_j - f(\vec{x}_j))^2 \tag{6.12}$$

is minimized. To find the minimum, the derivative of *RSS* is set to zero and solved for $\vec{\beta}$. Since the RSS is a quadratic function, the minimum is guaranteed to always exist.

6.3.1.2. Multivariate Adaptive Regression Splines (MARS)

Multivariate Adaptive Regression Splines (MARS) (Friedman, 1991) consist of piecewise linear functions comprised of *hinge functions*. Formally, the hinge functions with *knot* t are defined as $(x-t)_+ := \max\{0, x-t\}$ and $(t-x)_+ := \max\{0, t-x\}$. For model creation, let $\vec{x} = (x_1, \ldots, x_n)$ be the vector of independent variables as above, $H_i := \{(x_i - t_j)_+, (t_j - x_i)_+\}_j$ and $t_j \in T_i$, where T_i is the set of values of the i-th independent variable in the training data, i.e., $T_i := \{x_{j,i}\}_j$ for the training data defined as above, and $H := \bigcup_i H_i$. Then, MARS constructs a model f of the form

$$f(\vec{x}) = \beta_0 + \sum_{k=1}^{m} \beta_k h_k(\vec{x}) \tag{6.13}$$

with $h_k \in H$ and coefficients $\beta_0, \ldots, \beta_m$. Similar to the linear regression models, we explicitly distinguish between *MARS* and *MARS with interactions (IA)*. The latter also includes terms that are a product of one or more hinge functions in H.

The parameters β_i are determined based on the method of least squares, similar to the linear regression models. The model first grows greedily in a forward step. Starting from a constant function, the MARS algorithm iteratively adds the hinge functions in H that result in the highest reduction of the residual squared error. If interactions are allowed, the algorithm can also choose a hinge function as a factor, however, each variable can only appear once in a term, i.e., higher-degree powers of a variable are excluded. This process stops if a predefined number of maximum terms is reached or if the residual error falls below a predefined threshold. Then, the model is pruned in a second step to avoid overfitting. The terms that produce the smallest increase in residual squared error are removed iteratively until the model contains a predefined maximum number of terms after pruning. The pruning process may also consider the model complexity in combination with the residual squared error. This allows for a trade-off between accuracy and complexity of the model.

6.3.1.3. Classification and Regression Trees (CART)

Classification and Regression Trees (CART) (Breiman et al., 1984) create a model of the training data in form of a tree-based representation. CART models are binary trees with conditions in their inner, non-leaf nodes and constant values in their leaf nodes. For a given set of values of the independent variables, the evaluation starts at the root to determine the value of the dependent variable. The condition in the respective node is checked and one of the child nodes is followed depending on the evaluation of the node condition. This process is repeated until a leaf is reached.

The CART algorithm comprises a forward and a pruning step to create a model. In the forward step, an initial tree with a single node is created. The leaves in the tree are split iteratively at a certain splitting variable and a splitting condition. The splitting condition is determined greedily such that the residual squared error is minimized. The algorithm splits a leaf until it contains less samples of the training data than a predefined value. The forward step ends if no leaf can be split any further. In the pruning step, the tree is reduced using *cost-complexity pruning* (cf. Hastie et al., 2008). Let m be the m-th leaf, R_m be the region specified by the conditions to the m-th leaf, and $l(T)$ be the number of leaves in the tree T. Furthermore, for the training data $\{(\vec{x}_j, y_j)\}_j$, let the number of observations in a region $n_m = |\{\vec{x}_j \,|\, \vec{x}_j \in R_m\}|$, the mean of the observations values $\hat{c}_m = n_m^{-1} \sum_{\vec{x}_j \in R_m} y_j$, and the mean squared difference between each observed value and the mean of the observations values $q_m(T) = n_m^{-1} \sum_{x_j \in R_m} (y_j - \hat{c}_m)^2$. The cost-complexity criterion with parameter α is defined as

$$c_\alpha(T) := \sum_{m=1}^{l(T)} n_m q_m(T) + \alpha\, l(T) \tag{6.14}$$

that is to be minimized. The parameter α is a trade-off between complexity and goodness-of-fit to the training data. It is determined by the algorithm according to the residual sum of squares with cross-validation, which splits the training data into two partitions consisting of a learning and an evaluation set. For a given α, the tree is greedily pruned using *weakest link pruning*, where the nodes with the smallest per-node increase in $\sum_{m=1}^{l(T)} n_m q_m(T)$ are collapsed iteratively.

6.3.1.4. M5 Trees

Figuratively speaking, *M5* trees (Quinlan, 1992) combine CART trees with linear regression models. M5 models are also binary decision trees with conditions in their inner, non-leaf nodes. In contrast to CART trees containing constant values in the leaf nodes, the leaf nodes of M5 trees contain linear regression models. To evaluate a value, the conditions are evaluated starting in the root node until a linear regression model in a leaf is reached. This model is then used and evaluated.

Similar to the previous techniques, the M5 tree is first built in a forward step and then pruned afterwards. To build an M5 tree, the initial model consists of a tree T with a single node. The tree is split iteratively into subtrees T_i until a predefined maximum number of splits is reached. M5 splits the tree greedily at the condition that maximizes the expected reduction in error Δe with

$$\Delta e := \sigma(T) - \sum_i \frac{|T_i|}{|T|} \sigma(T_i), \tag{6.15}$$

where σ is the standard deviation of the observations values $\{y_j\}_j$ that are contained in the respective tree. After the creation of the tree, a linear regression model is created for each leaf. In the pruning step, the M5 model f is greedily simplified to decrease the complexity c with

$$c(T) := n^{-1} \sum_j |y_j - f(\vec{x}_j)| \cdot \frac{n+p}{n-p}, \tag{6.16}$$

where $\{(\vec{x}_j, y_j)\}_j$ is the training data (i.e., the observations), n is the number of samples in the training data and p is the number of parameters in the model. The term $\frac{n+p}{n-p}$ allows an increase in error if the complexity is decreased. For each leaf node, parameters of the linear model are removed, whereas for every non-leaf node, the node is collapsed if this reduces $c(T)$.

6.3.1.5. Cubist Forests

Cubist forests (RuleQuest Research Pty Ltd, 2012; Kuhn et al., 2012) are an extension of M5 trees. Cubist forests are based on rule-based model trees with linear regression models in the leaves. Cubist extends M5 by two aspects. First, it introduces a boosting-like approach, i.e., it creates multiple trees instead of a single tree. To obtain a single value, the tree predictions are aggregated using their arithmetic mean. Second, it combines *model-based* and *instance-based learning* (cf. Quinlan, 1993), i.e., it can adjust the prediction of unseen configurations by the values of the neighboring training data.

Before the algorithm begins, the maximum number of trees in the model is defined to construct a forest. The initial tree is created using the M5 algorithm. The following trees are created to correct the predictions of the training data by the previous tree $f_t(\vec{x})$. Each value of a training point y_i is adjusted by $\bar{y}_i := 2y_i - f_t(\vec{x})$ to compensate for over- and under-estimations. Then, the tree building is repeated and another tree is created using the M5 algorithm. For prediction, Cubist aggregates the values predicted by each tree using their mean value. Finally, the prediction of unseen configurations can be adjusted by the values of a possibly dynamically determined number of samples in the training data using *instance-based correction*, cf. Quinlan (1993). The prediction of a configuration $\vec{x}$ is adjusted by the weighted mean of its *neighbors*, i.e., the nearest samples, in the training data, with weight $w_{\vec{n}} := 1/(m(\vec{x},\vec{n}) + 0.5)$ for every neighbor $\vec{n}$, where $m(\vec{x},\vec{n})$ is the Manhattan distance of $\vec{x}$ and $\vec{n}$. M5 is a special case of Cubist with one tree and no instance-based correction.

6.3.2. Evaluation of Overhead and Complexity

As part of our selection process, we evaluate the computational overhead and the complexity of the considered regression techniques. For the evaluation, we analyze the following four dimensions:

1. *Model Creation and Evaluation Time*

   We measure the time required to create and evaluate a model with standard parameters.

2. *Prediction Time*

   We evaluate the time required to predict a set of data with the standard model.

3. *Optimization Overhead*

   We evaluate the optimization overhead for the techniques across their parameterization.

4. *Model Complexity*

   Finally, we discuss the algorithms w.r.t. their complexity and interpretability.

6.3.2.1. Setup

To measure the execution times for the dimensions, we run our evaluation process using a hyper-threaded Intel core i7 clocked at 2.66 GHz. The process is automated with the statistics framework *R* (R Core Team, 2013) and parallelized using the `doMC` library. Measuring the execution times is realized using the `rbenchmark` library, where the evaluations can be automatically replicated and the respective code is executed once before the time measurement begins. For all the techniques, we use the method `train` in the `caret` library, which serves as a façade to the actual implementations. During the model creation, the method `train` also evaluates the model using a 10-fold cross validation, such that 11 models are created in total for each method invocation. Thus, the model creation time also includes the model evaluation time, which helps to assess the quality of the model before actually employing it.

For the evaluation, we use two data sets from real measurements[1]:

1. Data Set I: The first data set consists of 576 measurement configurations and three independent variables for each model.

[1] The measurements from Data Set I and Data Set II are given in Table 9.5 and 9.6 in Chapter 9. The respective models and predictions are discussed in Section 9.4.

2. Data Set II: The second data set consists of 960 measurement configurations and five independent variables for each model.

Furthermore, four dependent variables are used for the evaluations for each data set, i.e., every model evaluation is inherently repeated 4 times – once for each dependent variable.

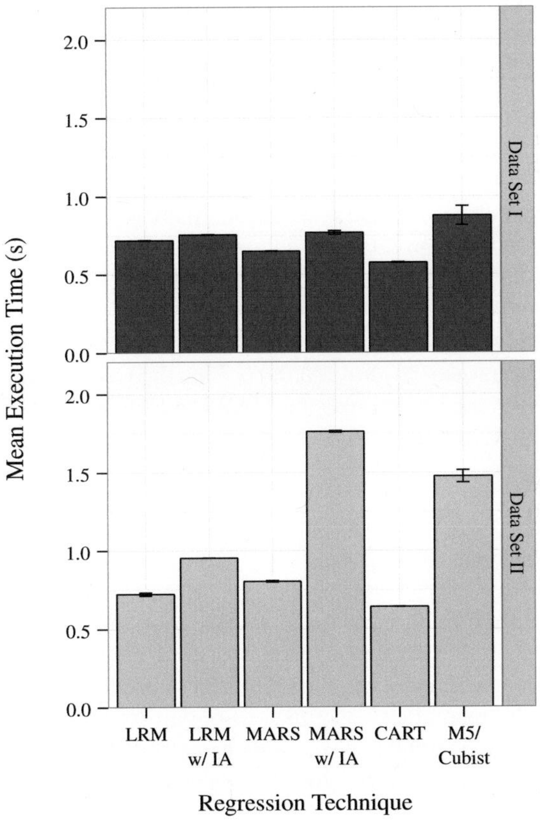

Figure 6.2.: Time Evaluation for Regression Model Creation and Evaluation

6.3.2.2. Model Creation and Evaluation Time

In this section, we measure the model creation and evaluation time with the considered regression techniques using their standard parameters and use 30 replications to obtain stable results, since the execution times are small. We use the two data sets and average the results for each technique across the repetitions and the four dependent variables. Furthermore, we distinguish for LRM and MARS between the models with and without interactions (IA). Finally, as Cubist equals M5 for the standard parameters, the two techniques are not distinguished.

The mean execution times for each model creation and evaluation are given in Figure 6.2, where the error bars (intervals) illustrate the standard error across the four models for each dependent variable, i.e., the distance from the lower end to the upper end is two times the standard error. Interestingly, while there are some trends, the regression techniques have similar runtimes for Data Set I. In general, the CART models are created fastest with 0.58 s, whereas the M5/Cubist models are created slowest with 0.88 s. For the more complex Data Set II, the trends indicated in the first data set become more apparent. While most techniques require around 0.75 s, the CART models are created again fastest with 0.64 s, whereas the MARS models with interactions and the M5/Cubist models with 1.76 s and 1.48 s, respectively, run more than twice as long as CART.

6.3.2.3. Prediction Time

In general, the required time to create a regression model outweighs the time for a model to predict data by several orders of magnitude. In this section, we evaluate for each model the time required to predict 100 random samples. We replicate the executions 30 times to obtain stable results for the short measurements and average the execution times for both data sets. The results are presented similar to the previous section and shown in Figure 6.3.

For Data Set I, there is a similar trend as in the previous evaluation. The predictions are generally fast, especially for LRM and CART models with 4.4 ms and 5 ms, respectively, for 100 samples. The slowest predictions originate from MARS with interactions and M5/Cubist models with 8.9 ms and 7.1 ms, respectively. Regarding Data Set II, the general trend is similar, where fastest predictions can be made with LRM and CART models having a prediction time of 5.9 ms and 6.6 ms, respectively. For this data set, the MARS models with interactions are slowest with 25.3 ms and require over 2.5 times more time than the second slowest models, which are the M5/Cubist models.

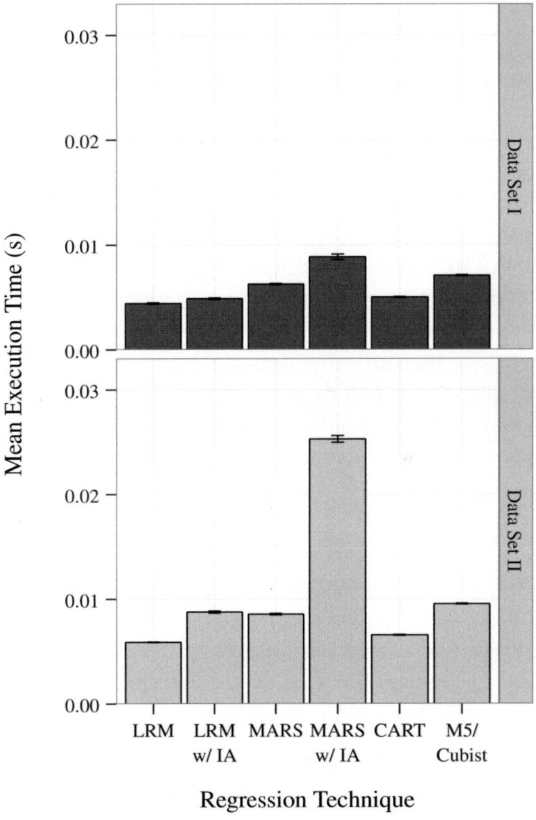

Figure 6.3.: Time Evaluation for Regression Model Prediction

6.3.2.4. Optimization Overhead

The two key factors for the optimization overhead are i) the model creation and evaluation time and ii) the number of model creations and evaluations. Regarding the former, the model creation time also depends on the parameterization itself, e.g., the number of trees created in a Cubist forest is a direct multiplier of the model creation time. For the latter, while the number of model creations and evaluations can be adjusted by the search configuration, cf. Theorem 1, an important factor is the overall number of parameters that are to be explored. As the parameters span the search space, the number of parameters affects the number of model creations and evaluations exponentially. Moreover, the actual parameters may vary depending on the implementation.

Keeping in mind that the optimization overhead can be adjusted through careful configuration based on the techniques' algorithms presented in Section 6.3.1, we will in this section measure the time required to optimize the regression techniques with a representative set of parameters chosen based on the recommendations in the `caret` library and the implementations of the techniques in R. We measure one optimization step as well as the average model creation and evaluation time using the S3 algorithm configured with $\zeta = 3$, $\eta = 1$, and $\theta = 1$. We will optimize the techniques using our two data sets with the following parameters:

1. LRM with/without interactions: The techniques have no apparent parameters, thus, they are not optimized.
2. MARS with/without interactions: The parameters are i) the maximum number of terms in the forward step, ii) the maximum number of terms after pruning, and iii) the minimum improvement in the goodness-of-fit (estimated by the coefficient of determination R^2) for a term to be added in the forward step.
3. CART: The two parameters are i) the minimum number of observations in a node for the respective node to be considered as a splitting candidate and ii) the minimum amount in lack of fit (estimated by the coefficient of determination R^2) a split must reduce for it to be considered.
4. M5: The only parameter is the maximum number of conditions, i.e., inner nodes.

5. Cubist: The parameters are i) the parameter of the M5 algorithm as well as ii) the number of trees in the forest and iii) the number of neighbors considered in the instance-based correction during prediction.

For the techniques that can be optimized, the measurement results are summarized in Figure 6.4 and Figure 6.5. As the search has a different number of evaluation points depending on the number of parameters (cf. Theorem 1), Figure 6.4 illustrates the average execution time per evaluation point in the optimization, whereas Figure 6.5 shows the total execution time for the optimization. Overall, CART and M5 show very fast execution times, since CART evaluations are very fast in general and we only optimized one parameter of the M5 algorithm. We can observe higher execution times for MARS, especially in Data Set II when the interaction terms are considered. The by far most computationally expensive algorithm appears to be Cubist. This is especially due to the fact that Cubist repeats the M5 algorithm for every tree in the forest.

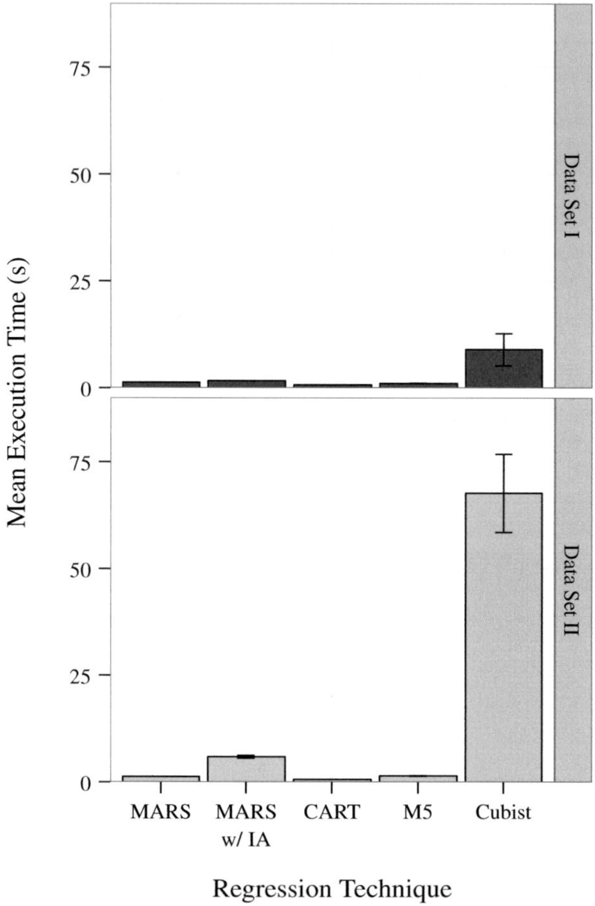

Figure 6.4.: Time Evaluation for Regression Model Optimization – Single Evaluation Time

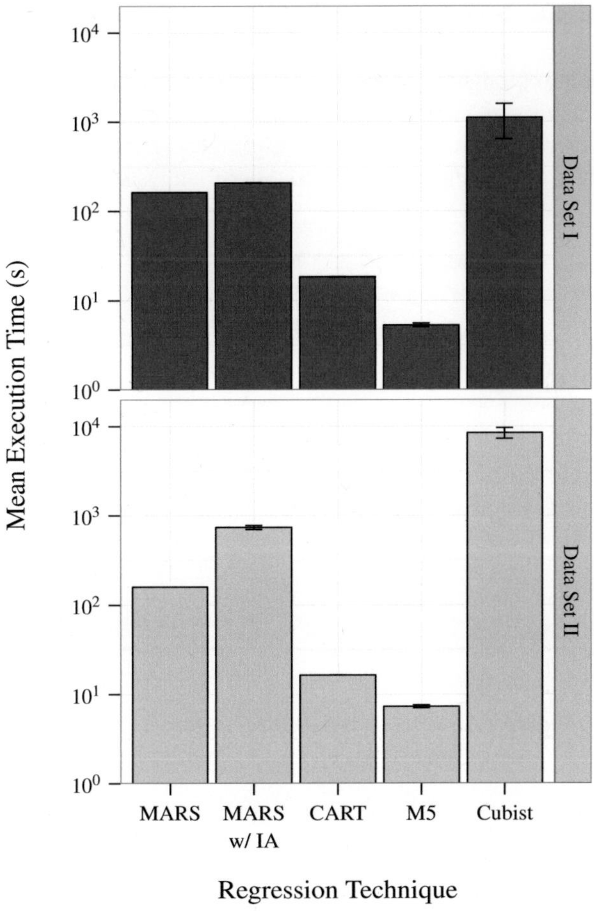

Figure 6.5.: Time Evaluation for Regression Model Optimization – Total Optimization Time (logarithmic y-axis)

6.3.2.5. Model Complexity

To evaluate the complexity of the regression techniques, more specifically, how simple the regression models can be interpreted by, e.g., an analyst, we discuss the considered regression techniques highlighting the relationships among them as illustrated in Figure 6.6 based on our analysis in Section 6.3.1.

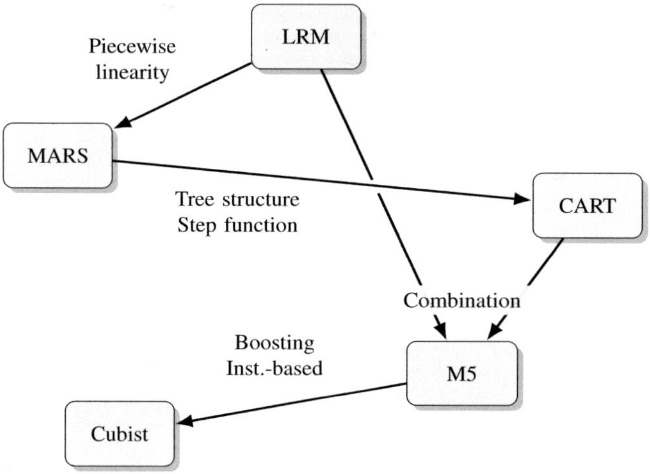

Figure 6.6.: Relation between the Regression Techniques

The basic models are LRM as well as LRM with interaction terms. The models have an inherently limited number of terms, i.e., $n+1$ and 2^n for the models without and including interaction terms, respectively, where n is the number of independent variables. Using these models, the effect and influence of a certain term on the overall modeled performance can be analyzed. The MARS algorithm can be seen as an extension of LRM by allowing piecewise linear terms. Unlike LRM, however, MARS models can grow arbitrarily large. If its parameterization permits, MARS models can contain up to one term for every measurement point. While this may be relatively easy to understand for an analyst if the dimensions are independent as the dimension can be analyzed in isolation, allowing interaction terms increases the number of terms exponentially as every combination of the terms may be included. In comparison, the algorithms of MARS and CART may seem very different, however, the forward step of MARS can be transformed into the one of CART by using a tree-based structure with step functions, cf. Hastie et al. (2008). By using a tree-based structure that group constant values, CART models are very popular because of their simplicity allowing to understand and visualize the information relatively easily. One of their weak points, however, is that CART models do not easily represent linear relationships among data as the predictions are merely constant values. To be able to capture a linear relationship for such data, a CART model would be overly branched. This issue may be overcome with the M5 algorithm, whose models can be seen as a combination of LRM and CART models. Algorithmically, M5 differs from CART in the error metric, the complexity criterion, and the pruning procedure. If the M5 models are not overly branched, they are easy to understand similar to the LRM and the CART models, otherwise it might become more difficult to understand the many separate subspaces and the effects of the independent variables. Finally, Cubist extends M5 by introducing a boosting-like approach and creating multiple trees whose predictions are aggregated. Furthermore, Cubist introduces an instance-based correction to take the training data into consideration for the prediction of unseen data. These extensions enable very powerful and complex models, however, this hinders the interpretability of the models significantly.

6.3.2.6. Overview

To summarize the evaluation results of the previous sections, Table 6.1 shows a compact overview of the regression techniques and their evaluation across the different aspects. Since the absolute evaluation also depends on the training data, the overview is to be understood as a ranking with relative scores on a 5-point scale, where more points indicate a better score. This evaluation can be used as a quick and an initial assessment of the regression techniques and, if required, can be refined with available training data to obtain absolute results using our evaluation process shown in the previous sections.

In general, LRM can be considered a simple and fast technique that does not require parameter optimization. Another simple and fast technique is CART, which can be quickly optimized. A more computationally expensive technique is MARS, especially MARS models with interaction terms can grow large. Similar, M5 models can be relatively simple and fast to create. Its extension, however, Cubist can grow significantly complex and is the most computationally expensive of the considered techniques to optimize.

Aside from the considerations that the regression techniques have an overhead to create an optimized model with a certain complexity, the key factor is the prediction error and the ability to generalize from observations, which is, however, dependent on the training data at hand and cannot be evaluated independently. For example, more complex relationships are more likely to be adequately captured by more complex regression techniques. Still, the overview in Table 6.1 is used as a basis guiding the regression model selection process presented in the next section.

Technique	Model Creation / Evaluation Time	Prediction Time	Optimization Overhead	Model Complexity
LRM	★★★★★	★★★★★	—	★★★★★
LRM w/ IA	★★★★☆	★★★★☆	—	★★★★★
MARS	★★★★★	★★★★☆	★★★★☆	★★★★☆
MARS w/ IA	★★★☆☆	★★☆☆☆	★★★☆☆	★★☆☆☆
CART	★★★★★	★★★★★	★★★★★	★★★★★
M5	★★★☆☆	★★★★☆	★★★★☆	★★★★☆
Cubist	★★★☆☆	★★★★☆	★☆☆☆☆	★☆☆☆☆

Table 6.1.: Evaluation Overview of Regression Techniques on a Relative 5-Point Scale

6.3.3. Process for Regression Model Selection

Guided by the analysis in the previous sections, we define a process for regression model parameterization and selection. The process is illustrated in Figure 6.7 and is comprised of the following steps:

1a. *Relative Ranking with Prepared Data*
For a quick or an initial assessment, the relative ranking shown in the previous section with the prepared data can be used as a criterion to evaluate the regression techniques. The ranking is created with representative and real measurement data and sufficient to characterize the computational cost and complexity of the regression techniques.

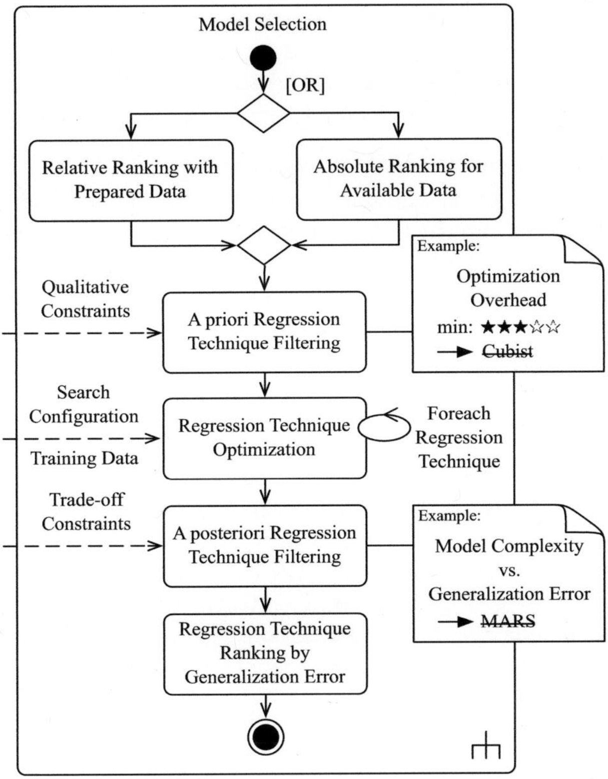

Figure 6.7.: Model Selection Process (dashed: data flow)

1b. *Absolute Ranking for Available Data*
Since the absolute evaluation, such as model creation and evaluation time, depends on the training data, the ranking approach of this chapter can be applied to available data to tailor the selection process to a given scenario. This allows to incorporate absolute constraints in the selection process.

2. *A priori Regression Technique Filtering*
From the set of candidate regression techniques, we use the evaluation and filter the techniques that are not applicable or that do not meet a

qualitative requirement. For example, if a simple model is needed, the more complex techniques can be discarded. Furthermore, techniques with a higher optimization overhead may be discarded to save resources required for finding their appropriate parameterization.

3. *Regression Technique Optimization*

   For each of the candidate regression techniques, the parameters are optimized for the training data at hand to minimize the generalization error of the models. Since this results in usually hundreds of regression model creations, the search configuration of the optimization algorithm is used to regulate the overall number of model creations. For the evaluation, the same fold (data partition) of the training data is used throughout the search as well as across the techniques to ensure a fair comparison.

4. *A posteriori Regression Technique Filtering*

   After the techniques are optimized and their generalization error for the given data is evaluated, they can be analyzed and the quality can be compared to their characteristics to possibly identify trade-offs. As also advised by Kuhn et al. (2013), for example, a more complex technique may be disregarded if it only provides a smaller decrease in generalization error than a simpler technique.

5. *Regression Technique Ranking by Generalization Error*

   The remaining techniques are ranked according to their quality, i.e., the generalization error for the data at hand. The techniques may be post-processed, e.g., to evaluate the goodness-of-fit of the models. Finally, the technique and its parameterization with the highest quality can be selected.

6.4. Process for Modeling of I/O Performance in Virtualized Environments

After the more general presentation in the previous sections, in the following we elaborate on how the regression model selection approach fits in the I/O performance modeling process. We have automated the process to a large extent using our performance evaluation approach introduced in Section 5.4.

Shown in Figure 6.8, the process is comprised of five steps, where steps 3 – 5 are fully automated:

1. *Modeling Target Specification*

   First, the system environment and configuration as well as the main modeling goals are specified. In general, we consider three scenarios: A first scenario is interested in a detailed analysis and evaluation of I/O performance-influencing factors, cf. Section 5.2. A second scenario focuses on a general view of an application workload having application-specific factors. A third scenario analyzes I/O performance interference among multiple virtual machines with a possibly mixed setup of the previous scenarios. For the first scenario when evaluating and modeling the I/O performance-influencing factors, we will show in Chapter 8 how such a model is integrated into software architecture-level performance modeling approaches as part of our big picture presented in Chapter 4. Furthermore, we demonstrate the three scenarios in separate case studies in Section 9.

2. *Measurement Space Configuration*

   Depending on the modeling goals and the system environment configuration, the *measurement space* or *configuration* is defined. This is used to perform the measurements in the next step, and based on it, the *independent variables* used in the following steps are determined as the configuration parameters that are explored in the measurement process.

3. *Systematic Measurements*

   After the measurement space and the scenario are identified, the measurement space is explored using systematic measurements. For the exploration, we use a full factorial design. At this point, heuristics to reduce the number of measurements, e.g., presented by Westermann (2014), could be integrated if required. The performance metrics, e.g., response time and throughput, are used as *dependent variables* in the following steps.

4. *Regression Model Selection*

   The measurements as well as the identification of independent and dependent variables are used as the training data for the regression model selection process, cf. Section 6.7. The selection process will provide a set of optimally parameterized regression techniques with their generalization error for the training data for each dependent variable. If the generalization error is acceptable, the process can continue, otherwise the source of the error needs to be identified and the process is repeated by either refining the measurement space configuration or, if applicable, allowing more complex regression techniques.

5. *Regression-based Performance Modeling*
   Finally, the performance models are created with the whole training data using the best regression technique, where a model is created for each dependent variable.

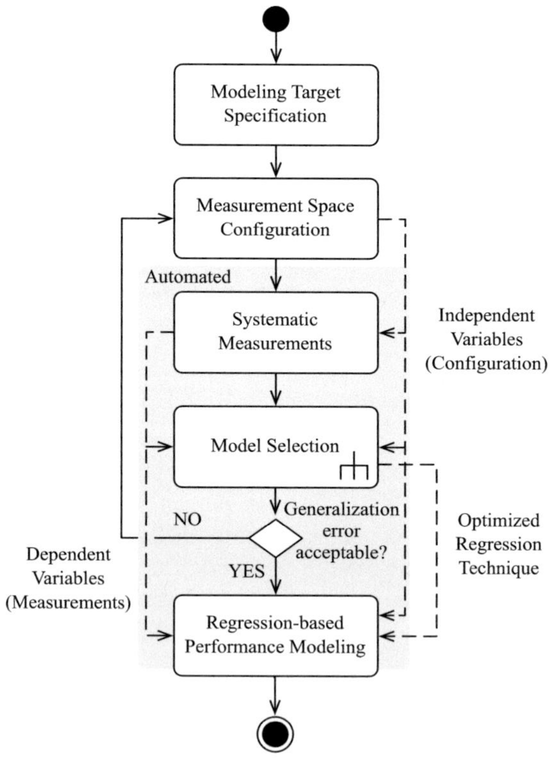

Figure 6.8.: Performance Modeling Process (dashed: data flow)

6.5. Summary

In this chapter, we developed an approach to model the I/O performance in virtualized environments with regression models in an automated process. The main idea is to choose a set of regression techniques, optimally parameterize the techniques for the available training data, and select the best resulting model. To this end, we first formulated the regression technique parameterization as an optimization problem based on k-fold cross-validation. We then developed Stepwise Sampling Search (S3), a deterministic and global search algorithm, to find an optimal parameterization. The benefit of the S3 algorithm is that the number of evaluations and computational complexity can be estimated in advance and adjusted using its configuration if required. Using k-fold cross-validation as a basis, which was our evaluation criterion for the quality of regression models, we analyzed a set of popular regression techniques for their computational overhead and complexity. The model selection process is developed with respect to the evaluated dimensions and chooses from a set of regression models the one with the highest quality. Finally for our I/O performance modeling approach, we constructed the process around the model selection approach automating the steps from i) measuring the system, to ii) optimally parameterizing and selecting a regression technique, through to iii) modeling the system from the measurements.

One notable aspect is the number of measurements required to create a regression model. Since the regression techniques learn the underlying structure of the measurements and create a statistical model, many measurements are needed to cover the measurement space and the possible configurations. In an ideal scenario, the measurements might be provided by the system manufacturer when the hardware infrastructure is developed. An alternative approach to creating the regression models is explicitly modeling the I/O performance of the considered environment, which is the goal of the next chapter. We will show in the following chapter how a complex environment can be analyzed and captured in queueing theory-based models that require more manual effort at first, but allow for reuse of the models with fewer measurements required for model calibration.

7. Using a Tailored Process for Queueing Theory-based Modeling of I/O Hardware and Scheduling Aspects

The previous chapter demonstrated how we optimally learn the I/O performance in virtualized environments from training data using statistical regression analysis. While this approach benefits from its high degree of automation, the caveat of such statistical modeling approaches is that they require a potentially large number of measurements as training data – for every modeled system. To not solely rely on the regression analysis-based models, we also use a queueing theory-based modeling approach to capture the I/O performance in virtualized environments. Such models require a higher amount of manual effort and expertise for their creation, but provide a deeper understanding of the modeled environment and higher reusability by recalibrating the model parameters if the performance in a similar system environment should be captured.

In this chapter, we present a general process tailored to virtualized environments for creating I/O performance models using queueing theory. The specific challenge is to cope with the increasing complexity of the system environment and, despite limited monitoring possibilities, yet to create practical and sufficiently accurate I/O performance models such that the models are able to abstract from the system details. We apply our process and show step-by-step how we use it to model our reference system environment and capture the I/O performance-relevant aspects using only few queueing stations in a queueing Petri net (QPN) model. The key idea is to create I/O performance models using the QPN formalism by observing the I/O performance with measurements and matching the observations to the performance-relevant factors of the system environment to capture them in the model. Overall, the process is demonstrated in a representative environment, but not limited to specific hardware or software.

Before we introduce our approach, in Section 7.1 we first highlight the scientific challenges of the chapter as well as the specific challenges when creating a queueing model of the I/O performance in virtualized environments. We then propose a general, three-phase methodology in Section 7.2 that we use for performance modeling. As part of our methodology, we revisit our reference system environment in Section 7.3 with a focused analysis highlighting the model-relevant aspects of the environment. Section 7.4 and Section 7.5 constitute the main part of this chapter applying our methodology to the system under study to create queueing models capturing the hardware and scheduling aspects, respectively, using the QPN formalism. The prediction accuracy achieved with our modeling approach is evaluated in Section 7.6. The chapter concludes with a summary in Section 7.7.

7.1. Scientific Challenges

The scientific relevance of this chapter is reflected by the publications (Noorshams et al., 2013d; Noorshams et al., 2014c) and the theses we supervised (Rostami, 2012; Rostami, 2014), on which this chapter is based. More specifically, we address the following scientific challenges in this chapter:

Challenge 1 — *What is an appropriate abstraction level for the I/O performance model?*

Finding a good trade-off between complexity and model accuracy is important. On the one hand, too fine-grained models might be difficult to create and calibrate in different environments. On the other hand, too coarse-grained models might be insufficient to predict the performance accurately. As indicated, the abstraction level is also reflected by the required calibration parameters of the model. If there are detailed system parameters and monitoring mechanisms required, for example, the model becomes more complex and this suggests that the model does not abstract enough from specific details.

Challenge 2 — *What is the process to create a queueing theory-based model of I/O performance in virtualized environments?*

In the literature, there are many high-level guidelines how to create a queueing model in general (e.g., Menascé et al., 1994). However, such guidelines are usually relatively abstract to be domain-independent and provide limited insight how to address the specific problem of creating an I/O performance model in virtualized environments, where there is a gap between the increasing complexity of the system environment and the limited monitoring possibilities that are both practically and technically feasible. Here, the challenge is to provide a reproducible, step-by-step process how to tackle this problem and create the I/O performance models.

Challenge 3 — *How can the I/O performance model be created independent from specific hardware environments or monitoring tools?*

Different vendors employ different virtualization architectures as well as monitoring tools with different granularity, details, and observed metrics. To maximize the applicability of our work, it is important not to depend on certain vendors and be independent from specific hardware and software as otherwise the approach might be limited to a specific type of environment.

Using these challenges as a basis, we investigate and demonstrate the following three hypotheses along this chapter:

H1: We can create queueing models that require a small amount of calibration parameters and we can calibrate the models using end-to-end response time measurements only.

H2: We can create queueing theory-based models of I/O performance in virtualized environments in an iterative process.

H3: We can realize the model building process without requiring in-depth or system-specific monitoring tools.

7.2. Methodology

Creating explicit, queueing theory-based I/O performance models in virtualized environments is a non-trivial task. The systems employed in such an environment are typically comprised of multiple physical tiers and even more logical abstraction layers. At the same time, it is often impractical and usually impossible to monitor the entire system environment and the activities inside the layers in full detail.

In this section, we present a step-by-step methodology tailored to the specific problem of I/O performance modeling in virtualized environments. The goal is to provide a reproducible approach for creating the I/O performance models. The main concept is a systematic, iterative process that starts from a simple model and extends it stepwise to capture more and more application scenarios. We will later employ our methodology and demonstrate how it can be used by creating QPN models of our reference system environment. We use the QPN formalism because of its expressive power combining queueing models with Petri net models (cf. Section 3.3). Our three-phased methodology is illustrated in Figure 7.1, where the phases are depicted as gray areas, and is based on established approaches from Menascé et al. (2004) and Bolch et al. (2006). After a system environment analysis and a planning phase, we create an initial model that we iteratively extend to account for more complex scenarios. Each iteration follows the common generic steps in classical performance engineering comprised of performance model *creation*, *calibration*, and *validation* (cf. Kounev, 2006; Menascé et al., 2000; Menascé et al., 2004).

The first phase of our methodology comprises a system environment analysis. We analyze the system setup and identify the performance-relevant system aspects that need to be captured in the model. Typically, these comprise hardware resources, e.g., storage tiers, as well as logical resources, e.g.,

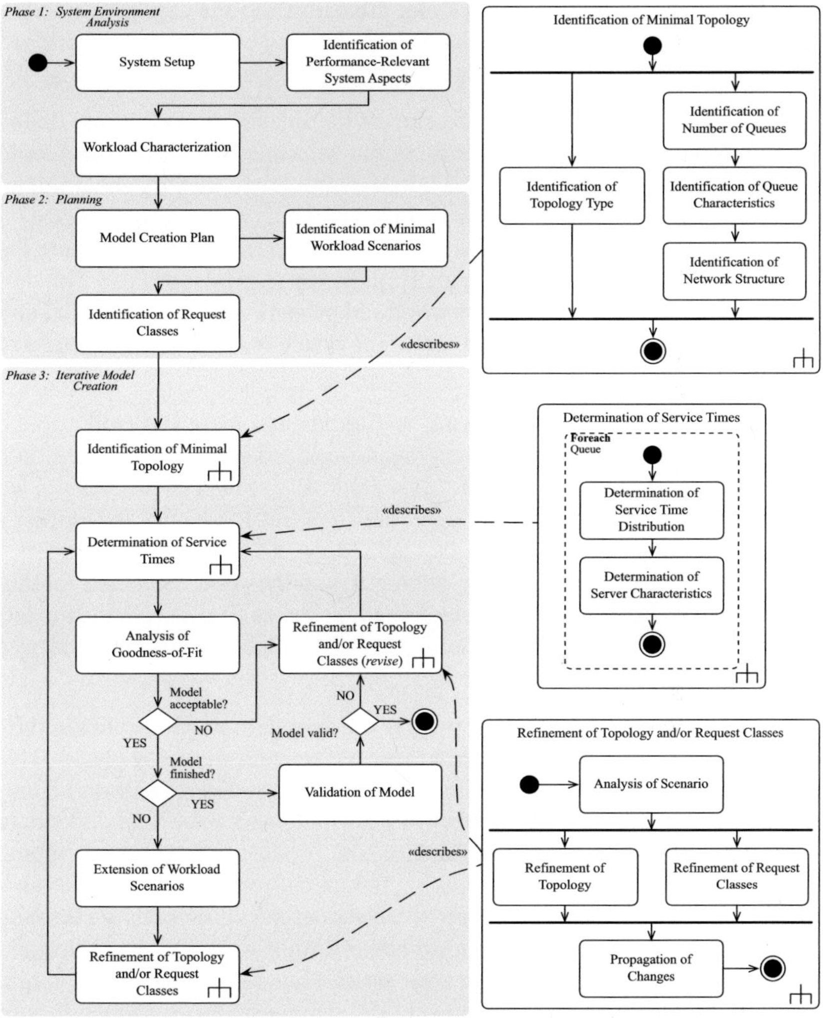

Figure 7.1.: Performance Model Building Methodology in Three Phases

I/O schedulers within the layers along the path from the application to the physical storage. The phase concludes with deriving an appropriate workload characterization.

In the next phase, we plan the creation of the queueing models and define the iterations in the process describing the workload scenarios that should be captured in the models. For the initial iteration, we identify the minimal workload scenarios that should be included in the model as a start. Based on the identified workload scenarios described in the iterations, we define the request classes of the model. Typically, different request types (e.g., read or write requests) as well as further workload properties (e.g., sequential and random requests or requests from different virtual machines) are mapped to different classes.

Finally in the third and main phase, we iteratively create and calibrate the performance model. Based on the minimal workload scenarios and the resulting performance-relevant resources that are involved in their processing, we create an initial QPN model topology. This requires to identify the topology type (i.e., open or closed model), the required queues and their characteristics (e.g., the capacity and scheduling strategy), and the connection and routing between the queues (i.e., the transitions and incidence functions in the model). For each queue, the scheduling strategy is determined either empirically or based on heuristics.

After the structure of the QPN model is created, the model is calibrated by quantifying the service times of each request type at the queueing places. This requires to estimate the service time distribution as well as the server characteristics of the queues, e.g., number of load-independent or load-dependent service stations. To conclude the iteration, the goodness-of-fit of the resulting QPN model is analyzed by comparing the model results with the measurements used to calibrate the model. If the model fits sufficiently well to the measurements, it can be extended to cover further workload scenarios and respective resources involved in their processing. Such extensions might require to refine the model topology and the request classes, which in turn might require to re-calibrate the model.

Finally, we validate the performance model by evaluating the prediction accuracy of the model for workload scenarios that have not been used during the calibration of the model. The workload scenarios typically include both interpolation and extrapolation scenarios using workload configurations within and beyond the calibrated ranges, respectively. We stop if the model is valid, i.e., if the performance predictions by the model reflect the measurements on the real system within a certain acceptable margin of error (Kounev, 2006; Menascé et al., 2004). We consider the model valid if the relative prediction error is below 30 % (cf. Menascé et al., 2000). Otherwise, the model needs to be analyzed and refined to better match the system behavior. If the QPN model is changed, it needs to be re-calibrated and re-validated.

7.3. System Environment Analysis

We next apply our methodology introduced in the previous section to create I/O performance models of our reference system environment introduced in Section 4.2 considering the generic performance-influencing factors identified in Section 5.2. To recall, our reference environment consists of the mainframe IBM System z and the storage server IBM DS8700, cf. Figure 4.2. In this section, we highlight the system setup and the aspects relevant for our I/O performance building process. Furthermore, we derive the workload characterization to consider in the next sections during model building.

7.3.1. System Setup

In our system environment, the storage system DS8700 contains 2 GB non-volatile cache (NVC) and 50 GB volatile cache (VC) and the data is stored in a RAID-5 array comprised of seven disks. Calibration and validation measurements are obtained in z/Linux VMs equipped with multiple shared cores and 4 GB of memory. In order to measure and model the I/O performance and not, e.g., the operating system cache and memory performance, we use direct I/O (using the *O_DIRECT* flag, cf. *open – Linux man page* n.d.) to focus our measurements on the storage performance.

For our calibration and validation measurements, we use the Flexible File System Benchmark (FFSB) (n.d.) because of its fine-grained configuration possibilities allowing the evaluation of specific workload effects on the I/O performance. FFSB runs at the application layer and measures the end-to-end response time covering all logical layers and physical tiers beginning from the application and operating system layers to the physical storage at the storage system. For any configuration, the measurements of FFSB run in two phases. First, a set of 16 MB files is created until the target file set size is reached. Then, the required workload threads are started and they begin to repeatedly issue the specified read or write requests to the previously created file set. The requests of each workload thread are comprised of 256 subsequent read or write requests of a specified size to a randomly chosen file within the file set. If the access pattern of a request type is configured to be sequential, the subsequent requests of each workload thread are directed to consecutive block addresses within the file. Each workload thread issues a request after the previous one has been completed. For any configuration of the measurements with FFSB, we use a measurement time of five minutes. During this time, the benchmark collects multiple millions of measurement samples, typically more than two million.

7.3.2. Identification of Performance-Relevant System Aspects

The performance-relevant aspects that need to be captured in the QPN model can be classified into two groups, physical hardware aspects, which process the requests and cause request queueing, and logical scheduling aspects, which affect the sequence in which the requests are processed. The hardware aspects of our system environment that should be represented in the model are the physical tiers schematically illustrated in Figure 4.2. We consider the two tiers comprised of the caches of the storage server and the RAID array.

The logical aspects can be identified on multiple layers. More specifically, I/O request scheduling typically occurs in the operating system I/O scheduler, the hypervisor, and the storage system. The I/O scheduler needs to be chosen carefully as the default schedulers are not necessarily best suited to virtualized environments (cf. Boutcher et al., 2010). Current understanding is to minimize the scheduling overhead at the operating system-level (cf. Ling et al., 2013). Instead, it is more efficient to use the hypervisor and storage system scheduling algorithms as they are more aware of both the sources of the overall I/O requests as well as the physical layout and topology of the storage tiers. Often, even the hypervisor leaves the scheduling of requests to the storage system because of the aforementioned reasons, which is also the case in our system environment.

Therefore, we split the QPN model building into two parts in the next sections, we model the physical hardware tiers in a homogeneous model first, and then extend it to the logical scheduling aspects of different request types and applications in a heterogeneous model.

7.3.3. Workload Characterization

From the analysis of the performance-influencing factors in Section 5.2, we can derive the general workload characterization as detailed in Section 5.3, which is summarized in Figure 7.2. In general, we characterize the workload along three general dimensions: the intensity of the workload, the requests the workload issues, and the locality of the workload. The workload intensity is accountable for the contention at the storage system, i.e., how many requests are competing for the storage resources. A given request is further characterized by the type of the request (i.e., read or write requests), the access pattern (i.e., sequential or random requests), and the request size. The locality of requests affects the storage caching effectiveness and can be estimated by the overall amount of data that is accessed in the workloads in combination with the access pattern of the requests. Assuming an approximately uniform distribution of requests among the files (or a dominant subset of the files), more specifically, that the requests address the data randomly, the amount of data affects the requests that can be served from cache and from the RAID array. A sequential access pattern of requests can negate this effect by allowing the storage system to anticipate the requested data and staging the data to cache before they are requested.

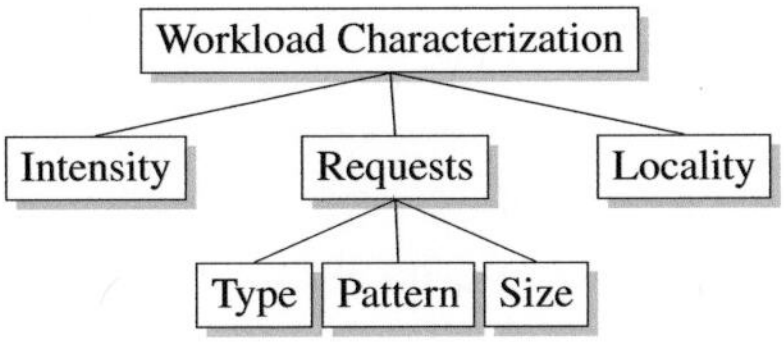

Figure 7.2.: Workload Characterization (simplified from Figure 5.1)

7.4. I/O Performance Models of Storage Hardware Aspects

After analyzing the system environment, in this section we apply our performance model building methodology to our system environment following the steps shown in Figure 7.1. In this section, we are first focused on modeling the physical hardware aspects of the system environment in homogeneous, i.e., single class, models. We will in the next section extend our model considering the scheduling aspects and create a heterogeneous model capturing the scheduling effects between different types of requests and VMs. For model solving, we use a simulation-based approach.

7.4.1. Planning

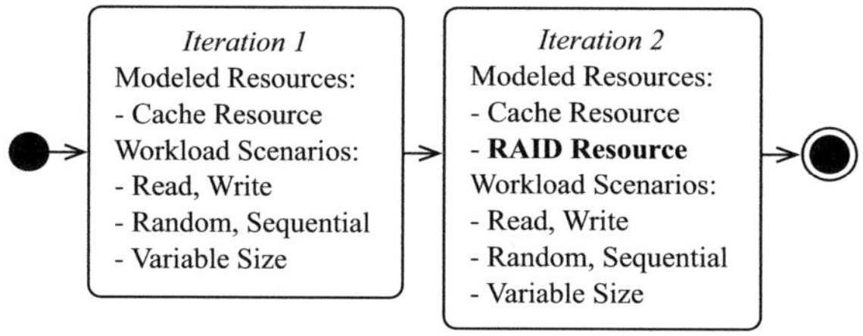

Figure 7.3.: Model Creation Plan for I/O Performance Models of Hardware Aspects

Before creating the performance models, we start planning the model building process. We develop a model creation plan to describe the iterations where we begin with a simple QPN model that is stepwise extended. Based on the results from the previous phase in Section 7.3, we follow the two-step model creation plan shown in Figure 7.3 to create the I/O performance models that capture the performance-relevant system behavior. We analyze the storage system tiers by evaluating the effect of the overall size of data accessed in our workloads on the observed performance. Initially, we only model the cache resource. We consider read and write as well as random and sequential requests. We then add the RAID resource to the models and extend the workload scenarios of the previous step by increasing the overall size of data accessed in the workloads, hereby decreasing the locality of the workload.

In every step, we create the QPN topology and stepwise scale the workload intensity, i.e., the number of clients (threads) configured repeatedly issuing the requests, for calibration.

To create the initial model, we first consider the minimal workload scenarios. We begin with a fixed request size, which we vary in the next step, and only distinguish the request type and the access pattern. To analyze the behavior of the cache resource, we configure the set of files accessed by the workload (i.e., the file set) to 1.25 GB so that it fits in the caches completely. Thus, for the models in this section, we use the following four classes to encode the requests of a given size:

- Random read requests, r_r
- Sequential read requests, r_s
- Random write requests, w_r
- Sequential write requests, w_s

7.4.2. Cache Resource Model

We begin creating the queueing model of the storage system by capturing the performance of the cache resource. More specifically, in this section we describe the first iteration of our model creation plan.

As network topology type, we use a closed model as indicated in Figure 7.4. In general, closed models are the most popular for software systems, since the interactions between application layers are subject to admission control or finite threading limits (W. Wang et al., 2013). The *Clients queueing place* with infinite server queue and service time equal to the client think time represents the arriving requests at the system. The *Storage System subnet place* captures the I/O performance in a separate queueing Petri net. Initially, this subnet consists of one *queueing place* with *unlimited capacity* and *First-Come-First-Served (FCFS)* scheduling strategy representing the cache resource, cf. Figure 7.5. The places are connected using *immediate transitions* that fire as soon as they are enabled.

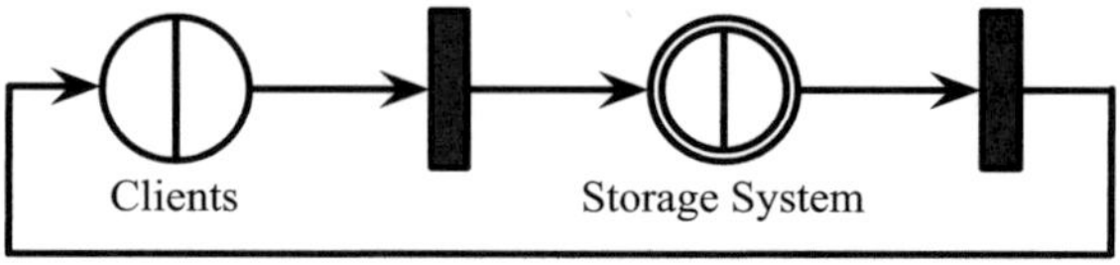

Figure 7.4.: General QPN Model

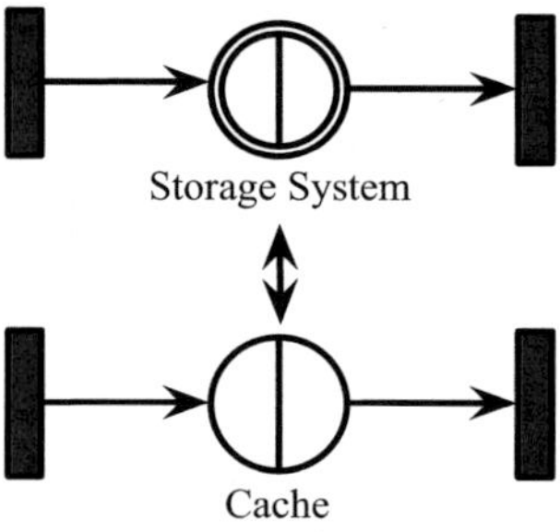

Figure 7.5.: Cache Resource Model

We model the read request and write request service times using *gamma distributions* whose parameters (k_ξ, θ_ξ) are estimated from the measurements for each request class ξ. To estimate the standard deviations σ_ξ, we measure the system under low workload intensity with one thread. Then, we scale the load up to 100 threads in steps of 10 for both read and write requests and vary the request size using 4 KB, 8 KB, 16 KB, 32 KB, and 64 KB requests, i.e., we use the set $\{(t_\xi, s_\xi) \mid \xi \in \{r_r, r_s, w_r, w_s\};\ t_\xi = 10, 20, \ldots, 100;\ s_\xi = 4\text{ KB}, 8\text{ KB}, 16\text{ KB}, \ldots, 64\text{ KB}\}$, where t_ξ and s_ξ are the number of requests and the request size, respectively, as configuration. Since the requests are served from the random access cache resource, we observe that the mean response times of random and sequential workload are approximately equal. Furthermore, we observe a strong correlation between the number of workload threads t_ξ, the request size s_ξ, and the mean read and write response time measurements ρ_ξ^m, respectively, with *coefficient of determination* R^2 of 0.9958 and 0.9966 for random and sequential read requests, respectively, and 0.9999 for random and sequential write requests in the form

$$\rho_\xi^m \approx \sum_{i\in\{0,1\}} \sum_{j\in\{0,1\}} c_{ij} t_\xi^i s_\xi^j \tag{7.1}$$

$$= \sum_{i\in\{0,1\}} a_i t_\xi^i \cdot \sum_{j\in\{0,1\}} b_i s_\xi^j, \tag{7.2}$$

$$a_i, b_i, c_{ij} \in \mathbb{R},$$

i.e., the measurements are linear in the request size s_ξ. Using *mean value analysis (MVA)*, we can estimate the mean read and write request service time $\mu_\xi(s_\xi)$, respectively, for a given request size s_ξ using the *arrival theorem*

$$\rho_\xi^m(t_\xi) = \mu_\xi[1 + \bar{t}(t_\xi - 1)], \tag{7.3}$$

where $\bar{t}(t_\xi - 1)$ is the average number of threads found in the queue by an arriving thread. Applying MVA to our topology and solving for μ_ξ, it holds that

$$\mu_\xi = \frac{\rho_\xi^m(t_\xi)}{t_\xi}. \tag{7.4}$$

We measure the read and write response times, respectively, for request sizes s_ξ of 4 KB, 8 KB, 16 KB, 32 KB, and 64 KB with a given value of t_ξ and fit the mean service times depending on the request size:

$$\mu_\xi(s_\xi) := \sum_{i\in\{0,1\}} c_i s_\xi^i, \; c_i \in \mathbb{R}. \tag{7.5}$$

Then, the parameters of the respective gamma distribution of read and write requests, respectively, are simply

$$k_\xi := \left(\frac{\mu_\xi}{\sigma_\xi}\right)^2 \text{ and } \theta_\xi := \frac{\sigma_\xi^2}{\mu_\xi}. \tag{7.6}$$

To evaluate the goodness-of-fit, Figure 7.6 shows the relative calibration error between the queueing model and the measurements on the system when the number of threads varies between 10 and 100 by increments of 10. For larger read requests (16 KB, 32 KB, 64 KB), the mean error (indicated by small crosses) is less than 7.5 %. For smaller read requests (4 KB, 8 KB), the error is up to approximately 18 %. This is because we use the method of least squares (cf. Section 6.3.1), which minimizes the absolute squared error, to fit the measurements to Equation (7.5), thereby reducing the relative error in these scenarios for larger request sizes at the cost of increased relative errors for smaller request sizes. However, since the measurements are in the range of a few milliseconds, the absolute calibration error for these request sizes is very small. For write requests, fitting the measurements results in very small deviations and the calibration error is always less than 2.5 %.

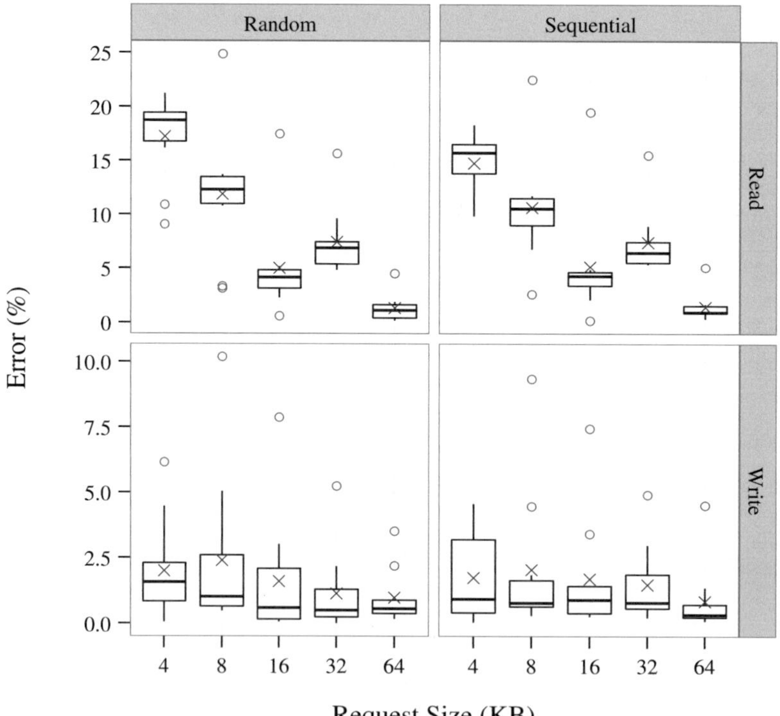

Figure 7.6.: Calibration Error for the Initial Model

7.4.3. Cache and RAID Resource Model

We next extend the cache resource model and describe the second iteration of our model creation plan in which the RAID system is integrated into the queueing model. The goal is to account for scenarios in which the requested data cannot be fully held in the cache. To analyze the behavior of the RAID resource, we configure the file set to be significantly larger (up to 180 GB) than the cache size so that the RAID system needs to be accessed frequently. Since the type of a request has an impact on the QPN topology and the service times, we show the extension stepwise for every request class.

7.4.3.1. Random Read Requests (r_r)

Random read requests are served from the cache if the requested data is available, otherwise they are served from the RAID system and the data is stored in the cache for future accesses. We thus extend the topology by a second queueing place with unlimited capacity and FCFS scheduling strategy representing the RAID resource. Initially, the requests arrive at the cache queue. After being served by the cache, two alternatives are possible for each request: Either the request arrives at the RAID queue with probability p_1 or the request is completed and leaves with probability $p_2 = 1 - p_1$. The topology is illustrated in Figure 7.7.

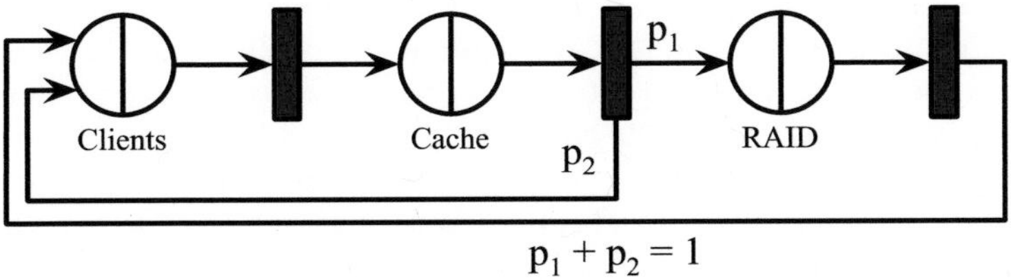

Figure 7.7.: Cache and RAID Resource Model for r_r

Recall that read requests are served by the 50 GB VC if possible. The exact cache hit rate of the workload, however, cannot be easily estimated because of the complex pre-fetching algorithm. Therefore, to estimate p_1 and p_2, we scale the workload up to 100 threads in steps of 10 and the file set size between 80 GB and 180 GB in steps of 20 GB. We observe two different situations, one for a number of threads between 1 and 30, and one for a number of threads between 40 and 100. If the number of threads is between 1 and 30, we observe that the response times follow two clearly separate distributions, one for requests served by the cache and one for requests served by the RAID array. The requests served by the cache can be identified by response times close to the response times when having a fully cached file set. Separating the distributions and calculating the relative number of requests for the two distributions leads to (p_1, p_2) of $(48.32\ \%, 51.68\ \%)$ on average with a standard deviation of 9.64 %. If the threads are between 40 and 100, however, we observe a significant change in the two distributions. If we apply the separation strategy as above, we obtain for p_1 a value of 99.91 % on average with a standard deviation of 0.03 %. We explain this behavior with the increased contention and the cache pre-fetching algorithm as the storage system tries to anticipate future requests and pre-fetches data from the RAID array to the cache. If the load is higher, which is the case for more than 30 threads, the requests served by the cache and RAID resources are no longer clearly distinguishable solely by the distribution of the response times, thus resulting in such a dominant value for p_1.

Before estimating the service times, we analyze the impact of the request locality in a preparation step. Therefore, we scale the file set size between 60 GB and 180 GB in steps of 20 GB such that it exceeds the volatile cache size. We then evaluate the mean response times for 50 and 100 threads with request sizes of 4 KB and 8 KB. For each number of threads and request size combination, interestingly, we observe a strongly natural logarithmic correlation between the file set size and the mean response time. For 50 threads, we observe an R^2 of 0.9902 and 0.9932 for 4 KB and 8 KB requests, respectively. For 100 threads, we observe an R^2 of 0.9803 and 0.9957 for 4 KB and 8 KB requests, respectively. To reflect this in the model, we include the file set size in the service times logarithmically as part of the next step.

To estimate the service times of the second queue, we measure the response times under low workload intensity and scale the intensity stepwise. We again model the second server with gamma-distributed service times. For the calibration, we distinguish between the two situations explained above when discussing the topology. More specifically, we distinguish between case S_1, where the number of threads is less than or equal to 30, and case S_2, where the number of threads is greater than 30. We analyze the response time distributions for number of threads t_{r_r}, request sizes s_{r_r}, and file set sizes f_{r_r} represented by the tuple set $\{(t_{r_r}, s_{r_r}, f_{r_r}) \mid t_{r_r} = 10, 30, 50, 80, 100;\ s_{r_r} = 4\text{ KB}, 8\text{ KB}, 16\text{ KB}, \ldots, 64\text{ KB};\ f_{r_r} = 80\text{ GB}, 100\text{ GB}, \ldots, 160\text{ GB}\}$. Note that the file set cannot be fully cached leading to regular cache misses. We separate the response time distributions in cache and RAID array response times. For each case S_1, S_2 and each queue, we parameterize the mean service times $\mu^c_{r_r}$, $\mu^R_{r_r}$ at the cache and RAID queue, respectively, with the file set size f_{r_r} and fit the mean service times to the cache and RAID response time measurements $\rho^{m,c}_{r_r}, \rho^{m,R}_{r_r}$ such that

$$\rho^{m,*}_{r_r} \approx \sum_{i\in\{0,1\}} \sum_{j\in\{0,1\}} \sum_{k\in\{0,1\}} c_{ijk} t^i_{r_r} s^j_{r_r} \cdot \ln(f_{r_r})^k;\ c_{ijk} \in \mathbb{R}. \qquad (7.7)$$

To simplify the service time parameterization, we prune insignificant terms, i.e., if the p-value of a term in the parameterization is greater than 0.05. We obtain R^2 values of 0.9327, 0.9937, 0.9951, and 0.9917 for the cache(S_1), cache(S_2), RAID(S_1), and RAID(S_2) queues and case S_i, respectively.

Evaluating the goodness-of-fit, Figure 7.8 shows the calibration error for 10, 30, 50, 80, and 100 threads and file set sizes between 80 GB and 160 GB in steps of 20 GB. The mean calibration error is between 8.01 % and 10.21 % depending on the request size, thus, indicating a good fit.

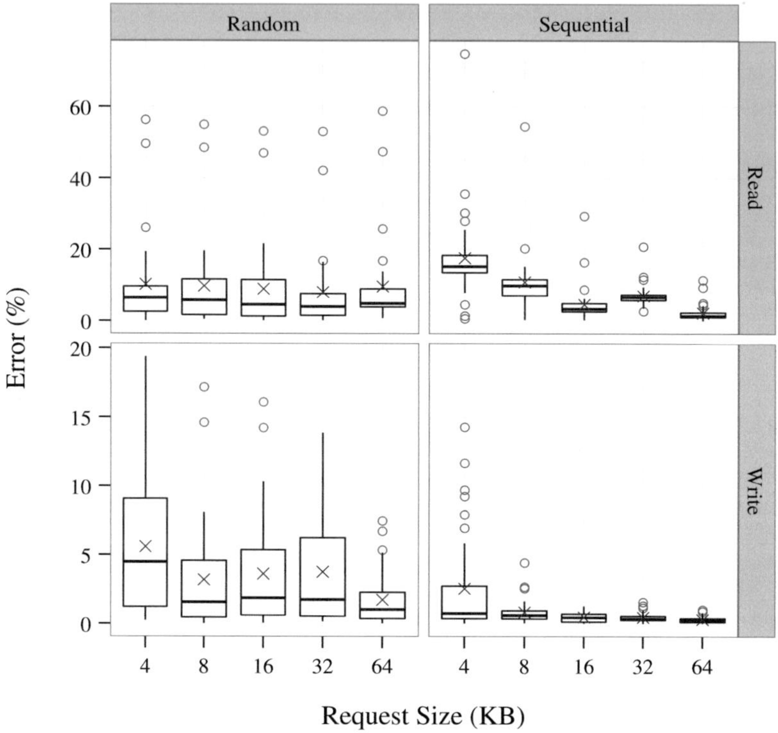

Figure 7.8.: Calibration Error for the Refined Model

7.4.3.2. Sequential Read Requests (r_s)

To determine the topology for sequential read requests, we analyze the effect of the file set size similar to the previous section and scale the file set size between 1.25 GB and until 160 GB by doubling the size. We observe that the requests appear to be almost entirely served by the storage server cache because of the effective pre-fetching algorithm. For large file set sizes significantly exceeding the storage cache, we observe only a slight decrease in performance due to some cache misses. Therefore, we model the system using two cases S_1 and S_2 representing the cache without pre-fetching (i.e., when the file set is fully cached) and the cache with pre-fetching and frequent RAID array accesses (i.e., when the file set size exceeds the cache size significantly), respectively. We use two separate queueing places to represent the cases each. The QPN topology is illustrated in Figure 7.9.

To parameterize the model, we analyze the mean response times similar to the previous analysis and use the tuple set

$$\{(t_{r_s}, s_{r_s}, f_{r_s}) \mid t_{r_s} = 10, 30, 50, 80, 100; \\ s_{r_s} = 4\text{ KB}, 8\text{ KB}, 16\text{ KB}, \ldots, 64\text{ KB};\ f_{r_s} = 80\text{ GB}, 100\text{ GB}, \ldots, 160\text{ GB}\},$$

where t_{r_s} is the number of threads, s_{r_s} is the request size, and f_{r_s} is the file set size.

The cases S_1 and S_2 apply for cached data and data exceeding the cache size significantly, respectively. For the queueing place in case S_1, we fit the mean service time of the server $\mu_{r_s}^{S_1}$ to the measurements $\rho_{r_s}^m$ in the form shown in Equation (7.1). For the queueing place in case S_2, we account for the cache misses due to the file set size f_{r_s} and fit the mean service time of the server $\mu_{r_s}^{S_2}$ to the measurements $\rho_{r_s}^m$ such that:

$$\rho_{r_s}^m \approx \sum_{i \in \{0,1\}} \sum_{j \in \{0,1\}} c_{ij} t_{r_s}^i s_{r_s}^j + c \cdot \ln(f_{r_s});\ c, c_{ij} \in \mathbb{R}. \tag{7.8}$$

Again, we prune insignificant terms and obtain R^2 values for the queues in cases S_1 and S_2 of 0.9962 and 0.9954, respectively.

For the measurement set used during calibration, we obtain an error as shown in Figure 7.8. While for 4 KB requests, the mean calibration error is 17.56 %, for larger requests, the error is less than 10.84 %. Since the absolute calibration error constitutes only a fraction of a millisecond, we can conclude that the model exhibits a reasonable fit.

7.4.3.3. Random Write Requests (w_r)

Unlike read requests, write requests are *always* served by the cache and stored asynchronously on the RAID array. We analyze this effect similar to the previous sections and measure the response times of random write requests while scaling the file set size between 1.25 GB and 160 GB by doubling the file set size stepwise. We observe that the cache is able to buffer the requests for a file set size of up to 5 GB without affecting the performance. If the file set size is exceeds the cache size further, the mean response time increases logarithmically. This effect is similar to the observed effect for sequential read requests. Therefore, we use the same QPN topology as depicted in Figure 7.9. For random write requests, the cases S_1 and S_2 define cached data (i.e., the file set size is up to 5 GB) and uncached data with frequent destaging (i.e., the file set size is greater than 5 GB), respectively.

For the service time estimation, we use the tuple set $\{(t_{w_r}, s_{w_r}, f_{w_r}) \mid t_{w_r} = 10, 20, \ldots, 100; s_{w_r} = 4\text{ KB}, 8\text{ KB}, 16\text{ KB}, \ldots, 64\text{ KB}; f_{w_r} = 1.25\text{ GB}, 2.5\text{ GB}, \ldots, 160\text{ GB}\}$. We parameterize the mean service times of the queue in case S_1 as shown in Equation (7.1). For the queue in case S_2, we use Equation (7.7). For both, we again prune insignificant terms. For the queues in cases S_1 and S_2, we obtain R^2 values of 1 and 0.993, respectively.

Figure 7.8 shows a very good fit of the model to the calibrated measurements with an average error of 5.89 % for 4 KB requests and less for larger requests.

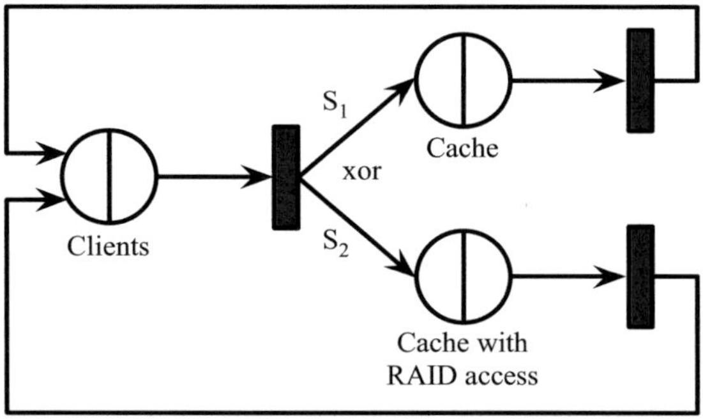

Figure 7.9.: Cache and RAID Resource Model for r_s, w_r

7.4.3.4. Sequential Write Requests (w_s)

Repeating the analysis of the previous section for sequential write requests, we observe that the requests are almost completely buffered by the cache even when we scale the file set size up to 160 GB. Therefore, we keep the QPN topology for sequential write requests as shown in Figure 7.5.

We calibrate the system using a number of threads t_{w_s}, request sizes s_{w_s}, and file set sizes f_{w_s} represented by the tuple set $\{(t_{w_s}, s_{w_s}, f_{w_s}) \mid t_{w_s} = 10, 30, 50, 80, 100;\ s_{w_s} = 4\text{ KB}, 8\text{ KB}, 16\text{ KB}, \ldots, 64\text{ KB};\ f_{w_s} = 1.25\text{ GB}, 2.5\text{ GB}, \ldots, 160\text{ GB}\}$ and fit the service times to the measurements of the similar form shown in Equation (7.8). We obtain an R^2 of 1.0000.

Overall, we obtain an almost perfect fit with a mean calibration error for each request size of up to 2.55 %, cf. Figure 7.8.

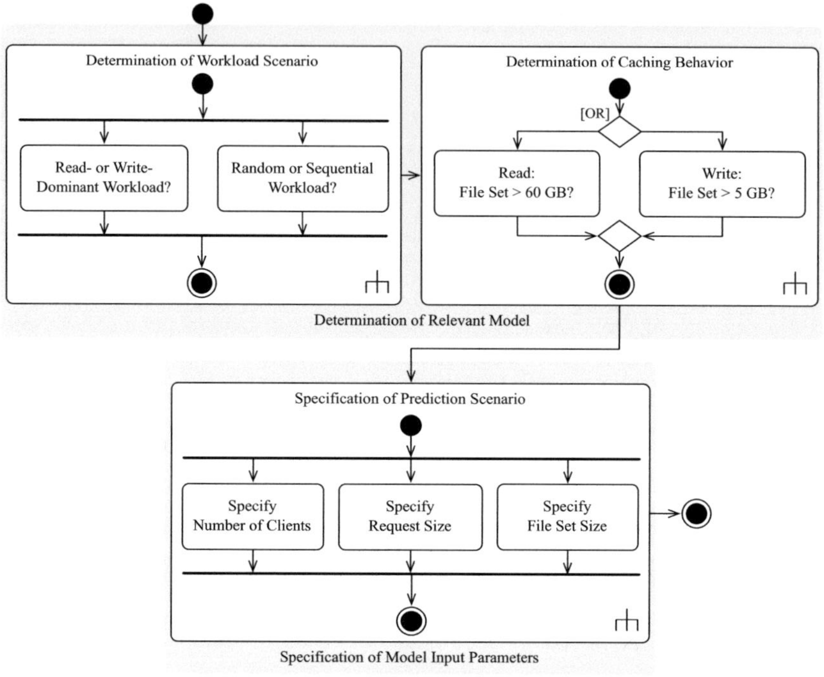

Figure 7.10.: Prediction Process for I/O Performance Models of Hardware Aspects

7.4.4. Prediction Process

After the models are created, Figure 7.10 illustrates the process when using the homogeneous QPN models for prediction. First the workload scenarios as well as the caching behavior needs to be determined to use the relevant model. Then, the prediction scenario has to be specified, which is comprised of the parameters used as input for the model.

The workload scenario can be read or write and sequential or random workload. The caching behavior is derived by the file set size. The empirically determined thresholds are 60 GB and 5 GB for read and write workloads, respectively. If the workload scenario comprises random write requests, for example, the relevant model is the w_r model as illustrated in Figure 7.9 with the respective service time parameterization for write requests. Furthermore, case S_1 applies for the QPN if the file set size is less than or equal to 5 GB; case S_2 applies otherwise.

The parameters used as input for the model are the number of clients, the request size, and the overall size of the file set accessed by the clients. The model then predicts the mean response time for the specified prediction scenario.

7.5. I/O Performance Models of Scheduling and Interference Aspects

In this section, we use the homogeneous QPN model as a starting point and iteratively extend it by applying our performance model building methodology shown in Figure 7.1 to account for scheduling effects among mixed workloads and multiple VMs with differing workload intensities. The goal is to predict the performance of mixed applications as well as to estimate how co-located workloads affect the performance of one another causing I/O performance interference. Before creating the model, we begin with a preparation step.

7.5.1. Planning

We again plan creating the performance models in multiple iterations as preparation for the modeling process. Building upon the model of the previous section, we stepwise extend the model to integrate the scheduling aspects of the environment across different request types as well as different VMs. The steps of the iterations are illustrated in Figure 7.11. Since our goal is to model the scheduling aspects between different types of requests, we can focus the model on capturing the cache resource of the storage system. Consequently, we do not need to distinguish between random and sequential workload as revealed during the model creation of the cache resource in the previous section. We first model mixed read/write requests of a fixed size from one VM. Then, we extend the model to account for workloads on two VMs. In the final step, we relax the request size restriction and account for different read and write request sizes. For each iteration, we create the QPN topology and scale the workload intensity stepwise to estimate the required parameters for calibration.

For the minimal workload scenario in the initial iteration, we consider read and write clients issuing random requests of a fixed size. We configure the set of files so that it fits into the caches. Overall, we distinguish the following aspects in different request classes having all combinations as a given request class:

- VM of the request
- Type of the request (read or write)
- Read and write request size

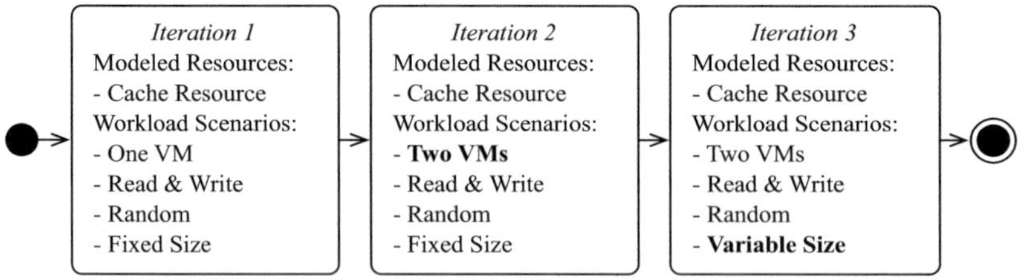

Figure 7.11.: Model Creation Plan for I/O Performance Models of Scheduling Aspects

7.5.2. Heterogeneous Workload Model

The starting point for our heterogeneous I/O performance model is the homogeneous, single-class queueing model as extracted in Section 7.4 and shown in Figure 7.4 and Figure 7.5. In this section, we extend the QPN model to account for performance and interference effects of mixed read/write requests, where we consolidate read and write workloads with different workload intensities, i.e., number of threads. We use the service times estimated as described in Section 7.4.2 and extend the network topology of our initial QPN model.

The workload that is used to create the model consists of different numbers of read and write threads t_r and t_w within one VM. Both are varied between 10 and 50, i.e., we use the set $\{(t_r, t_w) \mid t_\xi = 10, 20, \ldots, 50\}$ as configuration. At this point, we use a read and write request size s_r, s_w of 4 KB. The request size restriction is relaxed at a later stage of the model building process.

As previously mentioned, the request types are distinguished using different token classes. For the two request types, we first introduce separate client places for the tokens. When mixing the requests, we observe that the mean response time predictions of the read and write requests are systematically over- and underestimated, respectively, by the previous model (shown in Figure 7.5). We account for this observation in our QPN model by assigning relative priorities α and β to the read and write requests, respectively, during the processing of the respective request type. More specifically, if requests of both types are waiting to be served at the storage system, a read request is served with probability $\frac{\alpha}{\alpha+\beta}$ and similarly, a write request is served with probability $\frac{\beta}{\alpha+\beta}$. We realize this priority scheduling in the model by separating the queueing place of the storage system into a *Waiting* place and a *Storage* queueing place with a connecting transition whose modes of the incidence function are weighted. The complete topology is illustrated in Figure 7.12. The incidence functions of the two transitions at the storage queueing place are shown explicitly, where α and β are the firing weight that the respective mode of the incidence function fires if both are enabled, and $*$ denotes a wildcard token.

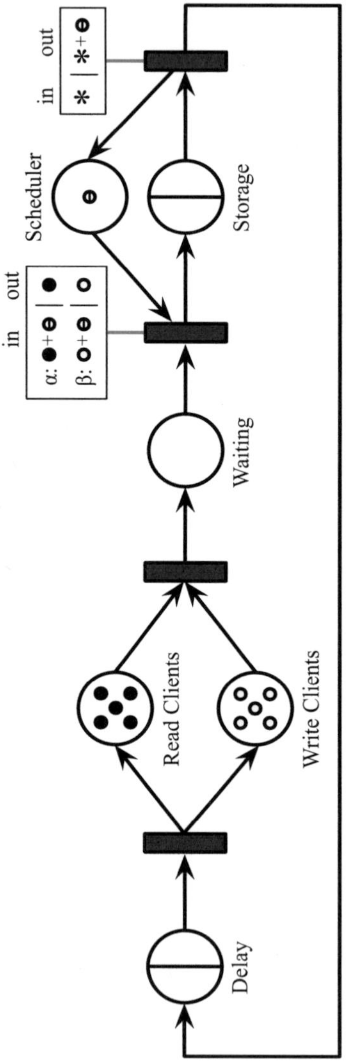

Figure 7.12.: QPN Model for Heterogeneous Workload

To determine α and β, we search for appropriate values using our iterative parameterization algorithm shown in Algorithm 3 for each configuration in our workload scenario. We iteratively search for values for α, β to account for systematic over- and underestimations of the respective mean read and write response times and adjust the priorities accordingly. As input to the algorithm, we use finite ranges $[\alpha_{min}, \alpha_{max}]$ and $[\beta_{min}, \beta_{max}]$ for α and β, respectively, which constitute the search space. While the ranges may be arbitrarily large, they help to focus the search. Furthermore, the search can be parameterized with a precision for the weights δ and a value for the acceptable error $error_{max}$. Similarly, both values can be used to reduce the time required for the parameterization. The search then finds values for α and β that minimize the average prediction error of the QPN model for the given measurement data by systematically correcting the weights, more specifically, the relative weight $\phi := \frac{\alpha}{\beta}$.

To predict the performance of configurations that were not used for calibration, we need a generalization for the weights, i.e., a function for α and β depending on the workload threads t_ξ of request type ξ. To build this function, we use a statistical modeling approach using *Multivariate Adaptive Regression Splines (MARS)*, cf. Section 3.2 and Section 6.3.1. As independent variable, we use the quotient $\frac{t_r}{t_w}$ and as dependent variable, we use the relative weight ϕ. Lines 21 and 22 in Algorithm 3 show how α and β are obtained from ϕ. We use MARS models and optimize the parameterization of the model creation using our S3 algorithm as explained in Section 6.2. For the MARS model, we obtain the function $\phi(t_r, t_w)$ with

$$\phi(t_r, t_w) := \lambda_0 + \sum_{i=1}^{n} \lambda_i h_i \left(\frac{t_r}{t_w}\right), \; \lambda_i \in \mathbb{R}, \tag{7.9}$$

where the h_i are the hinge functions.

For the evaluation of the goodness-of-fit of the resulting QPN model, Figure 7.13 shows a very good fit of the model to the calibrated measurements with an average error of the mean response times of 3.36 % for read requests and 4.80 % for write requests.

Algorithm 3 Parameterization of Request Weights (based on Rostami, 2014)

`Configuration:`
$error_{max} \leftarrow$ Acceptable error
$[\alpha_{min}, \alpha_{max}]$ $(\subseteq A) \leftarrow$ Range for the read weight
$[\beta_{min}, \beta_{max}]$ $(\subseteq B) \leftarrow$ Range for the write weight
$\delta \leftarrow$ Weights precision
  // Measurement data:
t_r, t_w $(\in T) \leftarrow$ Read and write clients
s_r, s_w $(\in S) \leftarrow$ Read and write request sizes
ρ_r^m, ρ_w^m $(\in P) \leftarrow$ Mean read and write response time measurements
  // $A, B, P, S, T \subseteq \mathbb{R}_{>0}$

`Definition:`
$\Psi : T^2 \times S^2 \times A \times B \rightarrow P^2$
  // Prediction function to predict mean read and write response times
  // for a given configuration with the QPN model

`Algorithm:`
$\phi_{min} \leftarrow \frac{\alpha_{min}}{\beta_{max}}$
$\phi_{max} \leftarrow \frac{\alpha_{max}}{\beta_{min}}$
$\phi \leftarrow \frac{1}{2}(\phi_{min} + \phi_{max})$ *// Pivot*
$error_{cur} \leftarrow error_{new} \leftarrow \infty$
do
  $\alpha \leftarrow \lfloor \phi \cdot 10^{\delta} + 0.5 \rfloor$
  $\beta \leftarrow 10^{\delta}$
  $(\rho_r^s, \rho_w^s) \leftarrow \Psi(t_r, t_w, s_r, s_w, \alpha, \beta)$
  $error_{cur} \leftarrow error_{new}$
  $error_{new} = \frac{1}{2}\left(\left|\frac{\rho_r^m - \rho_r^s}{\rho_r^m}\right| + \left|\frac{\rho_w^m - \rho_w^s}{\rho_w^m}\right|\right)$
  if $error_{new} < error_{cur}$ **then**
    if $(\rho_r^m > \rho_r^s)$ **and** $(\rho_w^m < \rho_w^s)$ **then**
      $\phi_{max} \leftarrow \phi$
      $\phi \leftarrow \frac{1}{2}(\phi_{min} + \phi_{max})$
    else if $(\rho_r^m < \rho_r^s)$ **and** $(\rho_w^m > \rho_w^s)$ **then**
      $\phi_{min} \leftarrow \phi$
      $\phi \leftarrow \frac{1}{2}(\phi_{min} + \phi_{max})$
    else
      break *// Exit do-while loop*
    end if
  end if
while $error_{new} < error_{cur}$ **and** $error_{new} > error_{max}$
return (α, β)

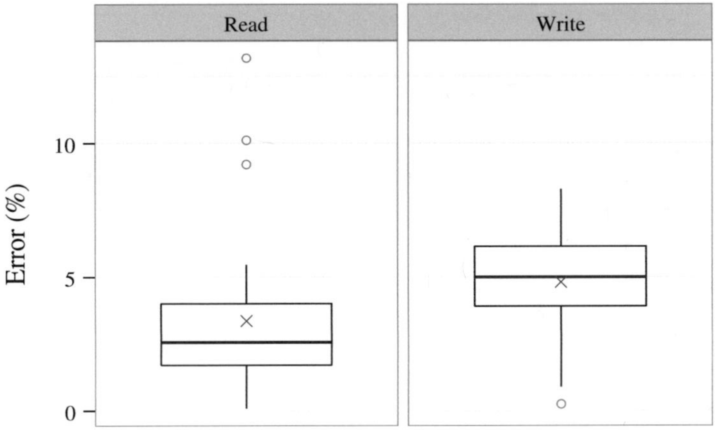

Figure 7.13.: Calibration Error for Heterogeneous Workload Model

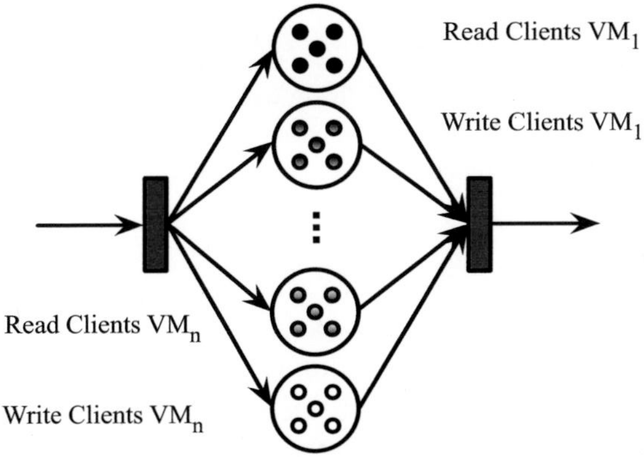

Figure 7.14.: Client Places in Multi-VM Model

7.5.3. Multi-VM Model

We will next extend our model to reflect workloads from multiple VMs and predict their performance behavior. We evaluate the interference how the consolidation of multiple workloads affects the performance of the different requests. To calibrate the model at this point, we use measurements from two virtual machines. We vary the number of threads of each request type and each VM between 10 and 30 in steps of 10. More formally, we use the configuration set $\left\{\left(\vec{t}_r := (t_r^j)_j, \vec{t}_w := (t_w^j)_j\right) \mid t_\xi^j = 10, 20, 30\right\}$, where $j \in \{1, \ldots, v\}$ and v is the number of VMs. The request sizes s_r, s_w of 4 KB are used for the request types.

We extend our topology that is illustrated in Figure 7.12 to integrate the multiple request types of each VM into our model, each modeled as a separate tokens class. Therefore, we will replace the read and write client places with multiple client places for each request type and each VM as shown in Figure 7.14. As a consequence, we have multiple scheduling priorities, i.e., firing weights $\vec{\alpha} := (\alpha_j)_j$ and $\vec{\beta} := (\beta_j)_j$, that define the priority of a read and write request, respectively, of VM j to be served at the storage system.

To obtain an initial estimation of the firing weights, we use the statistical model shown in Equation (7.9), where we use the aggregated number of threads $t_\xi := \sum_j t_\xi^j$ as configuration parameters such that $(\alpha, \beta) = \phi(\sum_j t_r^j, \sum_j t_w^j)$ and obtain $\vec{\alpha} := (\alpha, \ldots, \alpha)$ and $\vec{\beta} := (\beta, \ldots, \beta)$. We observe in the measurements that the mean response time of requests within a request class with more clients are overestimated and vice versa. To account for this observation, we adjust the weights individually for each request class using Algorithm 4 such that requests from request classes with more clients have a higher weight. We use sorting permutation to order the weights according to the number of the corresponding clients. Then, we reduce the weights proportionally depending on the initial weight estimations to have a descent between the request priorities.

The resulting calibration error is summarized in Figure 7.15. For read requests, the average error is 18.05 %. For write requests, the average error is 17.08 %. Generally, the model exhibits a good fit to the measurements obtained using two VMs. In the evaluation, we will extrapolate the number of VMs to evaluate the prediction accuracy of the model.

Algorithm 4 Parameterization of Multi-VM Request Weights (based on Rostami, 2014)

`Configuration:`
$\vec{t}_r, \vec{t}_w \ (\in T^\nu) \leftarrow$ Read and write clients $\quad$ *// $T \subseteq \mathbb{R}_{>0}$*
// Pre-calculation:
$\alpha, \beta \ (\in A, B) \leftarrow$ Read and write weight determined with the statistical model,
i.e., $\phi(\sum t_r^j, \sum t_w^j)$ $\quad$ *// $A, B \subseteq \mathbb{R}_{>0}$*
`Definition:`
$\pi_r, \pi_w : \{1, \ldots, \nu\} \to \{1, \ldots, \nu\}$, $\pi_\xi(\vec{t}_\xi) := (t_\xi^{\pi_\xi(j)})_j$,
such that $\pi_\xi(k) < \pi_\xi(l) \implies t_\xi^{\pi_\xi(k)} \geq t_\xi^{\pi_\xi(l)}$
// Sorting permutations, i.e., π_ξ^{-1} exists

`Algorithm:`
$\vec{\alpha} \leftarrow (\nu \cdot \alpha, \ldots, \nu \cdot \alpha)$
$\vec{\beta} \leftarrow (\nu \cdot \beta, \ldots, \nu \cdot \beta)$
$\vec{t}_r^* \leftarrow \pi_r(\vec{t}_r)$
$\vec{t}_w^* \leftarrow \pi_w(\vec{t}_w)$
if $\alpha = \beta$ **then**
  $\eta \leftarrow 1$
  for $i \leftarrow 2$ **to** ν **do**
    if $t_{r,i}^* \neq t_{r,i-1}^*$ **then**
      $\alpha_i \leftarrow \alpha_i - \eta$
      η++
    end if
  end for
  for $i \leftarrow 2$ **to** ν **do**
    if $t_{w,i}^* \neq t_{w,i-1}^*$ **then**
      $\beta_i \leftarrow \beta_i - \eta$
      η++
    end if
  end for
else
  if $\alpha > \beta$ **then**
    $\delta_r \leftarrow \frac{\alpha - \beta}{\nu}$
    $\delta_w \leftarrow \frac{\beta}{\nu}$
  else
    $\delta_r \leftarrow \frac{\beta}{\nu}$
    $\delta_w \leftarrow \frac{\beta - \alpha}{\nu}$
  end if
  $\eta_r \leftarrow \eta_w \leftarrow 1$
  for $i \leftarrow 2$ **to** ν **do**
    if $t_{r,i}^* \neq t_{r,i-1}^*$ **then**
      $\alpha_i \leftarrow \alpha_i - \delta_r \eta_r$
      η_r++
    else
      $\alpha_i \leftarrow \alpha_{i-1}$
    end if
    if $t_{w,i}^* \neq t_{w,i-1}^*$ **then**
      $\beta_i \leftarrow \beta_i - \delta_w \eta_w$
      η_w++
    else
      $\beta_i \leftarrow \beta_{i-1}$
    end if
  end for
end if
$\vec{\alpha} \leftarrow \pi_r^{-1}(\vec{\alpha})$
$\vec{\beta} \leftarrow \pi_w^{-1}(\vec{\beta})$
return $(\vec{\alpha}, \vec{\beta})$

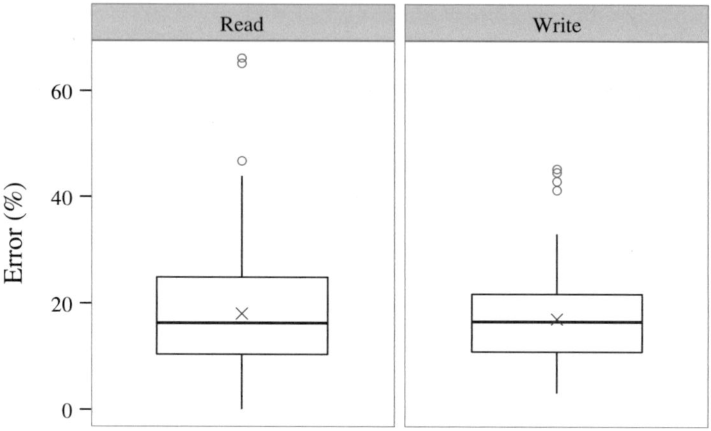

Figure 7.15.: Calibration Error for Multi-VM Model

7.5.4. Variable Workload Model

Finally in the last iteration of our model building process, we will extend our model in this section and integrate variable request sizes. We start with increasing the read and write request sizes simultaneously using measurements in one VM. We then relax the restriction in the next step to allow for differing read and write request sizes. Finally, we extend the model to account for both differing request sizes and multiple VMs.

For the calibration measurements, we use up to two virtual machines and vary the number of threads of each request type and each VM between 10 and 50 in steps of 10 represented by the set

$$\left\{\left(\vec{t}_r := (t_r^j)_j, \vec{t}_w := (t_w^j)_j\right) \mid t_\xi^j = 10, 20, \ldots, 50\right\},$$

where $j \in \{1, \ldots, v\}$ and v is the number of VMs. The read and write request sizes s_r, s_w are both varied from 4 KB to 64 KB by doubling the request sizes, i.e., we use the tuple set $\left\{(s_r, s_w) \mid s_\xi = 4 \text{ KB}, 8 \text{ KB}, 16 \text{ KB}, 32 \text{ KB}, 64 \text{ KB}\right\}$.

Since the total configuration set is very large (5^6 configurations with 5 minutes measurement time each results in more than 7 weeks of total measurement time alone), we use a subset of 60 configurations representative for the configuration space to limit the time required for calibration. More configurations can be considered iteratively as required to further refine the model and improve the prediction accuracy.

The topology of the QPN model is extended similar to the previous extensions to integrate the different request types of each VM distinguishing the request classes and request sizes with separate tokens classes. We use multiple client places, one for each request type and each VM as illustrated in Figure 7.16. For the scheduling of the request classes, we have firing weights $\vec{\alpha} := (\alpha_j)_j$ and $\vec{\beta} := (\beta_j)_j$ that define the priority of a read and write request, respectively, of the j-th VM at the storage system.

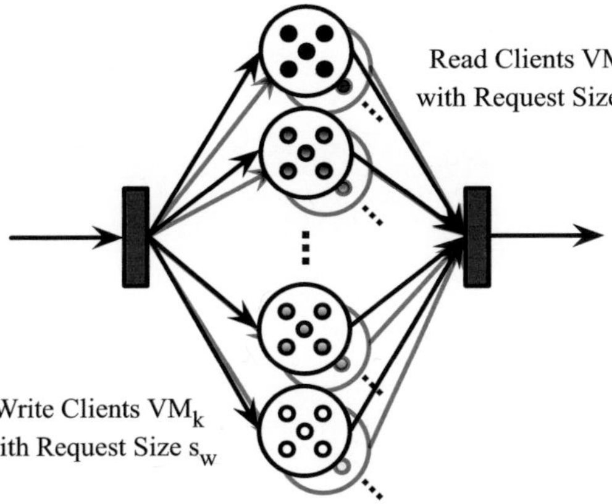

Figure 7.16.: Client Places in Variable Workload Model

As mentioned above, we first analyze measurements where $\frac{s_r}{s_w} = 1$ and $\nu = 1$ using the model obtained in the previous section and calibrate the model with service times obtained as described in Section 7.4.2. Interestingly, what was well-suited for the homogeneous model does not fit well for a mixed workload and we observe a systematic overestimation for increasing request sizes, which is especially significant for read requests. More specifically, the request size and the prediction error correlate logarithmically: $\frac{\rho_\xi^s - \rho_\xi^m}{\rho_\xi^m} \approx \sum_{i\in\{0,1\}} c_{\xi,i} \cdot \ln(s_\xi)^i,\ c_{\xi,i} \in \mathbb{R}$. We explain this observation with the internal optimizations in the storage system and the fact that two different physical caches are involved in the processing of the requests. The read requests affect only the volatile cache, while write requests affect both the volatile and the non-volatile cache, cf. Section 4.2 and Section 7.3. Thus, we account for this observation and re-adjust the modeled read and write service times μ_r, μ_w correcting the overestimation to better reflect the measurements:

$$\mu_\xi^*(s_\xi) := \mu_\xi(s_\xi) \cdot (1 - \Delta_\xi(s_\xi)), \text{ where} \qquad (7.10)$$
$$\Delta_\xi(s_\xi) := \sum_{i\in\{0,1\}} c_{\xi,i} \cdot \ln(s_\xi)^i,\ c_{\xi,i} \in \mathbb{R}.$$

Figure 7.17 shows that the recalibration was successful with a mean error of 8.19 % and 11.64 % for read and write requests, respectively.

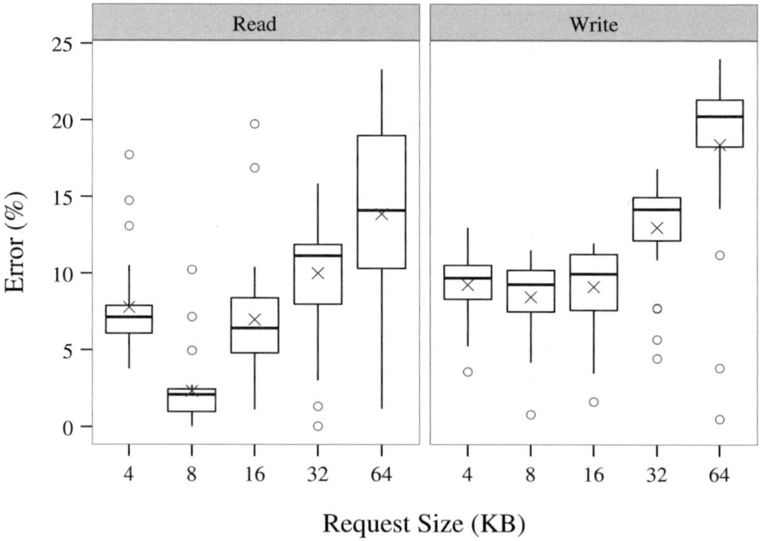

Figure 7.17.: Calibration Error after Service Time Recalibration

To allow differing read and write request sizes, we next also consider the measurements where $\frac{s_r}{s_w} \neq 1$. Similarly, we need to find α and β for the read and write requests, respectively. We will proceed as explained in the earlier section and apply Algorithm 3. To again generalize the weights for prediction, we again use the statistical modeling technique and create a MARS model with independent variables $\frac{t_r}{t_w}$ and $\frac{s_r}{s_w}$, and dependent variable ϕ. Thus, we obtain a relative weight depending on the number of clients and request sizes in the form

$$\phi(t_r, t_w, s_r, s_w) := \lambda_0 + \sum_{i=1}^{n} \lambda_i h_i \left(\frac{t_r}{t_w}\right) + \sum_{i=n+1}^{m} \lambda_i h_i \left(\frac{s_r}{s_w}\right) + \sum_{i=1}^{n} \sum_{j=n+1}^{m} \lambda_{ij} h_i \left(\frac{t_r}{t_w}\right) h_j \left(\frac{s_r}{s_w}\right), \quad (7.11)$$

$$\lambda_i, \lambda_{ij} \in \mathbb{R}$$

We also allow interaction terms in the model as shown above and again optimally parameterize the model creation.

Finally, we use measurements from two VMs. To estimate the priorities for the individual request classes that capture the performance interference effects across the workloads, we propose the calibration algorithm shown in Algorithm 5. The algorithm generalizes the observations similar to the idea of the previous algorithm and calibrates the weights by calculating local weights for each VM and adjusting the weights according to a global view of all workloads. In the algorithm, we use calibration coefficients ε and c that describe the performance interference effect of the read and write requests, respectively. The coefficients can be estimated from the measurements and we use $\varepsilon = 0.3$ and $c = 2$. After estimating the read weights, the algorithm adjusts the write weights of two special cases observed in the measurements, where either the sum of the clients differ in all VMs or there is a single VM with a low number of clients. In the first case, the write weights are adjusted if the weights are not in the same relative order as the aggregated number of clients. In the second case, the write weight of the VM with the single smallest number of aggregated clients is slightly increased.

As a final observation, we include a priority inversion effect we observed in the measurements. If the read request sizes are much larger then the write request sizes (by a factor of four), than the priority of the read and write requests of the VM with the smallest number of read clients are adjusted and inverted.

To conclude the model building process, we analyze the calibration error of the final variable workload model illustrated in Figure 7.18. Across the request sizes, the average error for read and write requests is 21.61 % and 19.11 %, respectively. Thus, the resulting QPN model fits sufficiently well to the measurements such that we can evaluate the models.

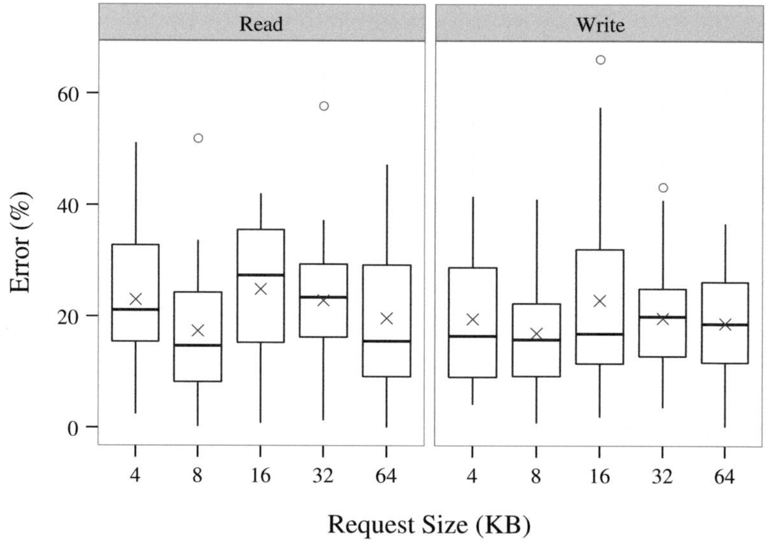

Figure 7.18.: Final Calibration Error for Variable Workload Model

Algorithm 5 Parameterization of Variable Workload Request Weights (based on Rostami, 2014)

`Configuration:`

$\vec{t}_r, \vec{t}_w \ (\in T^\nu) \leftarrow$ Read and write clients $\quad$ *// $T \subseteq \mathbb{R}_{>0}$*

$\alpha^g, \beta^g \ (\in A, B) \leftarrow$ *Global* read and write weight determined with the statistical model, i.e., $\phi(\sum_j t_r^j, \sum_j t_w^j, s_r, s_w)$ $\quad$ *// $A, B \subseteq \mathbb{R}_{>0}$*

$\vec{\alpha}^l, \vec{\beta}^l \ (\in A^\nu, B^\nu) \leftarrow$ *Local* read and write weights *within each VM* j determined with the statistical model, i.e., $\phi_j^l(t_r^j, t_w^j, s_r, s_w)$

$\varepsilon \ (\in (0,1)), c \ (\in \mathbb{N}^*)$ $\quad$ *// parameterization coefficients*

`Definition:`

$\pi_a : \{1,\ldots,\nu\} \to \{1,\ldots,\nu\}, \pi_a(\vec{t}^*) := (t^*_{\pi_a(j)})_j$, such that $\pi_a(k) < \pi_a(l) \Rightarrow t^*_{\pi_a(k)} \leq t^*_{\pi_a(l)}$,

$\pi_d : \{1,\ldots,\nu\} \to \{1,\ldots,\nu\}, \pi_d(\vec{t}^*) := (t^*_{\pi_d(j)})_j$, such that $\pi_d(k) < \pi_d(l) \Rightarrow t^*_{\pi_d(k)} \geq t^*_{\pi_d(l)}$, where $\vec{t}^* := \vec{t}_r + \vec{t}_w$

// Sorting permutations, i.e., π_ξ^{-1} exists

`Algorithm:`

$\vec{\alpha} \leftarrow 0^\nu$
$\vec{\beta} \leftarrow \vec{\beta}^l$
$\gamma \leftarrow \frac{\alpha^g}{\beta^g}$
$\alpha^{max} \leftarrow \gamma \cdot \max_i \{\beta_i^l\}$
$\beta^{max} \leftarrow \max_i \{\beta_i^l\}$
$I^\beta \leftarrow \{\iota \mid \beta_\iota^l = \max_i \beta_i^l\}$
$\alpha_{\iota^\beta} \leftarrow \alpha^{max}, \forall \iota^\beta \in I^\beta$
$\delta \leftarrow |\{t' \mid \exists i : t' = t_r\}| \cdot c$
$\delta_r \leftarrow \frac{\alpha^{max} - \beta^{max}}{\delta}$
$\vec{t}^* \leftarrow \pi_a(\vec{t}_r + \vec{t}_w)$
  // Fit read weights:
$\vec{\alpha} \leftarrow \pi_a(\vec{\alpha})$
$n \leftarrow \pi_a(\min I^\beta)$
if $n \neq 1$ **then**
  for $i \leftarrow (n-1)$ **to** 1 **do**
    if $t_i^* = t_{i+1}^*$ **then**
      $\alpha_i \leftarrow \alpha_{i+1}$
    else
      $\alpha_i \leftarrow \alpha_{i+1} + \delta_r$
    end if
  end for
end if
$n \leftarrow \pi_a(\max I^\beta)$
if $n \neq \nu$ **then**
  for $i \leftarrow (n+1)$ **to** ν **do**
    if $t_i^* = t_{i-1}^*$ **then**
      $\alpha_i \leftarrow \alpha_{i-1}$
    else
      $\alpha_i \leftarrow \alpha_{i-1} - \delta_r$
    end if
  end for
end if
for $i \leftarrow 2$ **to** $\nu - 1$ **do**
  if $\alpha_i = 0$ **then**
    $\alpha_i \leftarrow \alpha_{i-1}$
  end if
end for
  // Adjust write weights in special cases:
$\vec{t}^* \leftarrow \pi_d(\vec{t}_r + \vec{t}_w)$
$\vec{\beta} \leftarrow \pi_d(\vec{\beta})$
$\kappa \leftarrow |\{t' \mid \exists i : t' = t_i^*\}|$
if $\nu = \kappa$ **and** $\exists i, j : i \neq j \wedge t_i^* < t_j^* \wedge \beta_i \geq \beta_j$ **then**
  for $i \leftarrow 1$ **to** ν **do**
    $\beta_i \leftarrow \beta_i \cdot (1 - \varepsilon)$
    if $i > 1$ **then**
      $\varepsilon \leftarrow \varepsilon \cdot \frac{\kappa - 2}{\kappa - 1}$
    end if
  end for
else if $\kappa = 2$ **and** $\exists i \forall j : \beta_i \leq \beta_j \implies i = j$ **then**
  $\beta_\nu \leftarrow \beta_\nu \cdot (1 + \varepsilon)$
end if
$\vec{\alpha} \leftarrow \pi_a^{-1}(\vec{\alpha})$
$\vec{\beta} \leftarrow \pi_d^{-1}(\vec{\beta})$
return $(\vec{\alpha}, \vec{\beta})$

7.5.5. Prediction Process

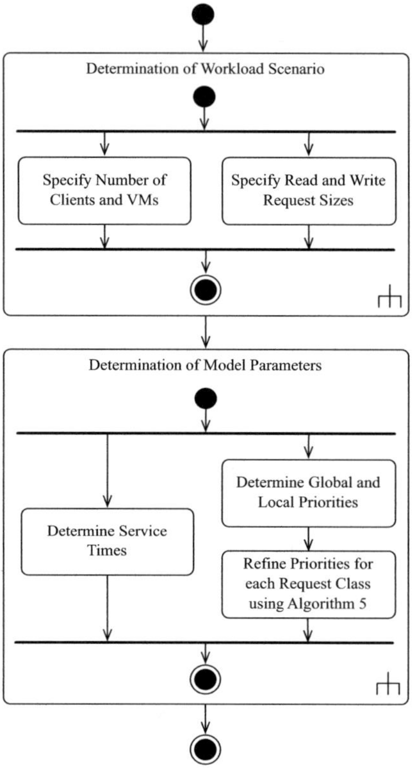

Figure 7.19.: Prediction Process for I/O Performance Models of Scheduling Aspects

The prediction process for using the QPN model is illustrated in Figure 7.19. First, the workload scenario has to be specified, which is used as input for the model. Then, the required model parameters need to be determined such that the model can be solved to obtain the results.

To determine the workload scenario, the number of read and write clients and the number of VMs as well as the read and write request sizes are specified. This information is used as input for the QPN model. For the requests of the workload scenario, the QPN model is parameterized with the service times using Equation (7.5) and Equation (7.10). To capture the scheduling effects with the request class prioritization, first the global and local priorities are determined using the weight model function in Equation (7.11) as indicated in Lines 3 and 5 of Algorithm 5. Finally, Algorithm 5 refines the priorities for the request classes. Using the workload scenario information as well as the model parameterization, the QPN model can be solved to predict the mean response times individually for each request class in the workload scenario. The prediction can be used to predict the performance of a given workload as well as its effect on the co-located workloads.

7.6. Evaluation

In this section, we evaluate our QPN models along multiple dimensions in different scenarios. Similar to the presentation of the I/O queueing models, the evaluation scenarios are grouped targeting the evaluation of the I/O queueing models capturing the hardware aspects and the scheduling aspects. Before presenting the evaluation, we formulate the goals of the evaluation and the questions we address.

7.6.1. Goals and Questions

The main goal of the evaluation is to confirm that the QPN models exhibit a sufficient prediction accuracy for unseen system configurations. Therefore, we set the following two goals regarding the two modeling aspects addressing the respective questions to evaluate the prediction accuracy in both interpolation and extrapolation scenarios:

Goal 1 — *Evaluation of the I/O performance models capturing the storage hardware aspects.*

- *Q1*: What is the response time prediction accuracy when varying the configurations within the calibrated ranges in interpolation scenarios?
- *Q2*: What is the response time prediction accuracy when varying the configurations beyond the calibrated ranges in extrapolation scenarios?

Goal 2 — *Evaluation of the I/O performance models capturing the scheduling and interference aspects.*

Q1: What is the response time prediction accuracy when varying the configurations within the calibrated ranges in interpolation scenarios?

Q2: What is the response time prediction accuracy when varying the configurations beyond the calibrated ranges in extrapolation scenarios?

7.6.2. I/O Performance Models of Storage Hardware Aspects

As indicated above, we evaluate the predictive power of our homogeneous I/O performance models in both interpolation and extrapolation scenarios. For the extrapolation scenarios, we consider extrapolation with respect to the number of clients and extrapolation with respect to the number of VMs. We present the results in full detail for the different request classes and explicitly distinguish between cached and uncached data. An overview of the results is given in Figures 7.20, 7.21, 7.22 and 7.23 as well as Table 7.5.

7.6.2.1. Interpolation

First, we evaluate the I/O performance models in interpolation scenarios where the workload configuration is within the calibrated ranges. For every evaluated workload scenario, we compare mean response time measurements of 200 completely random configurations within the ranges indicated in Table 7.1 with the simulation results obtained using the QPN models. Overall in this section, we evaluate 1200 completely random measurement configurations in total. Regarding the absolute response times, the mean read and write measurements are in the ranges of [0.51 ms, 30.58 ms] and [0.68 ms, 36.05 ms], respectively, depending on the configuration. The prediction results are illustrated in Figure 7.20 and Table 7.5.

For cached data of random read requests, i.e., if the file set size is up to 60 GB, we obtain a mean error of 8.40 %. There are a few higher error values occurring when the file set size is close to 60 GB. We conclude that

Parameter	Range
Request type	{read, write}
Access pattern	{random, sequential}
Request size	[4 KB, 64 KB] rounded to multiples of 512 bytes
Clients	[10, 100]
File set size	[1.25 GB, 180 GB] rounded to multiples of 16 MB

Table 7.1.: Interpolation Configurations for I/O Performance Models of Hardware Aspects

Parameter	Extrapolation Clients
Request type	{read, write}
Access pattern	{random, sequential}
Request size	{4 KB, 8 KB, 16 KB, 32 KB, 64 KB}
Clients	{125, 150}
File set size	{2.5 GB, 40 GB, 80 GB, 160 GB}

Table 7.2.: Extrapolation Configurations (Clients) for I/O Performance Models of Hardware Aspects

for some configurations, the caching effects can be observed already for such file set sizes. For uncached data, we observe a mean error of 8.25 %. A few higher error values can be observed, mainly occurring for low load when the number of threads is less than 20. For such configurations, every small absolute deviation results in a high relative error. For sequential read requests, the mean error is 5.00 %.

For cached data of random write requests, i.e., if the file set size is up to 5 GB, the model yields a mean error of 0.97 % for the evaluated configurations. For uncached data, the model exhibits a high prediction quality. The mean error is 5.19 %. For sequential write requests, the model exhibits a mean error of 1.02 %.

Parameter	Extrapolation 2 VMs
Request type	{read, write}
Access pattern	{random, sequential}
Request size	{4 KB, 8 KB, 16 KB, 32 KB, 64 KB}
Clients	{50, 75, 100}
File set size	{2.5 GB, 40 GB, 80 GB, 160 GB} / #VMs, rounded to multiples of 16 MB

Table 7.3.: Extrapolation Configurations (2 VMs) for I/O Performance Models of Hardware Aspects

Parameter	Extrapolation 2 VMs
Request type	{read, write}
Access pattern	{random, sequential}
Request size	{4 KB, 8 KB, 16 KB, 32 KB, 64 KB}
Clients	{33, 50, 100}
File set size	{2.5 GB, 40 GB, 80 GB, 160 GB} / #VMs, rounded to multiples of 16 MB

Table 7.4.: Extrapolation Configurations (3 VMs) for I/O Performance Models of Hardware Aspects

7.6.2.2. Extrapolation

We next evaluate the prediction accuracy of QPN models in two extrapolation scenarios whose configuration parameters exceed the calibrated ranges significantly.

Extrapolation Clients In the first extrapolation scenario, we increase the workload intensity and set the number of threads to 25 % and 50 % beyond the calibrated range. More specifically, we compare 160 mean response time measurements for all combinations of parameters shown in Table 7.2 against the simulation results obtained using the QPN models. Overall depending on the configuration, the mean read and write measurements are in the ranges of [2.74 ms, 44.86 ms] and [5.29 ms, 59.05 ms], respectively. The prediction results are shown in Figure 7.21 and Table 7.5.

For cached data of random read requests, the model yields a mean error of 7.98 %. It can be observed that in general, the model exhibits a higher accuracy for larger request sizes. Still, for small request sizes, the absolute error is less than 1 ms. For uncached data, the mean error is 4.41 %. For sequential read requests, the model yields a mean error of 5.76 %. The model again exhibits a higher accuracy for larger request sizes.

For cached data of random write requests, the model exhibits a high prediction accuracy. The mean error is 0.60 %. For uncached data, we observe a mean error of 4.11 %. Overall for sequential write requests, a mean error of 0.60 % shows that the model exhibits an excellent accuracy for this scenario.

Extrapolation VMs In this scenario, we increase the load on the system up to 300 % of the calibrated range by using two and three virtual machines. More specifically, we compare 480 mean response time measurements for all combinations of the parameters shown in Tables 7.3 and 7.4 against the simulation results obtained using the QPN models. Depending on the configuration, the mean read and write measurements are in the ranges of [2.12 ms, 90.33 ms] and [4.10 ms, 148.20 ms], respectively. The prediction results are given in Figures 7.22 and 7.23 and Table 7.5.

For cached data of random read requests, the model exhibits a mean error of 9.01 %. For uncached data, the model yields a mean error of 7.62 %. For sequential read requests, the model predicts also well with a mean error of 8.12 %.

For cached data of random write requests, the model exhibits an excellent prediction accuracy with a mean error of 0.62 %. For uncached data, the mean error is 6.32 %. Considering sequential write requests, the model yields a mean error of 0.59 %.

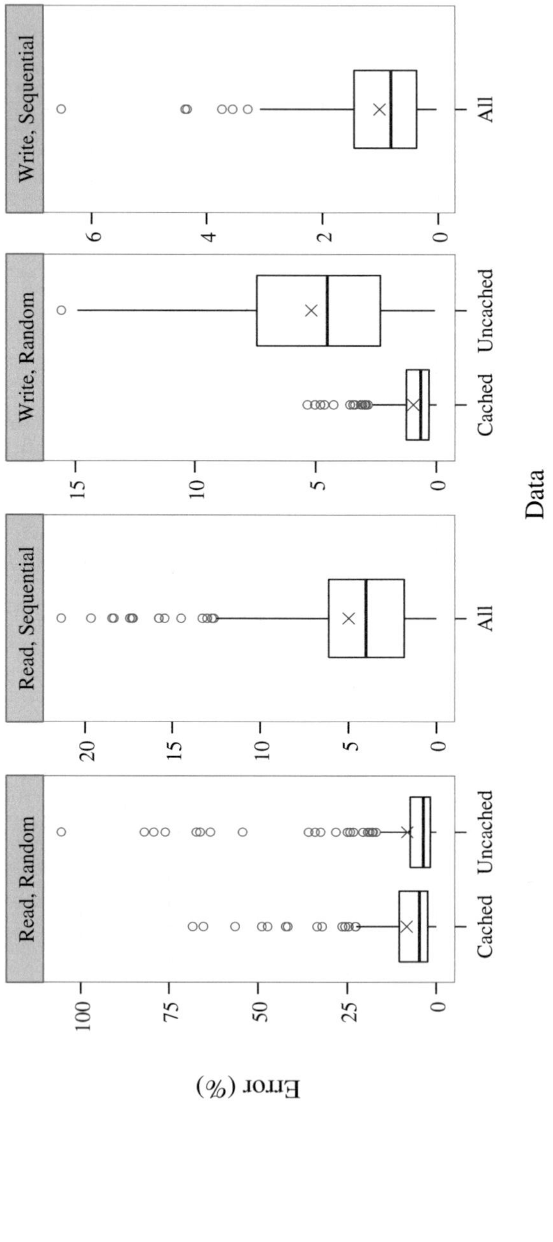

Figure 7.20.: Interpolation Error for I/O Performance Models of Hardware Aspects

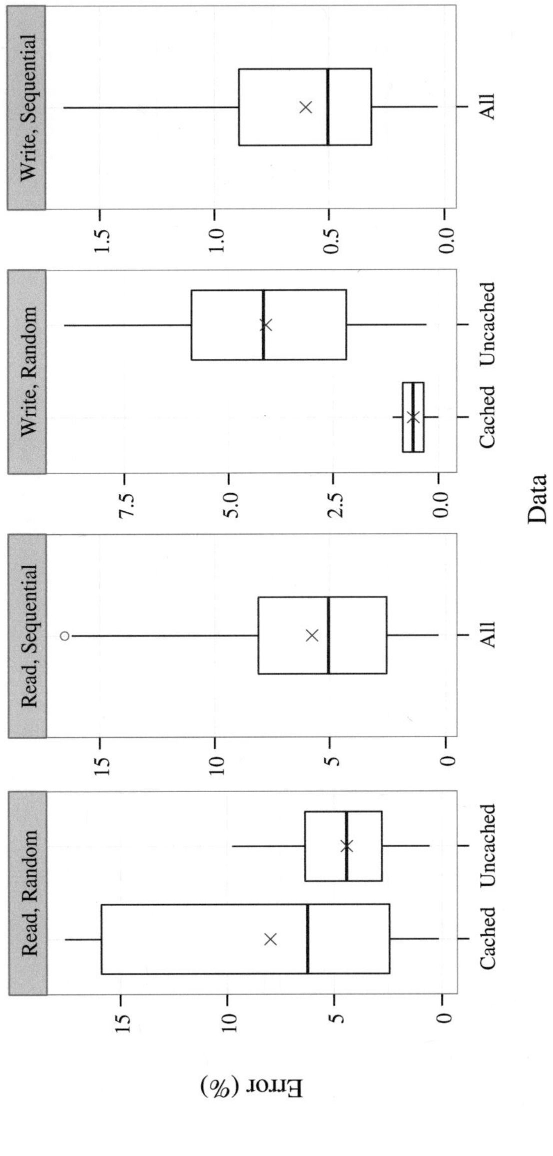

Figure 7.21.: Extrapolation Error (Clients) for I/O Performance Models of Hardware Aspects

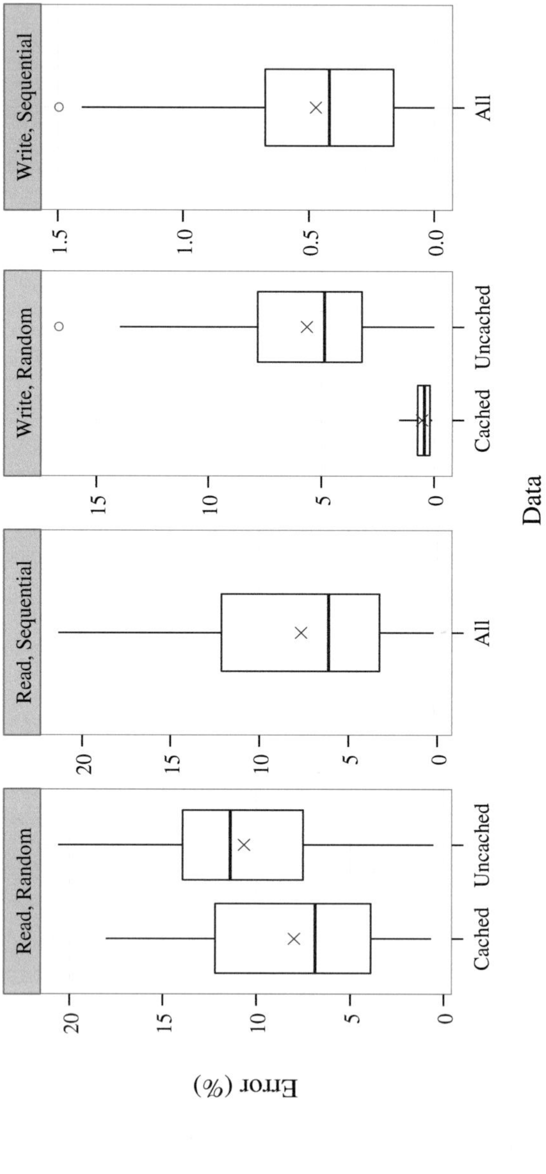

Figure 7.22.: Extrapolation Error (2 VMs) for I/O Performance Models of Hardware Aspects

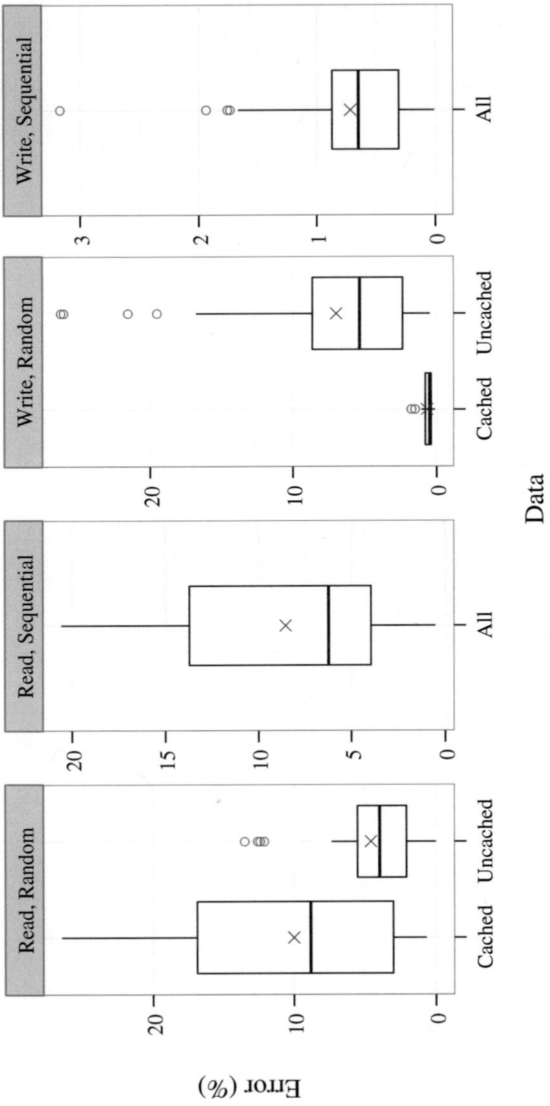

Figure 7.23.: Extrapolation Error (3 VMs) for I/O Performance Models of Hardware Aspects

Scenario	r_r Cached	r_r Uncached	r_s All	w_r Cached	w_r Uncached	w_s All	Mean – $\frac{1}{n}\sum$
Interpolation	8.40	8.25	5.00	0.97	5.19	1.02	4.81
Extrapolation Clients	7.98	4.41	5.76	0.60	4.11	0.60	3.91
Extrapolation 2 VMs	8.01	10.65	7.69	0.55	5.66	0.47	5.51
Extrapolation 3 VMs	10.02	4.59	8.55	0.68	6.98	0.72	5.26

Table 7.5.: Mean Prediction Error for I/O Performance Models of Hardware Aspects (%)

7.6.3. I/O Performance Models of Scheduling and Interference Aspects

Similar to the previous section, we present multiple interpolation and extrapolation scenarios to comprehensively analyze the heterogeneous QPN model. Note that since the workload is heterogeneous, the predictions are individual for each request class. For the sake of presentation, we evaluate the average prediction error across the request classes and present the average errors of the configurations for each scenario. The results are presented next, an overview of the results is given in Figures 7.24, 7.25, 7.26, 7.27 and 7.28 as well as Table 7.11.

7.6.3.1. Interpolation

To evaluate the interpolation quality of the model, we use random workload configurations whose parameters are within the calibrated ranges in the following two scenarios.

Parameter	Scenario I
VMs / Request types per VM	2 / 1
Clients per request type	[10, 50]
Read request size	[4 KB, 64 KB]
Write request size	[4 KB, 64 KB]
(Request sizes in multiples of 512 bytes)	

Table 7.6.: Interpolation Configurations for I/O Performance Models of Scheduling Aspects – Scenario I

Scenario I In our first scenario, we use two VMs each running a read-intensive and a write-intensive workload, respectively. As the VMs are sharing the resources, the I/O requests are mixed at the storage system. We compare mean response time measurements of 100 completely random configurations within the ranges indicated in Table 7.6 against results obtained using the QPN model. Depending on the configuration, the mean read and write measurements are in the ranges of [1.33 ms, 9.84 ms] and [2.72 ms, 23.29 ms], respectively. The prediction results are given in Figure 7.24 and Table 7.11. In this scenario, the QPN model exhibits a very high prediction accuracy. The mean prediction error for read and write requests is 6.49 % and 12.88 %, respectively.

Parameter	Scenario II
VMs / Request types per VM	2 / 2
Clients per request type	[10, 50]
Read request size	[4 KB, 64 KB]
Write request size	[4 KB, 64 KB]
(Request sizes in multiples of 512 bytes)	

Table 7.7.: Interpolation Configurations for I/O Performance Models of Scheduling Aspects – Scenario II

Scenario II In the next scenario, use two VMs with each running mixed read and write workloads competing for the shared storage system. We again compare mean response time measurements of 100 completely random configurations against simulation results obtained with the QPN model. The configuration ranges are shown in Table 7.7. The overall mean read and write measurements are in the ranges of [1.76 ms, 16.55 ms] and [3.27 ms, 62.16 ms], respectively. As shown in Figure 7.25 and Table 7.11, the QPN model also exhibits a high prediction accuracy in this scenario. The mean prediction error for read requests is 21.64 %, while it is 19.51 % for write requests.

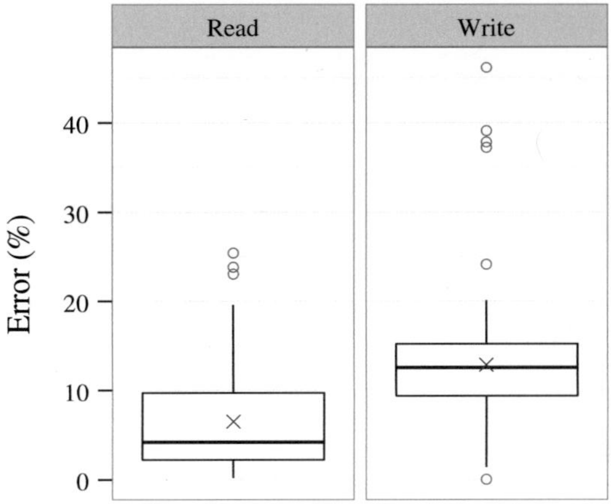

Figure 7.24.: Interpolation Error for I/O Performance Models of Scheduling Aspects – Scenario I

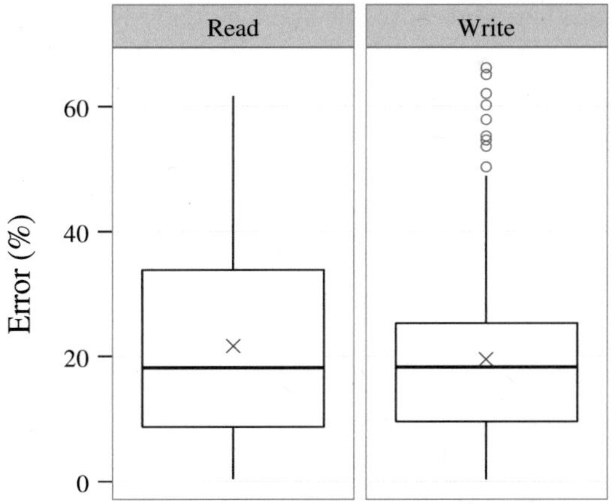

Figure 7.25.: Interpolation Error for I/O Performance Models of Scheduling Aspects – Scenario II

Parameter	Scenario III
VMs / Request types per VM	2 / 2
Clients per request type	(50, 90]
Read request size	[4 KB, 64 KB]
Write request size	[4 KB, 64 KB]
(Request sizes in multiples of 512 bytes)	

Table 7.8.: Extrapolation Configurations for I/O Performance Models of Scheduling Aspects – Scenario III

7.6.3.2. Extrapolation

To evaluate the extrapolation quality, we predict random workload configurations whose parameters exceed the configuration ranges used during calibration in three scenarios.

Scenario III To extrapolate the workload intensity, we increase the number of clients running in each of the VMs. We use 100 completely random configurations using two VMs with mixed workloads and their configuration ranges shown in Table 7.8. For the requests, the mean read and write measurements are in the ranges of [6.94 ms, 28.80 ms] and [24.98 ms, 121.20 ms], respectively. As illustrated in Figure 7.26 and shown in Table 7.11, the mean prediction error for read and write requests is 27.48 % and 27.93 %, respectively.

Scenario IV To extrapolate the number of VMs in this scenario, we add an additional VM, such that three VMs are running in total with mixed workloads each. Overall, we evaluate mean response time measurements of 100 completely random configurations in three VMs with the configuration ranges indicated in Table 7.9. The absolute mean read and write measurements are in the ranges of [3.06 ms, 25.40 ms] and [4.22 ms, 87.93 ms], respectively. For this scenario, the QPN model exhibits a decent prediction accuracy as shown in Figure 7.27 and Table 7.11. The mean read request prediction error is 29.03 %, while the error is 23.35 % for write requests.

Parameter	Scenario IV
VMs / Request types per VM	3 / 2
Clients per request type	[10, 50]
Read request size	[4 KB, 64 KB]
Write request size	[4 KB, 64 KB]
(Request sizes in multiples of 512 bytes)	

Table 7.9.: Extrapolation Configurations for I/O Performance Models of Scheduling Aspects – Scenario IV

Parameter	Scenario V
VMs / Request types per VM	2 / 2
Clients per request type	[10, 50]
Read request size	(64 KB, 128 KB]
Write request size	(64 KB, 128 KB]
(Request sizes in multiples of 512 bytes)	

Table 7.10.: Extrapolation Configurations for I/O Performance Models of Scheduling Aspects – Scenario V

Scenario V In our final scenario, we extrapolate the request sizes and run two VMs with mixed large requests. We use mean response time measurements of 100 completely random configurations with the configuration ranges indicated in Table 7.10. The absolute mean read and write measurements are in the ranges of [7.01 ms, 30.27 ms] and [21.47 ms, 107.50 ms], respectively. For large requests, the QPN model exhibits a good prediction accuracy as summarized in Figure 7.28. The mean read and write request prediction error is 20.11 % and 23.43 %, respectively, as also summarized in Table 7.11.

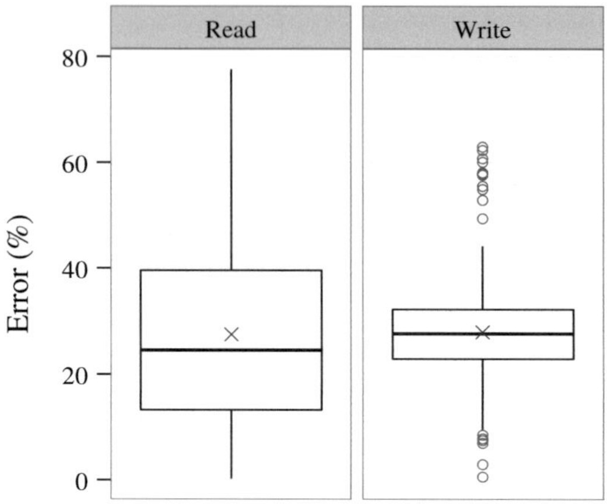

Figure 7.26.: Extrapolation Error for I/O Performance Models of Scheduling Aspects – Scenario III

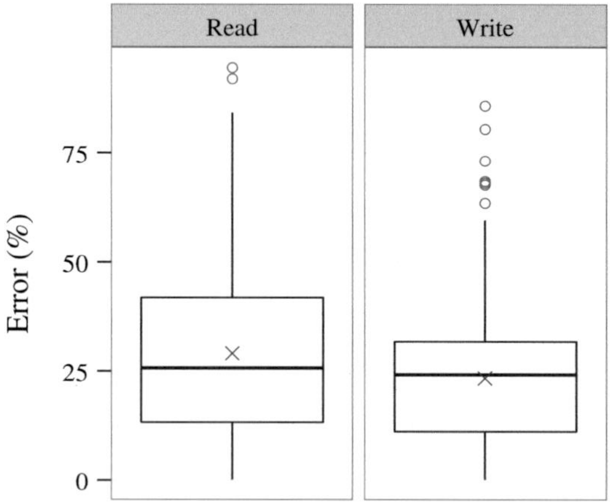

Figure 7.27.: Extrapolation Error for I/O Performance Models of Scheduling Aspects – Scenario IV

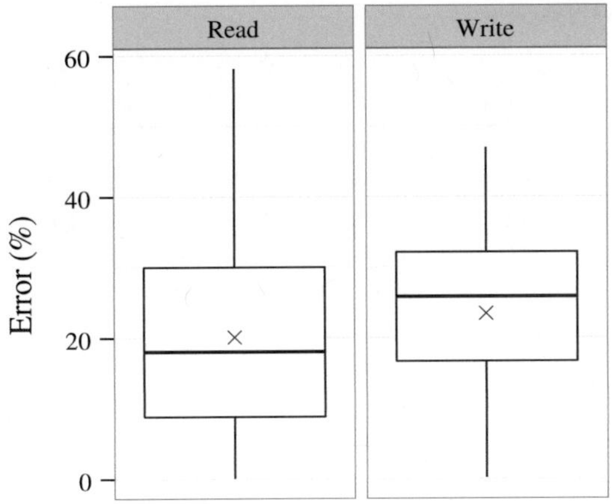

Figure 7.28.: Extrapolation Error for I/O Performance Models of Scheduling Aspects – Scenario V

Scenario	Read	Write	Mean – $\frac{1}{n}\Sigma$
Interpolation			15.13
Scenario I	6.49	12.88	9.69
Scenario II	21.64	19.51	20.58
Extrapolation			25.22
Scenario III	27.48	27.93	27.71
Scenario IV	29.03	23.35	26.19
Scenario V	20.11	23.43	21.77

Table 7.11.: Mean Prediction Error for I/O Performance Models of Scheduling Aspects (%)

7.7. Summary

In this chapter, we proposed a generic, step-by-step process to create explicit, queueing theory-based models of I/O performance in virtualized environment, where there is a limited amount of information for the creation and calibration of a performance model. We applied our process needing end-to-end response time measurements only and showed how it can be used to create QPN models capturing both the hardware aspects and the scheduling aspects between different request types and VMs observed in the considered system environment. The main idea throughout the model building process was to start from a simple model and iteratively extend it to capture more workload scenarios and system aspects. Overall, we were able to model a sufficiently complex system environment using only a few queueing stations and parameters that require calibration if a similar system environment should be captured.

We evaluated our QPN models to predict the mean I/O request response times in both interpolation and extrapolation scenarios for completely random, unseen configurations. Across the different scenarios, the mean prediction error for the I/O performance model capturing the hardware aspects was approximately 5 % in both interpolation and extrapolation scenarios. For the I/O performance model capturing the scheduling aspects, the mean prediction error was approximately 15 % and 25 % for the interpolation and extrapolation scenarios, respectively. Overall, the prediction accuracy is within the required range such that, in conclusion, the explicit model building process relying on measurement information successfully captured the I/O performance effects observed in the considered system environment and can be used as a guideline for creating similar models in other environments.

In this and in the previous chapter, we showed how to create models of the I/O performance in virtualized environments. In the next chapter, we will show how we can use such I/O performance models in approaches for software architecture-level modeling. More specifically, we show how our I/O performance models can be used when modeling software architectures, where there is limited information that can be provided to the models as input about the actual workload running in the environment. Thereby, the created I/O performance models will benefit from an increased applicability. The key question will be how to combine the two abstraction levels, the low-level I/O performance models and the high-level software architecture models.

8. Integrating Storage-level Models into Software Architecture-level Modeling Approaches

Model-based performance prediction approaches at the software architecture level have an increasingly high level of importance. They provide a powerful and practical mechanism for both evaluating design decisions and capacity planning because of the high modeling abstraction level and largely intuitive modeling constructs. The current state-of-the-art software architecture-level modeling approaches, however, struggle to account for the influencing factors of I/O performance in virtualized environments. They are not well-suited for the complex storage infrastructures employed in virtualized environments due to overly simplistic assumptions, which consequently lead to inaccurate performance predictions in that domain.

Our goal in this chapter is to overcome this issue and introduce a novel I/O performance modeling approach at the software architecture level. More specifically, we will focus on component-based software architectures for embedding our performance modeling and prediction approach in a modular and reusable manner. To this end, we employ the storage-level I/O performance models, i.e., the I/O analysis models, created in the previous chapters and combine them with a software architecture-level modeling approach. While, on the one hand, the software architecture model captures and represents the high-level structure of a software application, the I/O analysis model, on the other hand, captures and predicts the I/O performance at the low operating system, hypervisor, and storage infrastructure level. The main question is how to bridge the gap between the two abstraction levels to obtain performance results. For the solution of this discrepancy, we exploit the model-based performance prediction process, where a software architecture model is transformed into a target analysis model, which is a simulation model in our approach. This simulation model is then extended to use the I/O analysis model we developed. Finally, the two models are solved in combination to obtain performance predictions. In the following, the concepts of this combination are elaborated and demonstrated in this chapter.

The outline of this chapter is as follows: Similar to the previous main chapters, we first present the scientific challenges of this chapter in Section 8.1. We then in Section 8.2 introduce the general methodology for the combination of software architecture-level models and I/O analysis models using the model-based performance prediction process as a basis. In Section 8.3, we elaborate on the realization of the combination using the Palladio Component Model (PCM) as a representative software architecture-level performance modeling approach as example. In the end, Section 8.4 summarizes and concludes this chapter.

8.1. Scientific Challenges

Based on the publications (Noorshams et al., 2013c; Noorshams et al., 2014b) and thesis we supervised (Reeb, 2014), this chapter is concerned with the following challenges:

Challenge 1 — *How can software architecture models be combined with I/O analysis models?*

Combining software architecture models and I/O analysis models is not straightforward due to their different abstraction levels. While the software architecture model represents the high-level components and behavior of a software application, the I/O analysis model captures the performance of the low-level I/O requests to a virtualized storage system. They thus differ in the required parameterization and containing information and it is required to bridge the gap between the two model types. It is unclear if the two modeling abstractions can be combined to obtain accurate performance results or, if possible, one of the abstractions needs to be translated or automatically transformed to the other.

Challenge 2 — *How can the I/O analysis models be captured in the software architecture models to be encapsulated and to allow for reuse?*

While a translation or transformation approach might be successful as well, we aim to embed the I/O performance modeling concepts into component-based software architecture models in a combination approach. To this end, an appropriate component concept and interface need to be identified for using the I/O analysis model. This is to ensure the integrity and concepts of component-based software architectures. To increase component reuse, the system-relevant information should be decoupled from the general model with adequate mechanisms.

Challenge 3 — *What is the appropriate abstraction level to model I/O requests at the software architecture level?*

The interface of the I/O analysis model is invoked by I/O requests modeled at the software architecture level. On the one hand, an overly abstract interface specifying only few characteristics of the I/O requests is too coarse-grained to sufficiently parameterize the I/O analysis model and to obtain accurate prediction results. An example of an abstract interface is to specify the mere demand of the I/O request. On the other hand, an overly specific interface requiring too detailed characteristics of the I/O requests is too fine-grained to reasonably obtain the required information. An overly specific interface may require low-level information, such as the targeted device block addresses of the requested data, the mapping of the files to the device block addresses, and the mapping from virtual to physical device block addresses, for instance. Thus, the I/O requests need to be modeled at a balanced abstraction level to allow for their specification by software architects while still sufficient to allow for the derivation of the required parameters for the I/O analysis model.

Challenge 4 — *How can the combined model be solved to obtain performance results?*

Combining the software architecture model with the I/O analysis model might result in coupling different modeling formalisms that need to be solved to obtain performance predictions. Thus, an appropriate coupling of the model formalisms as well as a coupled solution mechanism are required. Such a coupling might require to solve the involved models individually and transfer the results of one model to the other, which can be an iterative process. Another approach might be able to solve the combined models in parallel to integrate the result of one model into the other.

Overall, we can formulate the following four hypotheses that are demonstrated in this chapter addressing the challenges:

H1: We can use the storage-level I/O performance models described in the previous two chapters as I/O analysis model within software architecture-level modeling approaches in a combined modeling approach.

H2: We can encapsulate the I/O analysis model in a well-defined component that can be accessed over its interface.

H3: We can model I/O requests at the software architecture level such that their specification does not require in-depth analysis or system-specific monitoring tools.

H4: We can map the I/O request information provided at the software architecture level on the required parameters of the I/O analysis model in a parallel, simulation-based model solution.

8.2. Methodology

Software architecture models describe the structural and behavioral aspects of an application at a high abstraction level. Performance-aware software architecture modeling approaches use such a description as well as the information on the system infrastructure and resource consumptions of the application, which may be estimated or measured, to predict the performance characteristics of the application. The PCM, as a performance modeling approach of component-based software architectures, uses such information in the model-based performance prediction process to estimate the performance of an application (cf. Section 3.4). Using model transformations to an analysis model, e.g., a simulation model or a queueing model, a PCM model is solved to predict the performance, for example, to evaluate design alternatives and to answer capacity planning questions.

In this chapter, we demonstrate our software architecture-level modeling approach of I/O performance in virtualized environments using the PCM as example, since it is a mature approach with a large amount of validation case studies, e.g., Becker (2008), Becker et al. (2009), Hauck et al. (2009), Huber et al. (2010), Krogmann (2010), and Kuperberg et al. (2008). In the PCM, storage resources are mapped to a single- or multi-server queue, typically with FCFS (First-Come-First-Served) scheduling strategy, and I/O requests are represented merely by their demands that need to be estimated manually for each request type. While this has been shown to be a reasonable degree of abstraction for basic hardware environments (cf. Becker, 2008), storage systems in virtualized environments are much more complex and have diverse influencing factors, cf. Section 5.2. In this section, as part of our big picture introduced in Chapter 4, we first describe how we extend the model-based performance prediction process to realize our approach. Then, we elaborate on how a software architecture model is transformed into a combined analysis model integrating an I/O analysis model as created in the previous chapters to obtain performance results.

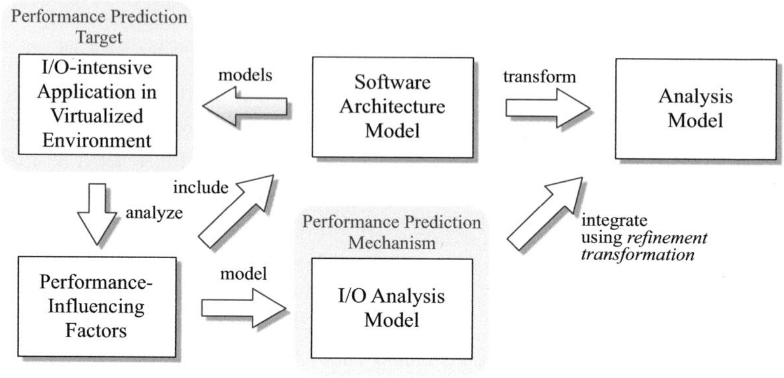

Figure 8.1.: Overview of Combining an I/O Analysis Model with a Software Architecture Model (cf. Figure 4.1)

8.2.1. Extending the Model-based Performance Prediction Process

Our goal is to allow performance modeling approaches at the software architecture level to predict the performance of an I/O-intensive application in a virtualized environment, which is our *performance prediction target*. To realize our goal, we extend the model-based performance prediction process as illustrated in Figure 8.1. More specifically, we combine the I/O analysis model created in the previous chapters, which is the required *performance prediction mechanism*, with the target analysis model of the software architecture model to obtain a combined, typically hybrid analysis model.

As part of our methodology, we start extending the process by analyzing I/O-intensive applications and the system environments to identify the influencing factors of I/O performance in virtualized environments. We then use the factors to create I/O analysis models that capture the performance effects of the factors. To evaluate the factors in the analysis model to which the software architecture model is transformed, the factors also have to be included into the software architecture model. This is achieved by allowing to specify both the static I/O-relevant information, e.g., the configuration of the operating system, and the dynamic I/O request information.

To exploit the additional information in the software architecture model, a prerequisite for the combination of the two modeling abstractions is the design of an *I/O interface* at the software architecture level. The I/O interface defines the I/O requests, whose performance is determined using the I/O analysis model combined with the target analysis model of the software architecture model. The I/O interface includes the required dynamic I/O request information in the software architecture model that is passed as input to the I/O analysis model (e.g., the distinction between read and write requests and their access patterns). Furthermore, the set of static I/O-relevant information is used to parameterize or choose the appropriate I/O analysis model. While the static information needs to be used only once, e.g., when initializing the I/O analysis model, the dynamic I/O request information needs to be passed with every I/O request.

For the combination approach of the high-level software architecture model and its target analysis model with the low-level I/O analysis model, we use refinement transformations described next in more detail.

8.2.2. Refinement Transformation for Performance Predictions

To obtain performance predictions with the software architecture model, we use a *refine transformation* approach as illustrated in Figure 8.2. The refinement transformation integrates the static I/O information into the software architecture model and transforms the software architecture model into an analysis model that is combined with the I/O analysis model. The overall process includes both i) a *completion* transformation (Woodside et al., 2002) enriching the software architecture model as well as ii) an *analysis transformation* to the target analysis model.

The completion transformation takes a software architecture model and generates a refined software architecture model. Here, the software architecture model is refined with the static I/O-relevant information and can be configured, e.g., using feature tree models (cf. Kapova et al., 2009). Depending on the required information, the completion may be realized using a sophisticated higher-order transformation (HOT) (Kapova et al., 2009) or by simply adding the static information where required.

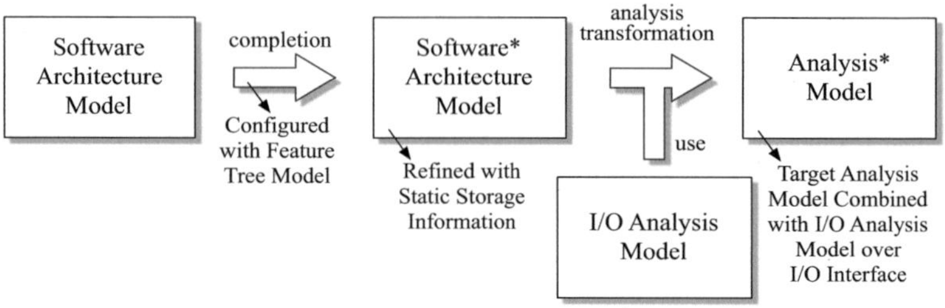

Figure 8.2.: Refinement Transformation from Software Architecture Model to Target Analysis Model

The analysis transformation uses the software architecture model and generates the target analysis model to predict the system performance as in the standard model-based performance prediction process, cf. Figure 3.8. This transformation is extended to use the refined software architecture model and to combine its target analysis model with the I/O analysis model. The combination is realized over the I/O interface using a bridge or adapter depending on the formalisms of the target analysis model and the I/O analysis model. Similar formalisms allow to bridge the requests, different formalisms require to adapt and translate the information of the one formalism to the other. Finally, the combined analysis model is analytically solved or simulated to obtain the performance results of the modeled software architecture.

8.3. Realization of I/O Performance Prediction in the PCM

After the schematic overview and presentation of the general approach, in this section we show how we realize our approach by combining a software architecture model with an I/O analysis model. We present the concepts of the realization using the PCM as example, however, as we do not depend on specific details or implementations of the PCM, our approach can generally be applied to any software architecture modeling approach supporting a model-based performance prediction.

The realization of our approach is structured along four aspects. We start by presenting the modeling concept in the PCM into which we embed our approach. Then, we revisit the I/O analysis model we created in the previous chapters and show how it is defined such that it can be integrated into the software architecture modeling approach. We show how the software architecture model is combined with the I/O analysis model and how it is solved to obtain performance results. Finally, we outline the process how to use our approach for performance prediction.

8.3.1. Modeling Concept

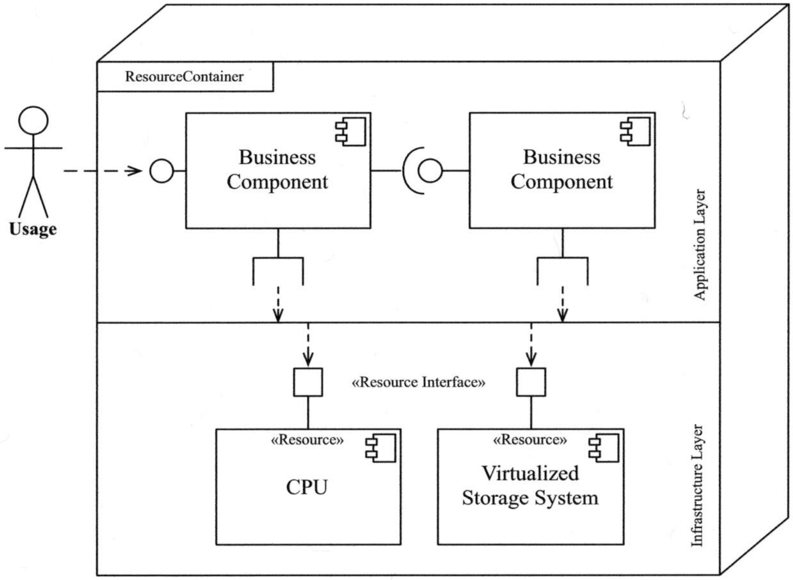

Figure 8.3.: Modeling Concept Overview (derived from Hauck et al., 2009)

To integrate our approach into the PCM, we use the modeling concept of *layered execution environments* of the PCM introduced by Hauck et al. (2009) and illustrated in Figure 8.3. In general for the components comprising the software architecture, we distinguish *business components* running at the *application layer* and *resource* components running at the *infrastructure layer*. The interface of one or more business components may be exposed to users accessing the application and issuing requests to the system. The business components, which capture the application logic, access the CPU and storage as well as further resources in the infrastructure layer using *resource interfaces*, represented by the square interfaces in Figure 8.3. We use the resource concept to capture a virtualized storage system, which accepts the I/O requests issued by the business components, as a storage resource providing its interface as the I/O interface introduced in the previous section to combine the software architecture model with the I/O analysis model.

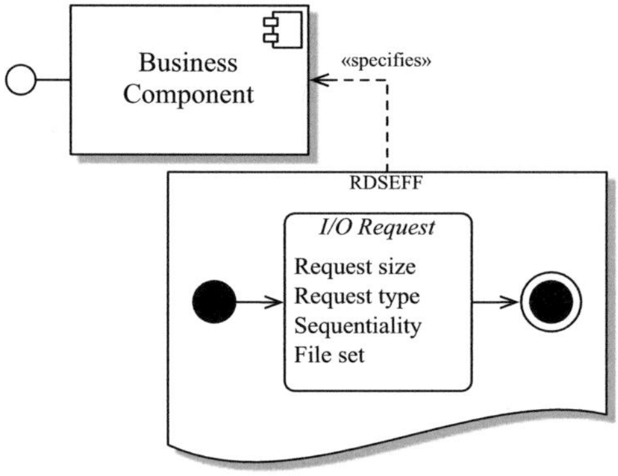

Figure 8.4.: Extended I/O Interface for I/O Requests

The I/O interface captures the representation of an I/O request of a business component. Before our extension, the requests were abstracted as one parameter, the demand to the storage resource. To use the I/O interface, which is extended for approach, the I/O requests of the business components are modeled in the RDSEFF as illustrated in Figure 8.4. Instead of specifying just the I/O demand, which was needed to be estimated manually, the I/O interface is designed comprising the following four parameters, which can be specified from the I/O requests of an application:

- *Request size*: the notion of I/O demand is represented by the I/O request size

- *Request type*: the type of an I/O request can be either a read or write request
- *Sequentiality*: the percentage (or probability) of a sequential access
- *File set*: the name and size of the file set the request is accessing

The need for the former two parameters is apparent, e.g., to distinguish between small read requests and big write requests. The latter two parameters are required to estimate the impact on the caching hierarchy at the storage system. For instance, the parameters indicate if the file set is too large to be held in the caches resulting in regular cache misses or if the requests are sufficiently sequential such that the requested data can be anticipated and pre-fetched by the storage system and the file set size affects the I/O performance only marginally, cf. Section 5.2. The four parameters of the I/O requests can usually be specified by analyzing the workload profile either manually or using monitoring and automated workload characterization techniques, cf. Section 5.4. Even if the application is not available, for example at software design time, because of the tangible nature of the parameters, they can be estimated more easily than the eventual demand the requests will induce at the storage resource.

The storage resource encapsulates the I/O analysis model that is used to capture the I/O performance of the modeled environment. The exact model and its parameterization depends on a number of factors, e.g., which target environment is used and how it is configured. As introduced in the previous section, we use a feature tree model to define the static I/O information, which in our case is used to determine and parameterize the appropriate I/O analysis model. The feature tree model we employ that leads to the I/O analysis model and parameterization is illustrated in Figure 8.5. The *system under study*, i.e., the virtualization architecture and hardware environment, and the *system setup*, i.e., *I/O scheduler* and *file system*, are relevant factors, cf. Section 5.2. Furthermore as shown in the previous chapters, the I/O analysis model can be created with different formalisms with different strengths and weaknesses (cf. Chapter 6 and Chapter 7).

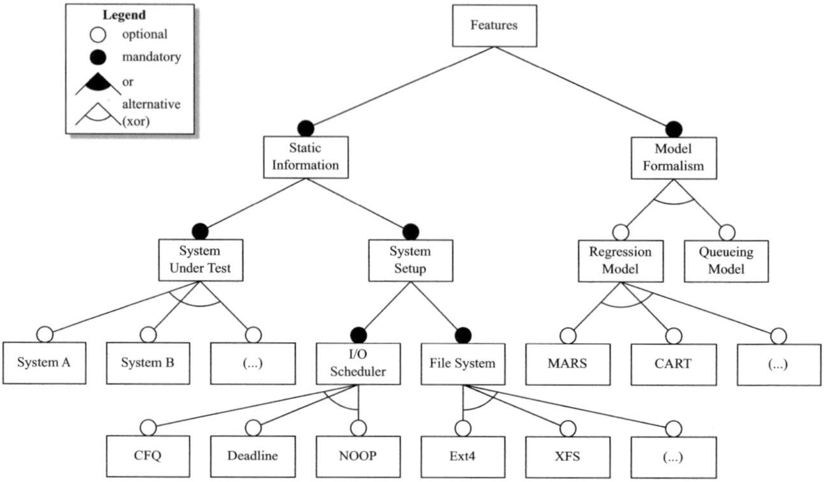

Figure 8.5.: Feature Tree of the I/O Analysis Model (cf. Section 5.2)

8.3.2. I/O Analysis Model

In Chapters 6 and 7, we showed how to create I/O performance models in virtualized environments using regression analysis and queueing theory, respectively. We use these models as I/O analysis models to enhance the software architecture model for performance prediction.

For the I/O analysis model, we identify the workload parameters we need to include based on the workload characterization in Section 5.3. To obtain the I/O analysis model, the performance model is created as presented in the previous chapters. The following eight parameters are captured as workload factors describing the I/O requests that access the storage resource. They are used as input for the I/O analysis models within the storage resource of the software architecture model:

- *Number of concurrent requests*: The contention at the resource is captured by specifying the pending requests as input.
- *Request type (read or write)*: The type of a request affects its scheduling impact and its demand at the storage resource.

- *Mean read request size*: Depending on the type of the currently analyzed request, this size indicates the average demand of either the same or the opposite requests.
- *Mean write request size*: similar as above
- *Read access pattern (random or sequential)*: Indicates if the request can be anticipated and possibly served from caches.
- *Write access pattern (random or sequential)*: similar as above
- *Read/write ratio*: Requests are typically scheduled and prioritized depending on the current request mix.
- *File set size*: Indicates if the accessed files can be possibly cached, thereby serving the requests from caches.

The output of the model is the prediction for the response time of the read and write requests of the modeled applications. This prediction constitutes the delay of the I/O requests including the contention at the storage resource.

8.3.3. Simulation for Solving the Analysis Model

For the two abstraction levels, the software architecture model describes the structure and behavior of the application, whereas the integrated I/O analysis model captures the I/O performance. On the one hand, the information provided at the software architecture level is in form of I/O request descriptions. On the other hand, the information required at the storage resource level is beyond a single I/O request and rather in form of workload currently accessing the storage. To obtain the performance results of the modeled application, it is required to bridge the gap between the two abstraction levels summarized in Figure 8.6. To this end, we use a simulation approach to solve the enhanced PCM model and map the information provided at the software architecture level on the information required at the storage resource level during simulation.

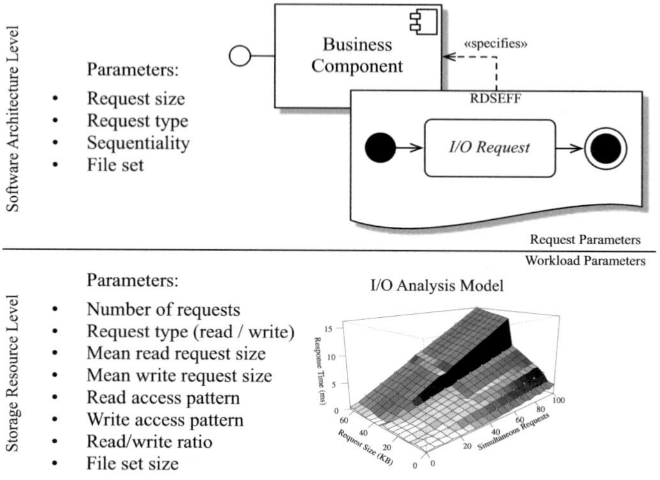

Figure 8.6.: Gap between the Abstraction Levels of the Models

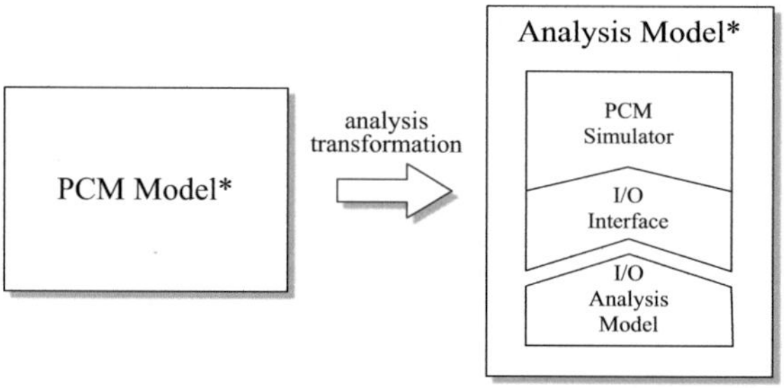

Figure 8.7.: Transformation of the PCM Model

As indicated in Figure 8.2 and realized as schematically shown in Figure 8.7, we transform the PCM Model, which was refined with the static I/O information as indicated by the *, during the analysis transformation to the target analysis model, which is a simulation model in our approach. In the simulation, we integrate the I/O analysis model that is used over the I/O interface to predict the I/O performance. More specifically, we have extended the PCM simulator SimuCom (Becker, 2008) by a virtualized storage system scheduler that maps the information provided by the software architecture model on the information required by the I/O analysis model as illustrated in Figure 8.8 to simulate the I/O delay at the storage resource. The simulation in the virtualized storage system scheduler is comprised of the following five steps:

I. Initially, the I/O requests of the business components issued in the application layer (which are modeled as shown in Figure 8.4 and Figure 8.6) arrive at the storage resource in the infrastructure layer. At this point, all the I/O requests accessing the same storage resource are consolidated even if they originate from different business components or VMs as long as they are sharing the resource component, cf. Figure 8.3.

II. The information of an arriving request is added to an internal *status list* maintained by the simulation, where the information of the last n requests is stored in order to determine and derive the current state of the I/O workload accessing the virtualized storage system (e.g., the current read/write ratio of all requests accessing the virtualized storage system from the application and across the VMs), since such information is not given by a single request itself. The value of n determines the *memory length* and can be estimated from the workload using the average I/O delay $delay_{I/O}^{avg}$ and the number of I/O requests arriving per time $requests_{I/O}^{Intensity}$ as

$$n := delay_{I/O}^{avg} \cdot requests_{I/O}^{Intensity}. \tag{8.1}$$

While this may not always be the best choice, the value of the memory length n can also be calibrated for a given application model.

III. The workload state information is calculated and passed together with the request information to the I/O analysis model. For the calculation, let Γ_r and Γ_w be the stored read and write request sizes, respectively, in the status list. Furthermore, let Π_r and Π_w be the sequentiality of the stored read and write request, respectively, in the status list. Apparently, it holds that

$$|\Gamma_r| + |\Gamma_w| = |\Pi_r| + |\Pi_w| \leq n. \tag{8.2}$$

The inequality holds in the beginning of the simulation, where the number of I/O requests has not reached n yet. From the n-th request on, the equation becomes an equality. The exact information (i.e., the workload parameters) required by the I/O analysis model as given in Section 8.3.2 and Figure 8.6 is passed and calculated from the arriving I/O requests as follows (cf. Section 5.3):

- *Number of concurrent requests*: currently active I/O requests, which are delayed at the storage resource at the current simulation time
- *Request type*: passed by the request
- *Mean read request size*: $\begin{cases} \frac{\sum_{j=1}^{|\Gamma_r|} \Gamma_{r,j}}{|\Gamma_r|}, & |\Gamma_r| > 0 \\ 0, & else \end{cases}$
- *Mean write request size*: $\begin{cases} \frac{\sum_{j=1}^{|\Gamma_w|} \Gamma_{w,j}}{|\Gamma_w|}, & |\Gamma_w| > 0 \\ 0, & else \end{cases}$
- *Read access pattern*: $\begin{cases} \text{sequential}, & |\Pi_r| > 0 \wedge \frac{\sum_{j=1}^{|\Pi_r|} \Pi_{r,j}}{|\Pi_r|} \geq 0.5 \\ \text{random}, & else \end{cases}$
- *Write access pattern*: $\begin{cases} \text{sequential}, & |\Pi_w| > 0 \wedge \frac{\sum_{j=1}^{|\Pi_w|} \Pi_{w,j}}{|\Pi_w|} \geq 0.5 \\ \text{random}, & else \end{cases}$
- *Read/write ratio*: $\frac{|\Gamma_r|}{|\Gamma_r| + |\Gamma_w|}$
- *File set size*: passed by the request

IV. The I/O analysis model, which is encapsulated by the resource component in the infrastructure layer, uses the parameters of the workload state and the arriving request to predict the actual I/O delay for the given request. The I/O analysis model can be the regression model or the queueing model as introduced in the previous chapters.

V. By using the workload state information of the storage resource, in particular the number of concurrent requests, the I/O analysis model inherently captures the contention at the storage resource. Thus, the predicted response time is assigned to the arriving request such that the I/O request is delayed by this calculated value.

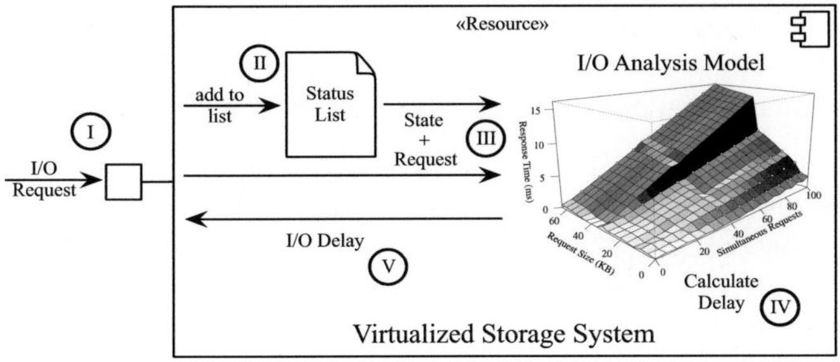

Figure 8.8.: Storage Resource Simulation

8.3.4. Prediction Process

Overall to use the extended PCM, Figure 8.9 illustrates the process to obtain performance predictions of a software architecture model with our approach. The process consists of the following five steps:

1. The initial step is creating the PCM model comprised of the software architecture and its abstract description of the application whose performance should be evaluated. The model is comprised of the four sub-models as before our extension specifying the components and their behavior, the software architecture, the resource environment, and the usage of the system (cf. Figure 3.7). In the description of the component behavior, the information on the I/O requests, which are the parameters of the I/O interface (cf. Figure 8.4), is added.
2. Using an instance of the feature tree model shown in Figure 8.5, i.e., a feature configuration, the required I/O analysis model is determined. The feature tree is used by evaluating the given system configurations and simply choosing the appropriate modeling formalism whose advantages and disadvantages have been highlighted in the previous chapters. For regression models, for instance, the models can be stored in a repository or created with measurements when they are needed, e.g., for a new environment or with another configuration. If a new model is created, it can be created incrementally by leaving some parameters fixed when measuring the environment. For instance, if an application

is known to access a file set of a certain size, this parameter and its effect are not needed to be fully evaluated and the exploration of the parameter can be postponed to save measurement time.

3. After the structural and behavioral model of the application is created, the resource demands of the non-I/O operations of the software architecture model need to be estimated and calibrated, e.g., for CPU resources. For existing applications, this can be achieved using existing techniques for resource demand estimation (cf., e.g., Spinner et al., 2014). Alternatively, the resource demands can be approximated by fitting them to the measured or expected response times of the operations.

4. Additionally, the parameters used for the resource component of the virtualized storage system as illustrated in Figure 8.8 might be calibrated for the application model, e.g., the memory length can be adapted if required.

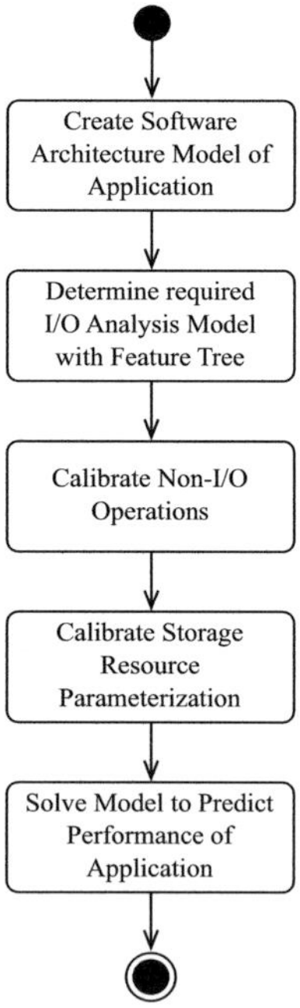

Figure 8.9.: Performance Prediction Steps

5. After the model creation and calibration steps have been completed, the transformation of the software architecture model to the simulation model, which is fully automated, can be triggered to simulate the combined model and obtain performance results. The results can be used to predict the performance of the application, e.g., to predict the effect of an increasing number of users on the application performance.

8.4. Summary

In this chapter, we introduced a generic approach for software architecture-level modeling and prediction of I/O performance in virtualized environments. The main idea is to extend the model-based performance prediction process employed in performance-aware software architecture modeling approaches and integrate I/O analysis models, which we created in the previous chapters, into the target analysis models generated from software architecture models. The degrees of freedom of the I/O analysis model can be expressed in form of a feature tree model, whose instance can be used to determine the required model and its parameterization.

We realized our approach by extending the Palladio Component Model (PCM), a model-based performance prediction approach for component-based software architectures. We introduced a scheduler for virtualized storage systems that uses the I/O analysis model to capture the behavior of I/O requests modeled at the software architecture level and to estimate the storage resource contention. We exploited the concept of layered execution environments employed in the PCM to encapsulate our virtualized storage system scheduler in a resource component that can be used over its resource interface. Based on the analysis of I/O performance-influencing factors in the beginning of this thesis, we identified the required parameters at the resource interface and at the I/O analysis model. To solve the model and obtain performance results, we use a simulation approach, where a PCM model is transformed into a simulation model. During the simulation, we calculate state information of the I/O workload currently accessing the storage (e.g., the read/write ratio) from the I/O requests. The state and the I/O request information is then used as input for the I/O analysis model to determine the delay of a given I/O request at the storage resource.

After this final chapter of our I/O performance prediction approach, we present the validation of this thesis in the next chapter. We present case studies along the path of the thesis contributions as indicated in the big picture of our approach. Put together, the case studies constitute the end-to-end validation starting from the validation of our workload characterization approach until the creation of the I/O analysis models and its integration into the software architecture-level modeling approach as presented in this chapter. Moreover, the validation chapter discusses the applicability of our work reflecting both the strengths and the limitations of our approach.

9. Validation

In this validation chapter, we evaluate our goal of this thesis to enable I/O performance predictions in virtualized environments. For the evaluation of our goal and this thesis, in the following we present multiple case studies along the overall steps of this work presented in the previous chapters beginning from the workload characterization, to the storage-level I/O analysis models, through to the software architecture-level models. A subset of the case studies have been part of our publications (Noorshams et al., 2013a; Noorshams et al., 2014a; Noorshams et al., 2014b; Busch et al., 2015) based on the theses we supervised (Bruhn, 2012; Busch, 2013; Reeb, 2014).

Before presenting the case studies in this chapter in full detail, Section 9.1 first introduces the goals and questions addressed in the case studies. Then, Section 9.2 gives an overview of the experimental setup of the case studies. The first part of the case studies is presented in Section 9.3 evaluating our workload characterization approach. Then, Section 9.4 presents case studies on the storage-level performance predictions based on regression analysis. In Section 9.5, we show a set of case studies for evaluating the performance predictions with our software architecture-level modeling approach. Finally, Section 9.6 discusses the scope and the applicability of our approach.

9.1. Goals and Questions

The goal of this thesis is to allow for performance predictions of I/O-intensive applications in virtualized environments with both practical performance engineering approaches and intuitive software architecture-level performance modeling techniques. We evaluate our approach in multiple case studies grouped into multiple parts. The case studies constitute the end-to-end validation of our work with explicit focus on the proposed aspects of our approach.

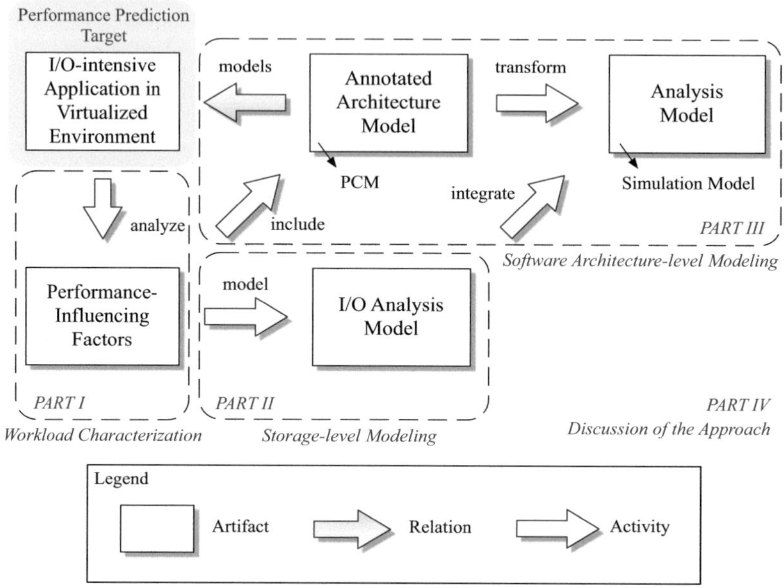

Figure 9.1.: Evaluation Overview (cf. Figure 4.1)

Figure 9.1 shows the four evaluation parts of this chapter along the steps of our big picture given in Chapter 4, where we have abstracted and simplified the big picture showing the extending steps of our work, which are evaluated in this chapter. We first evaluate the workload characterization we obtained from the performance-influencing factors in Part I. We then in Part II evaluate our I/O analysis model and the storage-level performance prediction with regression analysis-based models. Finally, we present case studies evaluating the performance predictions at the software architecture level in Part III. To conclude in Part IV, we discuss the scope of our work addressing the applicability and the limitations.

Each evaluation part is structured hierarchically as elaborated in the following to give an overview of the validation goals and the questions addressed in the validation:

PART I: Workload Characterization – Section 9.3

Goal 1 — *Abstraction level of the workload characterization.*

- *Q1*: Can the workload characterization of a running I/O-intensive application be extracted by the automated process?
- *Q2*: Is the chosen abstraction level of the workload characterization sufficient to capture the influences of an I/O-intensive application on the I/O performance?

Goal 2 — *Feasibility of performance evaluation using the workload characterization.*

- *Q1*: Can the characterized workload that is captured be used to estimate the performance of an I/O-intensive application?
- *Q2*: Can the characterized workload that is captured be used to estimate the performance of consolidated I/O-intensive applications?

PART II: Storage-level Modeling – Section 9.4

Goal 1 — *Prediction accuracy of the regression models.*

- *Q1*: What is the prediction accuracy for I/O performance when using different regression techniques?
- *Q2*: What is the prediction accuracy for I/O performance interference when using different regression techniques?

Goal 2 — *Regression technique optimization.*

- *Q1*: Is the regression technique optimization significantly increasing the model prediction accuracy?
- *Q2*: How many iterations are required to find an optimal parameterization for the regression techniques?

PART III: Software Architecture-level Modeling – Section 9.5

Goal 1 — *Prediction accuracy of the combined model for capacity planning.*

- *Q1*: What is the prediction accuracy for an increasing number of clients when calibrated for a certain number of clients?
- *Q2*: Can the combined model be used to predict the performance of multiple I/O-intensive applications that share the environment?

Goal 2 — *Model overhead and transferability.*

Q1: What is the modeling overhead to predict the performance of an application?

Q2: What is the modeling overhead if the system environment is changed?

PART IV: Discussion of the Approach – Section 9.6

Goal 1 — *Approach applicability.*

Q1: What are the aspects that increase the applicability of the approach?

Q2: What is the prediction accuracy *without* our approach?

Goal 2 — *Approach conclusions.*

Q1: What evaluation criteria of the approach are fulfilled?

Q2: What are the assumptions and limitations of the approach?

9.2. Experimental Setup

Before presenting our case studies, in this section we introduce the software as well as the system environments employed for the validation of our approach.

9.2.1. Tools and Benchmarks

The experimental evaluation in the case studies is fully automated and realized with the *Storage Performance Analyzer (SPA)* (Noorshams et al., 2015), cf. Section 5.4. SPA coordinates and controls the measurements and, if required, monitors the system environment during the measurements. The collected measurements are stored for analysis and used to create regression models in an automated process as needed. SPA has integrated the two benchmarks that are used in the case studies, both use direct I/O (using the *O_DIRECT* flag, cf. *open – Linux man page* n.d.) to specifically measure the I/O performance.

For measurements with fine-grained configurations, we use the *Flexible File System Benchmark (FFSB) (n.d.)* because of its configuration possibilities allowing to evaluate the effects of the I/O performance-influencing factors (cf. Section 5.2). Furthermore, we use FFSB as a basis for the I/O analysis model that is integrated into the PCM, which is the software architecture-level model used in this work (cf. Section 3.4), since the benchmark allows to evaluate the required parameters. Running at the application layer, FFSB measures the end-to-end response time in two phases. First, the target file set of the required size is created using 16 MB files. Then, the specified number of workload threads (clients) are started and they start issuing read or write requests to the file set, where any thread issues a request after its previous one has been completed. The requests of each workload thread are comprised of 256 subsequent read or write requests of a specified size to a randomly chosen file. For a sequentially configured access pattern of a request type, the subsequent requests of the workload threads are directed to consecutive block addresses within a file.

To evaluate composite application workloads, we use the *Filebench (n.d.)* framework. Filebench employs a workload definition language to define and emulate typical I/O-intensive applications. The application workload is comprised of a sequence of file system operations, e.g., a file in a file set is opened, read, and then closed. The sequence is executed repeatedly by a number of workload threads (clients) during the measurement period. To define the application workload, Filebench uses, among others, the following operations:

- *openfile:* Opens a randomly chosen file in the file set.
- *closefile:* Closes an opened file.
- *createfile:* Creates an empty file.
- *deletefile:* Deletes a randomly chosen file.
- *statfile:* Requests the meta information of a file.
- *readwholefile:* Reads a file in one request.
- *writewholefile:* Writes a file in one request.
- *appendfilerand:* Appends a random amount of data (with specified mean size) to a file.

Listing 9.1: File Server Workload

```
File set:
  - number of files = 10000
  - mean file size = 128 KB
  - file preallocation = 80 %
Threads:
  - 50 (default)
Operations:
  - createfile
  - writewholefile
  - closefile
  - openfile
  - appendfilerand, mean size = 16 KB
  - closefile
  - openfile
  - readwholefile
  - closefile
  - deletefile
  - statfile
```

In the case studies, we use a *file server* and a *mail server* application that are defined using the above operations as shown in Listing 9.1 and Listing 9.2, respectively. In contrast to FFSB, the file sets of the workloads in Filebench are not necessarily fully created before the workload threads start issuing the requests.

9.2.2. System Environments

In the case studies, we use two representative, state-of-the-art server environments to validate our approach: A *Sun Fire* environment and an *IBM System z* environment introduced in the next two sections.

Listing 9.2: Mail Server Workload

```
File set:
  - number of files = 50000
  - mean file size = 16 KB
  - file preallocation = 80 %
Threads:
  - 16 (default)
Operations:
  - deletefile
  - createfile
  - appendfilerand, mean size = 16 KB
  - closefile
  - openfile
  - readwholefile
  - closefile
  - openfile
  - appendfilerand, mean size = 16 KB
  - closefile
  - openfile
  - readwholefile
  - closefile
```

9.2.2.1. Sun Fire

The first environment is a Sun Fire X4440 x64 server system and is schematically shown in Figure 9.2. The server contains four 6-core processors and 128 GB of main memory. The storage subsystem consists of a RAID array with 8 Serial Attached SCSI (SAS) hard disks. The array contains a 256 MB battery-backed, non-volatile cache (NVC) for write requests. The system is virtualized using a Citrix XenServer hypervisor and the applications run in Linux guest VMs. The scheduler of the hypervisor manages the access of the guest VMs to the resources. In contrast to accesses to the CPUs, XenServer uses for I/O requests accessing the storage resource a privileged host VM (Dom0) able to access the physical devices. The guest VMs are equipped with multiple cores and sufficient memory. The file system is configured to the de facto standard *EXT4* and as I/O scheduler, we use the default scheduler in virtualized environments (Ling et al., 2013).

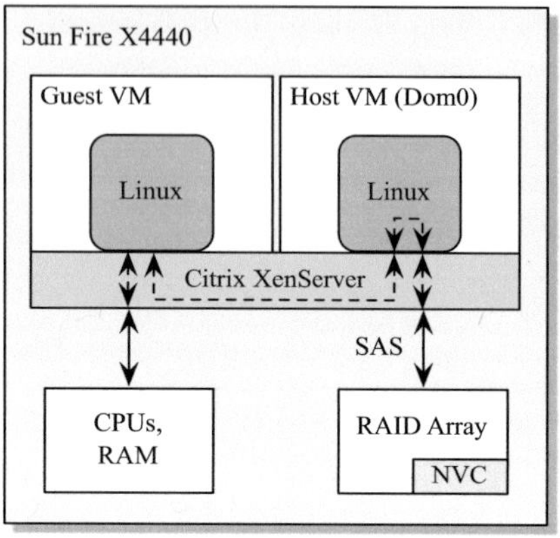

Figure 9.2.: Schematic Illustration of Sun Fire X4440

9.2.2.2. IBM System z

The second environment is based on the IBM mainframe System z and the storage system DS8700 first introduced in Section 4.2. To briefly summarize, Figure 9.3 illustrates that the System z provides processors and memory resources and the DS8700 provides storage space. The environment is virtualized using the *Processor Resource and System Manager (PR/SM)* hypervisor creating logical partitions (*LPARs*, i.e., VMs) that use the resources. To optimize I/O performance, the storage system DS8700 contains a storage server having a volatile cache (VC) and a non-volatile cache (NVC) that are enhanced with several pre-fetching and destaging algorithms for increased performance (Dufrasne et al. (2010), cf. Section 4.2). In our environment, the DS8700 contains 2 GB NVC and 50 GB VC with a RAID-5 array containing seven HDDs and measurements are obtained in z/Linux LPARs equipped with multiple cores. The I/O-related operating system configurations are similar to the ones of our previous environment.

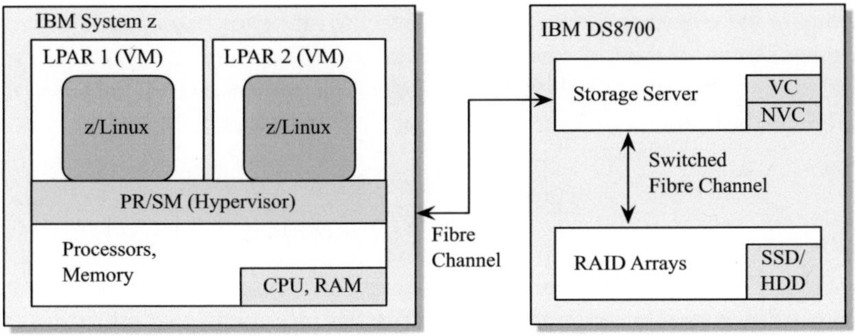

Figure 9.3.: Schematic Illustration of IBM System z and DS8700

9.3. Case Studies on Workload Characterization

In this section, we evaluate our workload characterization introduced in Chapter 5. We focus on our two evaluation goals to analyze the abstraction level of the workload characterization as well as its performance evaluation possibilities. The workload characterization steps shown in the following two case studies are fully automated. Before we begin with the case studies, we introduce the overall evaluation process. After presenting the case study results, we summarize and discuss the evaluations.

9.3.1. Overview

The general process for the case studies is illustrated in Figure 9.4 and is comprised of the following five steps: i) We analyze an I/O-intensive application, e.g., a file server, whose users generate a *high-level* workload, e.g., by uploading and downloading files. ii) The high-level workload translates to *low-level* I/O workload comprised of simple read and write operations. iii) We observe and monitor this low-level workload to calculate the metrics of our workload characterization, cf. Section 5.3, where we use a closed workload intensity characterization. iv) We use the calculated metrics as input for a reference benchmark to mimic the captured low-level workload. v) We finally compare the response times obtained using the reference benchmark with the response times of the low-level I/O workload of the application. For every run (i.e., repetition), we calculate the *response time difference* ΔRT between the reference benchmark and the application's I/O workload using

$$\Delta\text{RT} := \left| \frac{RT^{App} - RT^{Ref}}{RT^{Ref}} \right|, \tag{9.1}$$

where RT^{App} and RT^{Ref} denote the mean response time of the application and the reference benchmark, respectively. For the I/O-intensive application, we use *Filebench* to measure the considered application workloads as introduced in Section 9.2. Furthermore, we use FFSB as reference benchmark. In the case studies, we use our two system environments comprised of the IBM System z and the Sun Fire system, cf. Section 9.2. All measurements, monitoring, and data collection are automated and the measurements are repeated 20 times each running five minutes with a warm-up period of one minute.

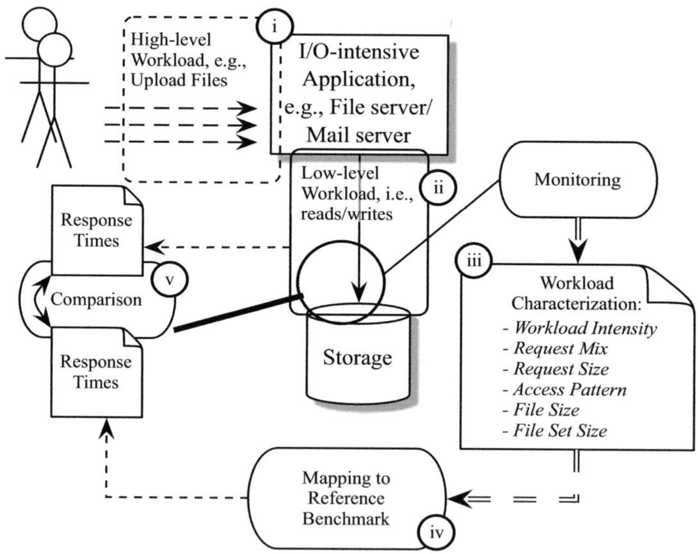

Figure 9.4.: Workload Characterization Overview

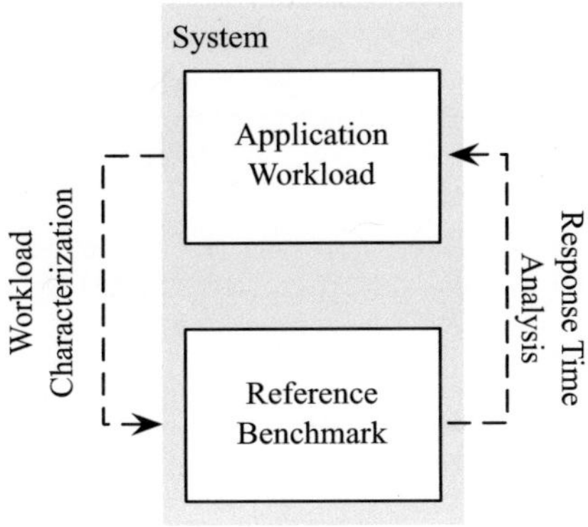

Figure 9.5.: Workload Characterization Process

9.3.2. Case Study I: Workload Characterization

In our first case study, we characterize the two considered applications, a file server and a mail server application measured using Filebench. In this case study, we use our IBM System z and IBM DS8700 environment. The evaluation process as introduced in Section 9.3.1 is realized in this case study as schematically illustrated in Figure 9.5. To characterize the application workload, the application is first run and monitored to extract the performance and workload characteristics for the configuration of the reference benchmark. Then, we run the reference benchmark and compare its response times with the response times of the original workload to evaluate the difference.

The application workloads comprise a set of file system operations, e.g., a file is opened, read, and finally closed, where the file server and the mail server workload are defined as shown in Listing 9.1 and Listing 9.2, respectively. Running the two application workloads and extracting the workload characteristics, Tables 9.1 and 9.2 show both the average of the mean characteristics as well as the standard deviation of the mean characteristics across the 20 repetitions for the considered workloads. Furthermore, the table indicates that we obtain a stable characterization across all metrics given the small standard deviations in relation to the mean values.

	File server	
	Mean	Std. dev.
File Size	129.76 KB	3.91 KB
File Set Size	1163.49 MB	5.91 MB
Workload Intensity	50 Threads	0 Threads
Request Size Read	105 152.00 B	166.67 B
Request Size Write	80 473.09 B	190.77 B
Request Mix	41.85 %	0.37 %
Access Pattern Ratio (Read)	97.00 %	2.30 %
Access Pattern Ratio (Write)	99.23 %	0.27 %

Table 9.1.: Workload Characterization for the File Server across 20 runs

	Mail server	
	Mean	Std. dev.
File Size	16.62 KB	0.74 KB
File Set Size	683.68 MB	58.37 MB
Workload Intensity	16 Threads	0 Threads
Request Size Read	14 151.17 B	31.63 B
Request Size Write	15 639.04 B	81.59 B
Request Mix	55.96 %	0.11 %
Access Pattern Ratio (Read)	28.74 %	0.52 %
Access Pattern Ratio (Write)	57.24 %	1.22 %

Table 9.2.: Workload Characterization for the Mail Server across 20 runs

Next, we use the characteristics obtained from the applications in Tables 9.1 and 9.2 as input for the reference benchmark. We run our reference benchmark and compare the response time measurements with the results obtained using Filebench. For the file server application, the response time measurements of the I/O operations are shown in Table 9.3. For the file server workload, we have two types of write operations, write and append. For the read and write operations, we obtain a mean response time of 11.21 ms and 11.65 ms, respectively. Mimicking the file server application with our reference benchmark, we measure a mean response time of 11.67 ms and 18.48 ms with a mean standard deviation $\overline{\sigma}$ (i.e., the standard deviation averaged over the 20 runs) of 21.13 ms and 20.77 ms for the read and write requests, respectively. Overall across the repetitions, we obtain a response time difference ΔRT in the ranges of [1.18 %, 9.62 %] and [33.89 %, 41.06 %] for the read and write requests, respectively. While the response time difference is very low for read requests, it is higher for write requests because of the mixed write/append operations of the application. Illustrated in Figure 9.6, the mean response time difference is 3.93 % and 36.96 % for the read and write requests, respectively. The response time measurements of the I/O operations of the mail server application are shown in Table 9.3. Here, each operation is measured twice as shown in the workload description (cf. Listing 9.2). For the read and append (i.e., write) operation, we obtain a mean response time of 0.98 ms and 0.83 ms, respectively. Now, using FFSB with the extracted configuration to mimic the application, we obtain a mean read response time of 0.81 ms with a mean standard deviation $\overline{\sigma}$ of 2.78 ms. Further, we obtain a mean write response time of 1.29 ms with a mean standard deviation $\overline{\sigma}$ of 2.94 ms. In comparison, the response time difference ΔRT for read requests is in the ranges of [17.01 %, 25.87 %] and in the ranges of [31.25 %, 38.54 %] for write requests. Since the absolute response times are relatively small, the results are considered acceptable. On average, as shown in Figure 9.6, the response time difference is 20.82 % and 35.72 % for the read and write requests, respectively. The results show that the I/O workload characterization of the considered workloads can be obtained in an automated process and are sufficient to capture the key characteristics of the I/O workloads and their I/O performance.

Workload	Operation	Resp. Time	Std. dev.
File server	ReadWholeFile	11.21 ms	0.26 ms
	AppendFileRand	9.36 ms	0.25 ms
	WriteWholeFile	13.93 ms	0.47 ms
Mail server	ReadWholeFile	0.98 ms	0.03 ms
		0.98 ms	0.03 ms
	AppendFileRand	0.66 ms	0.01 ms
		1.00 ms	0.03 ms

Table 9.3.: Mean and Standard Deviation of the Mean Response Times

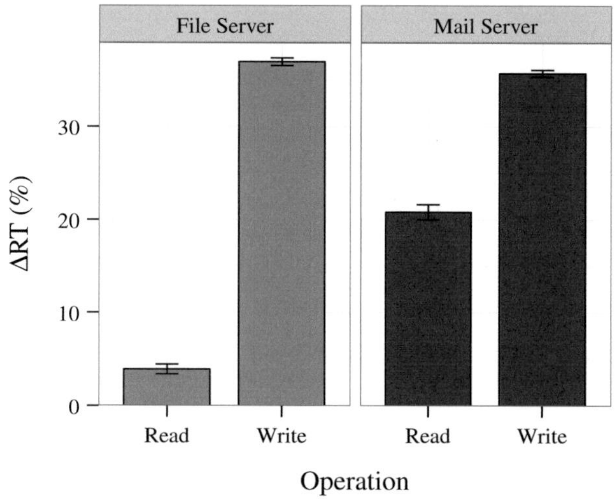

Figure 9.6.: Mean Response Time Difference ΔRT with Standard Error in Case Study I

9.3.3. Case Study II: Workload Migration & Consolidation

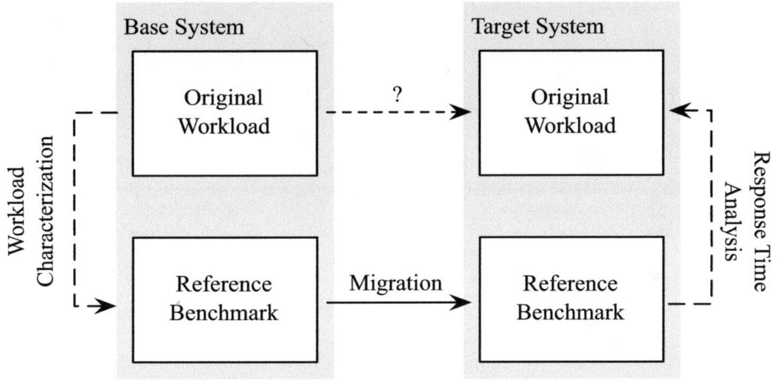

Figure 9.7.: Workload Migration Process

In this case study, we use our workload characterization to estimate the impact of migrating an application from a *base* to a *target system*. We employ the process described in Section 9.3.1 in two scenarios in this case study as schematically illustrated in Figure 9.7 and Figure 9.8. As the base system, we use the IBM System z and IBM DS8700 environment. We use the Sun Fire environment as the target system. In our migration scenario, we characterize our application on the base system. In particular, we use the file server application in this scenario. Then, we use our reference benchmark and migrate to the target system. We run the reference benchmark and, finally, we use the response times obtained with our reference benchmark to estimate the response times of the original workload on the target system. In our consolidation scenario, we characterize two applications on the base system in isolation, where we use both the file and the mail server application in a heterogeneous scenario, i.e., using two different applications. We then use the reference benchmark and migrate to the target system, where we run two instances of the benchmark in two virtual machines in consolidation. Finally, we use the measurements of the reference benchmark to estimate the impact of consolidating the applications in respective virtual machines on the target system. We use the workload characterization of the applications in isolation obtained in our first case study as shown in Tables 9.1 and 9.2.

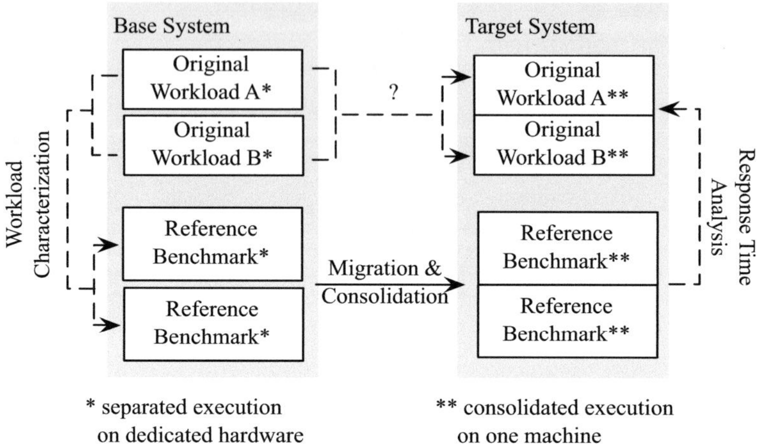

Figure 9.8.: Workload Consolidation Process

We configure the reference benchmark with the workload characterization to estimate the performance of the applications in the target environment in the migration and consolidation scenario. For both scenarios, we calculate the response time difference as shown in Equation (9.1).

Workload Migration. The response time measurements of the application's I/O operations in the migration scenario are shown in Table 9.4. Having again two write operations in the file server application, in the target environment we obtain a mean response time of 67.21 ms and 33.32 ms for the read and write requests, respectively. Using the reference benchmark in the target environment, the mean response time is 55.29 ms ($\overline{\sigma}$ = 20.61 ms) for the read requests and 42.21 ms ($\overline{\sigma}$ = 14.49 ms) for the write requests. Overall, the response time difference of the file server workload for read requests is in the ranges of [19.12 %, 28.02 %] and for write requests in the ranges of [12.77 %, 24.12 %]. Averaging the response time difference, we obtain a mean response time difference of 21.59 % for read request and 20.98 % for write request as shown in Figure 9.9.

Workload Consolidation. For the two applications in consolidation, the response times of the I/O operations are shown in Table 9.4. The read and write operations are averaged and we obtain a mean response time of 77.75 ms and 59.71 ms for the read and write requests, respectively. For the measurements of our reference benchmark, the mean response time is 89.34 ms for the read requests and 79.12 ms for the write requests. Comparing the response time measurements, the response time difference for read requests is in the ranges of [9.23 %, 17.32 %], while it is in the ranges of [21.46 %, 28.28 %] for write requests. Overall, the mean response time difference is 12.95 % and 24.51 % for the read and write requests, respectively, cf. Figure 9.9.

In both scenarios, the measurement results between the workloads show sufficient agreement such that, in conclusion, we are able to automatically obtain the I/O workload characterization of an application and can use it to successfully estimate the impact of workload migration and consolidation.

Workload	Operation	Resp. Time	Std. dev.
File server	ReadWholeFile	67.21 ms	0.55 ms
	AppendFileRand	34.96 ms	0.44 ms
	WriteWholeFile	31.68 ms	0.47 ms
File and Mail Server	AppendFileRand	85.00 ms 30.57 ms 29.94 ms	2.08 ms 0.87 ms 0.69 ms
	WriteWholeFile	93.43 ms	2.46 ms
	ReadWholeFile	139.48 ms 47.67 ms 46.11 ms	2.56 ms 1.22 ms 1.20 ms

Table 9.4.: Mean and Standard Deviation of the Mean Application Response Times

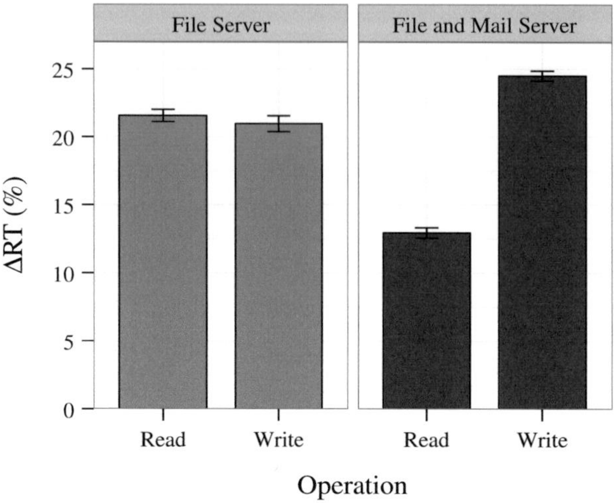

Figure 9.9.: Mean Response Time Difference ΔRT with Standard Error in Case Study II

9.3.4. Summary and Discussion

In this section, we presented two case studies to show that our workload characterization of I/O-intensive applications is a reasonable abstraction of an application workload. In two case studies, we extracted the workload characterization of a mail and a file server application measured with Filebench in an automated manner. We compared the applications' response times to the ones obtain with our reference benchmark FFSB that uses the workload characterization as input to mimic the application. Addressing Goal 1 of the evaluation, the first case study demonstrates the automated applicability and appropriateness of our workload characterization approach to capture performance-relevant aspects of the considered applications. We measured the two considered applications in our System z environment, obtained the workload metrics while monitoring the environment, and evaluated the response time difference between the application and the reference benchmark. While the response time difference was relatively low for read requests and higher for write requests, the response time difference was mostly caused by abstracting the variations in the requests and request sizes simply using averaged request sizes with our reference benchmark. This can cause higher variations when having multiple different operations of one workload type, for instance, having multiple append and write file system operations that are translated to write requests at the storage level. Still, the response times of the application and the reference benchmark were in the same order of magnitude for both types of requests, thus, the characterization provided a reasonable abstraction of the more complex workloads considered in the case study. In our second case study, we addressed both the first and the second goal of the evaluation. We showed that the workload characterization approach is able to capture the performance-relevant aspects of the considered applications in an automated process. Furthermore, we showed how our approach can be used to estimate the impact of application migration and consolidation as we estimated the I/O performance of the applications in a migrated, new environment. For this estimation, our approach is more flexible as, for instance, a simple record/replay mechanism, since we are able to capture an application as well as vary specific parameters (e.g., the workload intensity) if required, which would be difficult and sometimes impossible for production workloads. In the case study, we were able to reuse the characterization of the previous case study, thus, there was no additional overhead for the process as we migrated to another environment. Overall, the performance estimation in the unknown environment was acceptable, even when the workloads were mixed and different applications consolidated with response times of operations between 30 ms and 140 ms and a maximum response time difference of 25 %. While, in general, the estimation accuracy could be improved with a more fine-grained representation and characterization, it would introduce additional complexity and our approach showed to be a reasonable compromise between complexity and accuracy to use for automated performance evaluation.

9.4. Case Studies on Storage-level Modeling

In the following, we evaluate our storage-level modeling approach using the regression analysis-based performance prediction introduced in Chapter 6. We address our two evaluation goals and analyze the prediction accuracy achieved with our approach as well as the reduction in prediction error with our regression technique parameterization approach. Overall, the measurements as well as the regression modeling steps shown in the case studies are fully automated. In this section, we present three different case studies using our IBM System z environment for the evaluation. We first present a brief overview of the approach and conclude with a summary and discussion of the results after the case studies.

9.4.1. Overview

In our case studies, we employ the I/O performance modeling process introduced in Section 6.4, where in the case studies we will first specify the respective modeling target. For each case study, we choose a representative measurement space configuration, which is then explored with measurements in an automated manner. We then select a set of regression models and search for their optimal configuration. From the set of studied regression techniques, we choose to create models using MARS with interaction terms, CART, and Cubist, since MARS models can be seen as an extension of linear regression models and the Cubist models are a direct extension of M5 trees. Furthermore, the Cubist algorithm is equal to the M5 algorithm for Cubist's standard parameterization. To search for the optimal configuration, the regression technique parameterization step is configured reasonably (S3 algorithm with number of splits $\zeta = 4$, number of explorations $\eta = 5$, and maximum number of iterations $\theta = 10$). The considered parameters of the regression techniques are described in Section 6.3. Finally, for each regression technique we use the measurement data to create the regression models, which are finally evaluated with new configurations that are not used in the modeling process. For the evaluation, we calculate the prediction error as the

$$relative\ error := \left| \frac{metric^M_{avg} - metric^P_{avg}}{metric^M_{avg}} \right|, \tag{9.2}$$

where the *metric* is either response time or throughput, such that we compare the measured average performance $metric^M_{avg}$ with the average predicted performance $metric^P_{avg}$.

I/O scheduler	CFQ, NOOP
Threads	100
File set size	1 GB, 25 GB, 50 GB, 75 GB, 100 GB
Request size	4 KB, 8 KB, 12 KB, 16 KB, 20 KB, 24 KB, 28 KB, 32 KB
Access pattern	random, sequential
Read percentage	0 %, 25 %, 30 %, 50 %, 70 %, 75 %, 100 %

Table 9.5.: FFSB Experimental Setup Configuration

9.4.2. Case Study I: Modeling Performance-influencing Factors

In our initial case study, we model major I/O performance-influencing factors introduced in Section 5.2. To this end, we employ the FFSB benchmark to systematically measure the system environment with the required fine-grained configurations and use the measurements to create optimized regression models. The explicit setup configuration is chosen representatively and given in Table 9.5. The parameter space is explored in a full factorial design leading to a total of 1120 measurement configurations. For each configuration, in the measurements we use a one minute warm-up and a five minute measurement phase. In one minute, the benchmark collects approximately 575 000 measurement samples on average and between approximately 90 000 and 2 800 000 measurement samples depending on the configuration. Overall, the mean response times of the read and write requests are in the ranges of [2.2 ms, 70.4 ms] and [2.8 ms, 60.7 ms], respectively, and the throughputs of the read and write requests are in the ranges of [4.02 MB/s, 386.70 MB/s] and [2.99 MB/s, 171.1 MB/s], respectively.

For each of the considered regression techniques, we create four different models to capture the I/O performance: A read response time model (RT_r), a write response time model (RT_w), a read throughput model (TP_r), and a write throughput model (TP_w). Thus using the three regression techniques, we create a total of 12 regression models. We evaluate 100 measurement configurations with parameter values chosen completely randomly within the configured ranges (e.g., 90 GB file set size, 30 KB request size, etc.). For each configuration, we compare the model predictions with measurements on the real system. For the 100 configurations, Figure 9.10 illustrates the prediction errors, the mean prediction errors are shown in the bars in the upper part and as the small crosses in the lower part. Overall, the models perform very well and especially MARS and Cubist have a high prediction quality with less than 7 % and 8 % mean prediction error, respectively. After the parameterization of the models, the CART trees are highly branched, but their prediction accuracy with approximately 10 % mean error is good. Averaging the four models of the techniques, the mean of the 95th percentile of the prediction error is 20.89 %, 24.32 %, and 27.48 % for MARS, Cubist, and CART, respectively.

Finally, we evaluate the improvements in prediction accuracy achieved with our optimized regression parameterization and compare the optimized models with models created with standard parameters. We evaluate the performance prediction error for each model with the 100 completely random configurations similar to the evaluation above. In summary, especially MARS and CART benefit significantly from the parameter optimization approach and show an average reduction in prediction error of 66.30 % and 74.08 %, respectively. The reduction in prediction error for Cubist is 15.7 %. To support these results, we evaluate the statistical significance of the reduction in prediction error in a set of *paired t-tests*. In these tests, the p-value of both MARS and CART is less than $2.2e^{-16}$ and the p-value of Cubist is $3.39e^{-4}$, hereby confirming that the parameter optimization is statistically significant for every considered regression technique. In conclusion, our parameter optimization approach is key to significantly reduce the prediction errors of the regression models.

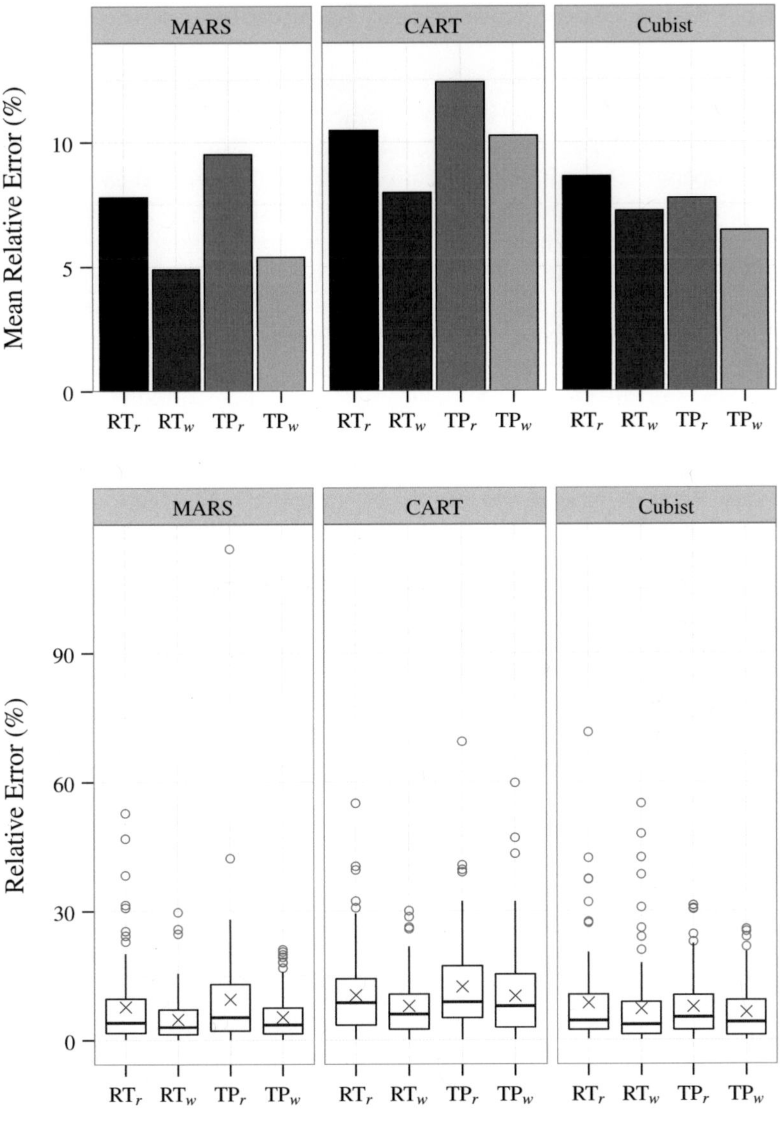

Figure 9.10.: Prediction Quality (Case Study I)

9.4.3. Case Study II: Modeling Application Workload

For our second case study, we use Filebench to measure and model an application workload and predict its I/O performance. We use a mail server workload with configurations as indicated in Table 9.6 triggering a set of mixed file system operations, such as file creation and deletion as well as whole file reads and append operations of random size, cf. Listing 9.2. We evaluate all configuration combinations and vary the number of clients (threads), the number of files, and the mean file sizes as shown in Table 9.6 in a full factorial design leading to a total of 576 measurement configurations. Similar to the previous case study, we use a one minute warm-up phase and a five minute measurement phase for each measurement configuration. During the measurements, the benchmark collects approximately 980 000 read and append samples on average and between approximately 825 000 and 1 100 000 samples depending on the configuration. Furthermore, the absolute mean response times of the read and append requests are in the ranges of [0.36 ms, 2.74 ms] and [0.40 ms, 1.70 ms], respectively, and the throughputs of the read and append requests are in the ranges of [5.95 MB/s, 62.95 MB/s] and [5.60 MB/s, 7.60 MB/s], respectively.

Using each considered regression technique, we create different models for each I/O performance metric: A read response time model (RT_r), an append response time model (RT_a), a read throughput model (TP_r), and an append throughput model (TP_a) resulting in a total of 12 regression models. Each model is evaluated using 100 measurement configurations with parameter values chosen randomly within the configured ranges. For each configuration, we compare the model predictions with measurements on the system. Figure 9.11 illustrates the prediction errors for the various models. Overall, the models exhibit a very high prediction accuracy and especially MARS shows excellent results with less than 4 % mean error. The Cubist and CART models perform also very well with approximately 7 % and 8 % mean prediction error, respectively. Across the four I/O performance metrics, the mean of the 95th percentile of the prediction error is very good for MARS with 9.66 %. It is higher for Cubist and CART with 20.78 % and 20.88 %, respectively.

Workload type	Mail server workload
Threads	16(*), 32, 48, 64, 80, 96
Files	1000(*), 5000, 10000, 20000, 30000, 40000, 50000, 60000, 70000, 80000, 90000, 100000
Mean file size	4 KB, 16 KB(*), 32 KB, 48 KB, 64 KB, 96 KB, 128 KB, 192 KB
	(*) default value

Table 9.6.: Filebench Experimental Setup Configuration

To again evaluate the improvements in model accuracy achieved with our optimized regression parameterization, we compare the accuracy of the models when using the optimized regression parameters with those configured with the standard parameters. We evaluate the performance prediction error of the models with 100 random configurations similar to the evaluation above. For this case study, the optimization approach reduces the prediction error by 4.2 %, 27.3 %, and 8.7 % for MARS, CART, and Cubist, respectively. Evaluating the results in a *paired t-test*, the p-value of MARS, CART, and Cubist is $5.26e^{-4}$, $9.63e^{-14}$, and $2.19e^{-3}$, respectively, thus confirming that the reduction in prediction error is again statistically significant for every considered regression technique.

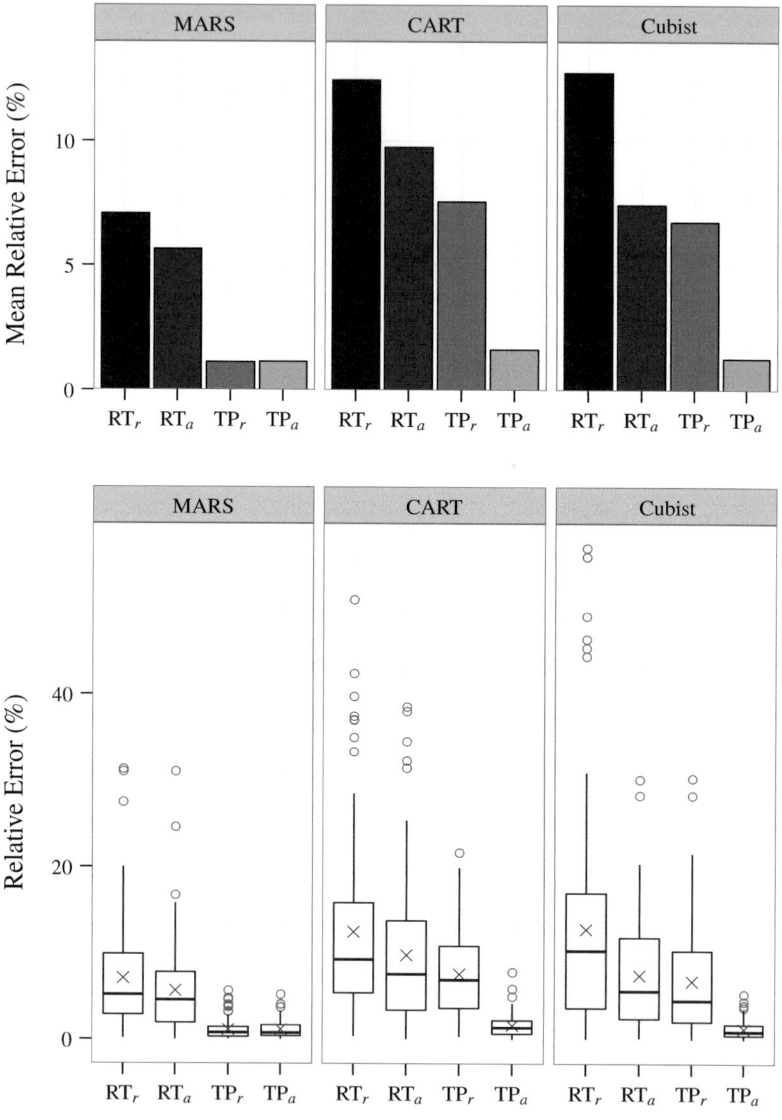

Figure 9.11.: Prediction Quality (Case Study II)

Filebench Workload Parameters @VM1	
Workload type	File server workload
Threads	50$^{(*)}$
Files	10000$^{(*)}$
Mean file size	128 KB$^{(*)}$
FFSB Workload Parameters @VM2	
Threads	50
File set size	1 GB, 2 GB, 5 GB, 10 GB
Request size	4 KB, 8 KB, 16 KB, 32 KB, 64 KB
Access pattern	random, sequential
Read percentage	10 %, 30 %, 50 %, 70 %, 90 %
	$^{(*)}$ default value

Table 9.7.: Hybrid Experimental Setup Configuration

9.4.4. Case Study III: Modeling Performance Interference

In the final case study of this evaluation part, we analyze the I/O performance interference between applications running in separate VMs, i.e., we analyze how the performance of one application is directly affected by the workload of an application running in a co-located VM as the applications are sharing the storage resources. In this case study, we focus on applications with a constant and equal workload intensity and vary the workload type (e.g., read- or write-intensive workload) in one VM to evaluate how the performance is affected by the characteristics of the workload. In general, I/O performance isolation in virtualized environments is widely an open issue, thus varying the workload intensity would lead to obvious performance interference. For the measurements, we use both the FFSB benchmark and Filebench running a file server workload, which consists of mixed file system operations, such as file creation and deletion as well as whole file reads, whole file writes, and append operations of random size, cf. Listing 9.1. The workloads run in two separate virtual machines with the configurations chosen representatively as listed in Table 9.7. We evaluate all combinations in a full factorial design leading to a total of 200 measurement configurations. Similar to our previous case studies, we use a one minute warm-up phase and a five minute measurement phase.

Before modeling the performance interference, we analyze the absolute number of operations and the I/O performance. An initial indication for the performance interference between the applications is the number of read, append, and write operations of the file server workload generated with Filebench in VM1. Depending on the configuration of the FFSB workload in VM2, the number of operations in VM1 varies between approximately 375 000 and 700 000 with a mean of approximately 550 000 operations, while the number of operations in VM2 varies between approximately 420 000 and 3 100 000 with a mean of approximately 1 300 000 operations. For VM1, the mean response times of the read, append, and write requests are in the ranges of [13.08 ms, 34.08 ms], [11.63 ms, 32.12 ms], and [17.90 ms, 52.81 ms], respectively, and the throughputs of the read, append, and write requests are in the ranges of [54.80 MB/s, 108.30 MB/s], [3.40 MB/s, 6.20 MB/s], and [55.30 MB/s, 109.10 MB/s], respectively, depending on the configuration. For VM2, the mean response times of the read and write requests are in the ranges of [4.34 ms, 26.75 ms] and [7.45 ms, 37.59 ms], respectively, and the throughputs of the read and write requests are in the ranges of [1.38 MB/s, 218.00 MB/s] and [2.21 MB/s, 95.20 MB/s], respectively, depending on the configuration. These values indicate that the performance of both applications strongly depends on the type of workloads running in the VMs, which is obvious for the workload that is changed (VM2), but also applies to the co-located workload that remains constant (VM1).

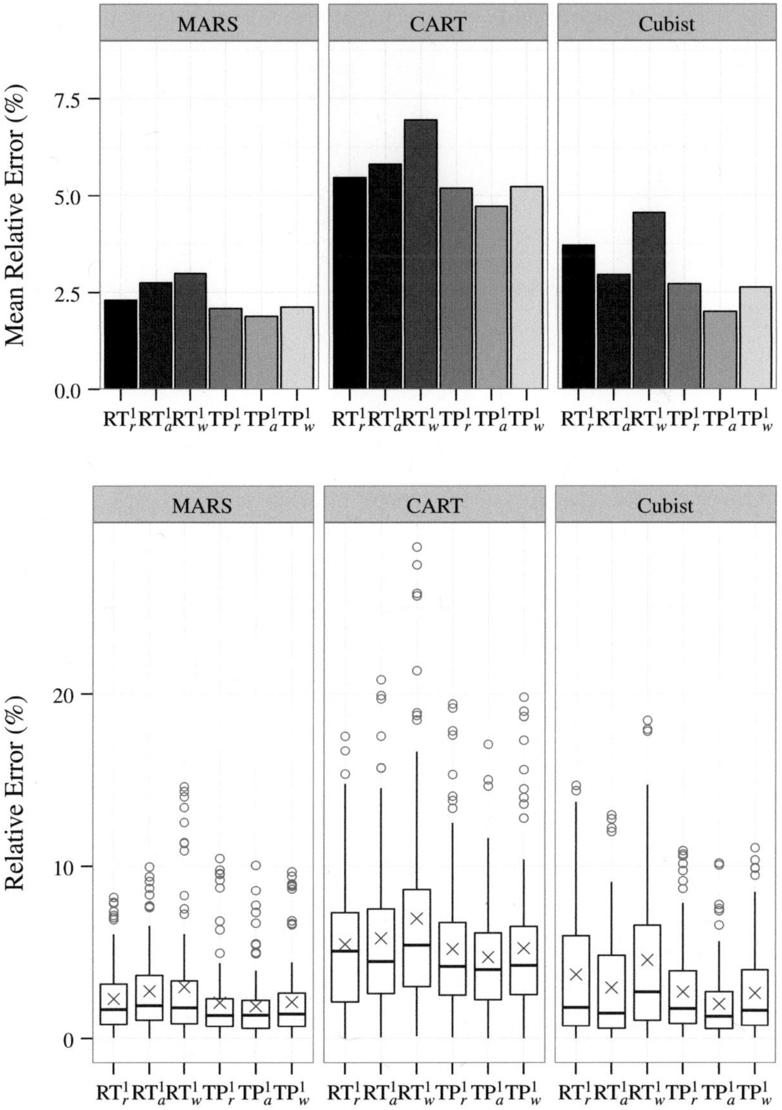

Figure 9.12.: Prediction Quality VM1 (Case Study III)

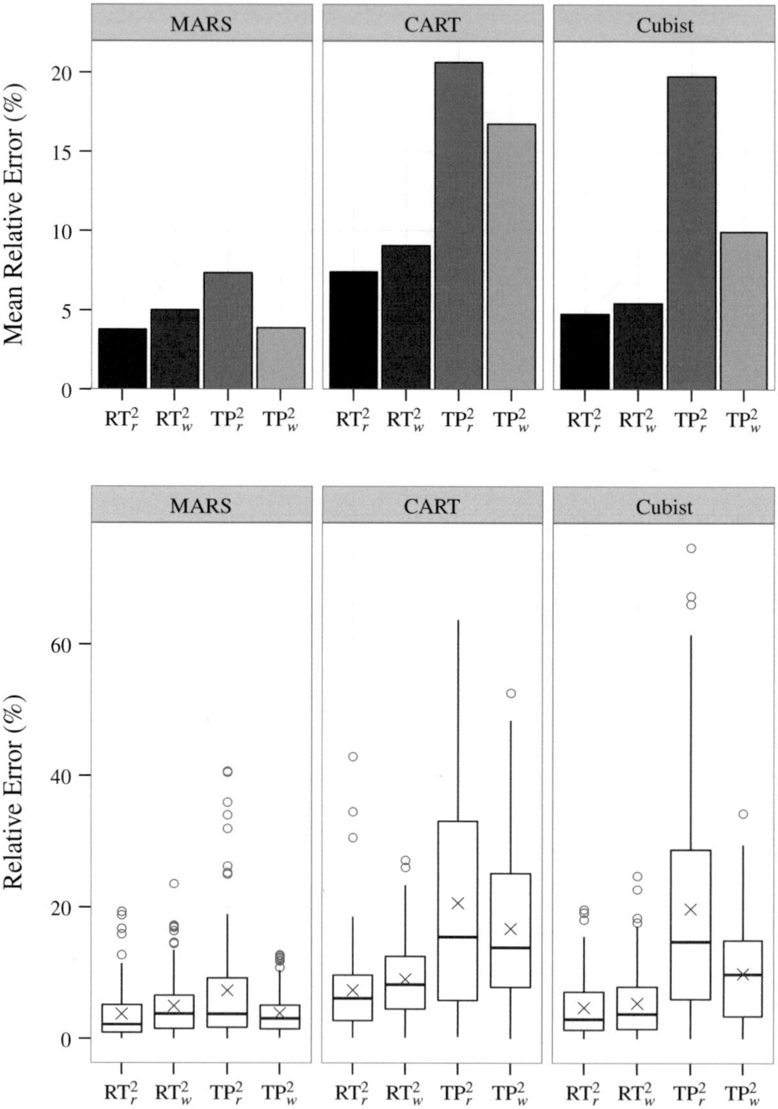

Figure 9.13.: Prediction Quality VM2 (Case Study III)

Modeling the interference effects with the considered regression techniques, we create a total of 10 models for each technique: For VM1, we use the configuration in VM2 as independent variables and create a read response time model (RT_r^1), an append response time model (RT_a^1), a write response time model (RT_w^1), a read throughput model (TP_r^1), an append throughput model (TP_a^1), and a write throughput model (TP_w^1). Since the configuration in VM1 remains constant in this case study, for VM2 we do not need to use the configuration in VM1 as independent variables explicitly. We create a read response time model (RT_r^2), a write response time model (RT_w^2), a read throughput model (TP_r^2), and a write throughput model (TP_w^2) using the configuration in VM2 as independent variables. Thus, we create a total of 30 models and evaluate 100 configuration scenarios with parameter values chosen randomly within the configured ranges. We use these random parameter values as configuration for the FFSB benchmark and predict both the performance of the FFSB benchmark and the performance interference on the co-located VM running the file server application. For each scenario, we compare the model predictions with measurements on the real system. The prediction results are given in Figures 9.12 and 9.13 for the various models. Particularly interesting are the prediction errors shown in Figure 9.12 indicating that the models are able to predict very accurately how different workload types (e.g., read-intensive or write-intensive) affect the application performance on the co-located VM. This is not obvious, since the performance interference is significant as analyzed above. As illustrated in Figure 9.14, even if the workload remains constant, the response times of the I/O operations spread by between 261 % and 295 % depending on the workload produced by the co-located VM. Overall, the models exhibit a very high prediction accuracy for both VMs. In general, the MARS models show the highest performance prediction accuracy with approximately 2.1 % and 5.0 % mean prediction error for VM1 and VM2, respectively. The Cubist models also exhibit low prediction errors with approximately 2.6 % and 10.0 % mean prediction error for VM1 and VM2, respectively. Finally, the CART models appear to have the highest error in this case study with approximately 5.2 % and 13.5 % mean prediction error for VM1 and VM2, respectively. For VM1, the mean of the 95th percentile of the prediction error across the six models is very low for MARS and Cubist with 8.39 % and 9.99 %, respectively, while it is slightly higher with 15.14 % for CART. For VM2, the mean of the 95th percentile of the prediction error across the four models is 16.15 %, 27.39 %, and 34.00 % for MARS, Cubist, and CART, respectively.

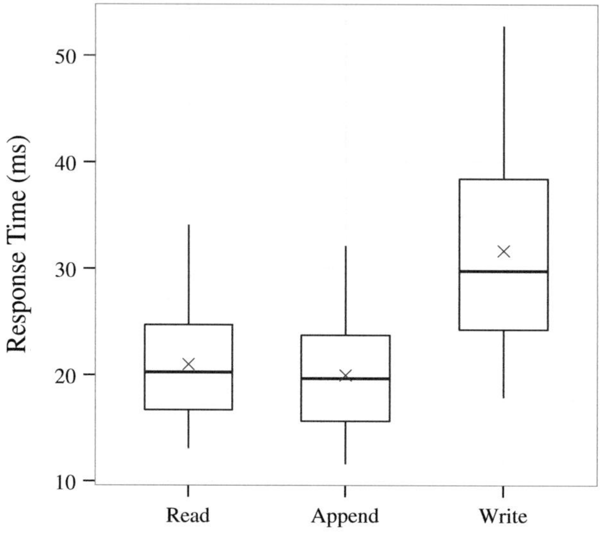

Figure 9.14.: Performance Interference Impact

Finally, we evaluate the improvements in model accuracy achieved through our optimized regression parameterization approach comparing the accuracy of the models when using the optimized regression parameters with the models created with standard parameters. We evaluate the performance prediction error for each model with 100 random configurations similar to the analysis above. Depending on the scenario and the regression technique, we obtain a reduction in prediction error with the optimization approach between 5.0 % and 32.3 %. Furthermore, the p-value is at most $1.46e^{-3}$, thus confirming that the optimization is statistically significant for every considered regression technique.

9.4.5. Summary and Discussion

In this section, we presented three case studies on the creation of optimized regression models using three regression techniques to analyze and predict the I/O performance and interference effects in virtualized environments. We evaluated the prediction accuracy in the case studies creating performance models with two different I/O benchmarks. The three case studies comprised models of major I/O performance-influencing factors, of application workloads, and of I/O performance interference effects of workloads sharing the storage resources. We used our IBM System z environment and created the performance models in a fully automated process. Overall, we effectively created performance models with high predictive power. Notably, out of the three considered regression techniques, MARS exhibited the highest prediction accuracy in comparison with CART and Cubist in every case study. The mean prediction error of MARS was between 2.1 % and 7 % in the case studies, while it was between 5.2 % and 13.5 % for CART and between 2.6 % and 10 % for Cubist. In summary, we can conclude with regard to our first evaluation goal that we are able to extract accurate regression models with low prediction errors.

In the case studies, the low prediction errors are especially due to our regression parameter optimization approach reducing the error of MARS, CART, and Cubist by up to 66.3 %, 74.08 %, and 21.9 %, respectively. Furthermore, the regression parameter optimization approach reduced the prediction error of every considered technique with statistical significance in every case study. Elaborating on our second evaluation goal, the optimization was key to obtain the accurate models. For the optimization runs, Figure 9.15 summarizes for all the case studies the earliest iterations in which the best regression parameterizations for the regression models were found. Here, we can observe some interesting aspects. First, the Cubist optimization rarely required all ten iterations to find the best optimization, which is particularly relevant, since the optimization of Cubist is computationally expensive (cf. Section 6.3). However, Cubist was also optimized along discrete parameters, which means that if interesting candidates are found, the adjacent areas can be evaluated exhaustively, i.e., the search will not continue infinitely as in the case for continuous parameters. The second observation is that the best parameterization for CART was for multiple models the initial starting point (Iteration 0), which results in the most branched, most complex CART model. This may be because the CART models were not able to sufficiently abstract and model the underlying structure of the data for these scenarios[1]. If we set aside these cases, the CART parameterization was then usually requiring more iterations, which is however not overly computationally expensive (cf. Section 6.3). The final observation for MARS is that the best parameterization is often found in later iterations. In 14 out of 18 cases, the earliest iteration with the best parameterization was Iteration 7 or above. Overall, if the regression techniques have continuous parameters, the optimization process might require more iterations to find the best parameterization. The parameter values, however, might not differ significantly in the later iterations as the step widths in the search decrease, such that a good enough model might also be found and considerable within fewer iterations of the optimization. Overall, merely ten iterations of our S3 algorithm sufficed to significantly improve the prediction accuracy of the regression techniques in our case studies.

[1] Actually, these are not the only scenarios in which the CART models are highly branched, however, this can only be seen by analyzing the resulting regression parameter values and is not obvious from Figure 9.15.

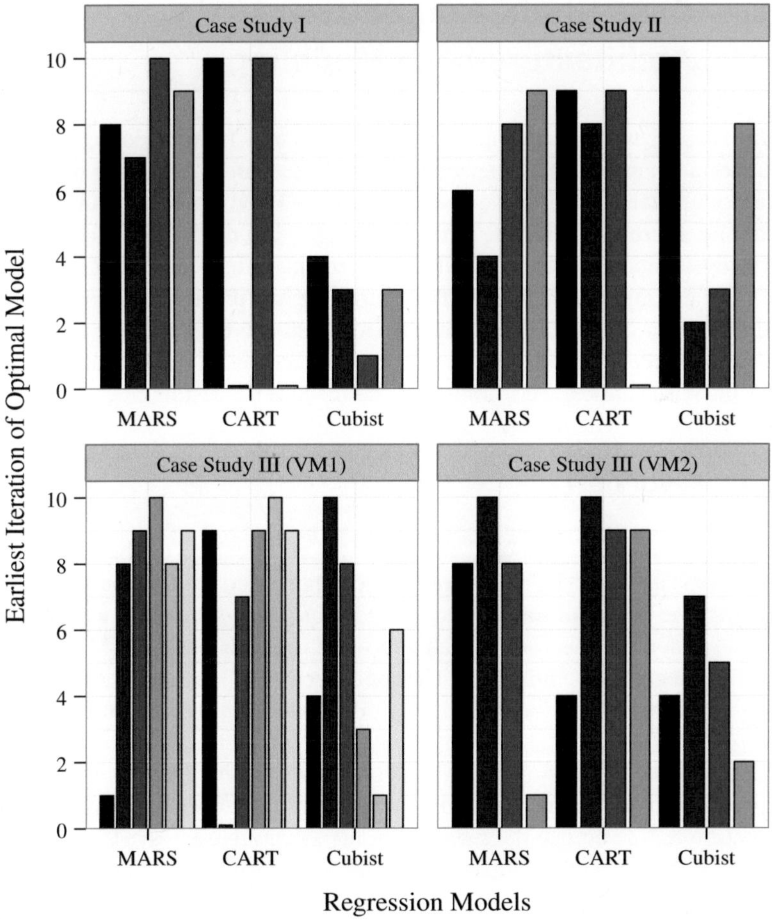

Figure 9.15.: Optimization Length Summary

9.5. Case Studies on Software Architecture-level Modeling

In this section, we evaluate our software architecture-level modeling approach detailed in Chapter 8 with respect to our two evaluation goals, the prediction accuracy and the modeling overhead. We use the PCM as software architecture modeling approach. We have integrated regression models into the PCM as I/O analysis model to capture the I/O performance, since they can be obtained in a fully automated manner. In the following, we present four case studies using our two considered system environments to evaluate our combined modeling approach. We first give a brief overview of the evaluation next. After the case studies, we summarize and discuss the results.

9.5.1. Overview

In the case studies, we model the software architecture of the considered applications using the PCM, where we have integrated the I/O analysis model to predict the delays of the I/O requests. As I/O analysis model, we use separate regression models for the read and write requests based on Multivariate Adaptive Regression Splines (MARS), cf. Section 6.3, as they have been the best predicting regression techniques in this domain in our case studies in Section 9.4. In general, however, the approach is not limited to the MARS models and the regression modeling formalism as I/O analysis model. We use FFSB to measure the required parameters of the I/O analysis model listed in Section 8.3.2 and use the measurements to create the regression models, whose parameters are optimized using our S3 algorithm (cf. Section 6.2).

For our measurements of the applications that are modeled with the PCM, we use the file server and the mail server applications provided by Filebench deployed in our two system environments based on the Sun Fire as well as the IBM System z servers, cf. Section 9.2. We run the applications multiple times with one minute warm-up time and five minutes measurement time and then average the measurements across the repetitions. We use three repetitions, where the measurements exhibit sufficiently stable results in our environments. We model the applications as well as the system environments with the PCM. For the requests of the applications, we model the create and delete operations as requests to the CPU resource. We model the open, close, and stat operations as requests to a Delay resource (infinite server resource). We model the I/O operations read, write, and append as requests to the virtualized storage system resource whose performance is captured by the I/O analysis model.

To evaluate the prediction accuracy, we use the following two metrics, i) the mean I/O response time prediction error $err^{I/O}$ and ii) the end-to-end response time prediction error err^{E2E} that are defined as

$$err^{I/O} := \frac{1}{n}\sum_{i}^{n}\left|\frac{opsIO_i^M - opsIO_i^P}{opsIO_i^M}\right| \tag{9.3}$$

and

$$err^{E2E} := \left|\frac{\sum_i ops_i^M - \sum_i ops_i^P}{\sum_i ops_i^M}\right|, \tag{9.4}$$

respectively, where $opsIO_i^M$ and $opsIO_i^P$ is the measured and predicted response time of the i-th I/O operation (i.e., read, write, or append), respectively, and ops_i^M and ops_i^P is the measured and predicted response time of the i-th operation, respectively.

9.5.2. Case Study I: File Server on Sun Fire

In our initial case study, we measure and model the file server application in the Sun Fire environment. To get an impression of the PCM model, Figure 9.16 illustrates the modeled application using the PCM in two simplified views, which are captured in the PCM in different submodels (cf. Section 3.4). Figure 9.16a shows the components and resources as well as the interface of the application, which is exposed to the users. The interface of the application is modeled according to the operations provided by Filebench. The application component maps the operations on the respective resource, where we employ a CPU, a Delay, and the Virtualized Storage System resource. Operations to the CPU and Delay resource specify their demand, which is a simple decimal number (`double`), operations to the storage resource are determined by the extended parameters, which also include more complex data types such as enumerations (`enum`) and composite data types (`composite`). Figure 9.16b illustrates the usage model describing the sequence in which the users invoke the operations of the application. This model is obtained from the Filebench workloads, where in the file server we have a population of 50 users with no think time, which describes a closed workload. Furthermore, the sequence of operations in this case study is determined from the workload definition as given in Listing 9.1. The operations are either calibrated with their demand or parameterized according to the workload definition.

To capture the application in the PCM, we calibrate the architecture model of the file server with 40 clients (threads), which is a value below the default value to also predict the default number of clients. To this end, we calibrate the resource demands of the operations using the CPU and Delay resource as well as the memory length for the I/O analysis model and the passed parameters. For the prediction, we increase the number of clients and evaluate both the mean I/O response time prediction error as well as the end-to-end response time prediction error.

We increase the number of clients up to 70 and observe that the end-to-end response time measurements increase from 103.09 ms (40 clients) to 188.51 ms (70 clients). For the configurations, Figure 9.17 illustrates the prediction error with the software architecture model. In general, the architecture model exhibits a very high prediction accuracy in this case study with approximately between 5 % and 8 % prediction error for both the mean I/O response time and the end-to-end response time. The prediction accuracy is notably high especially considering the fact that two different types of write operations, i.e., 128 KB write and 16 KB append requests, are predicted using the same I/O analysis model in the simulation that takes as input the mean write request size of requests currently accessing the storage, cf. Section 8.3.

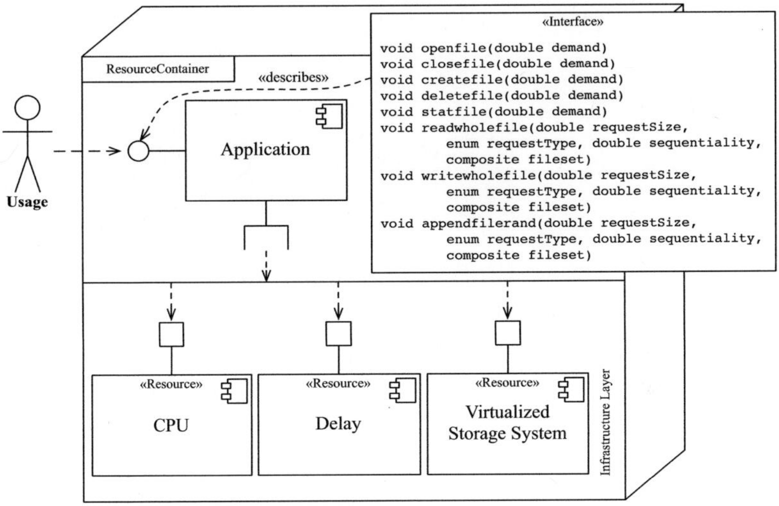

(a) Components and Resources (cf. Figure 8.3)

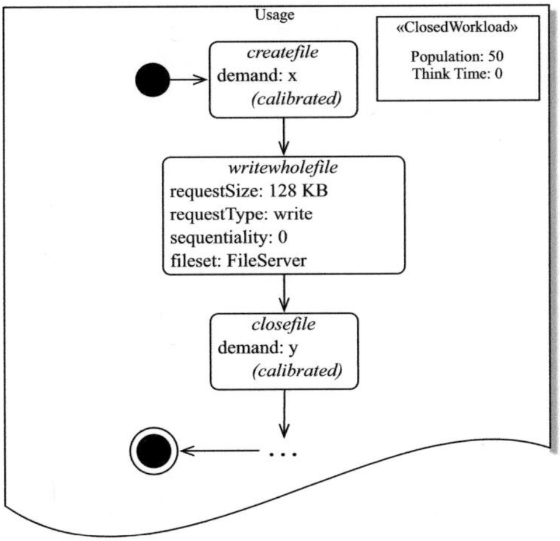

(b) Interaction of the Users with the System

Figure 9.16.: Illustration of the Application Modeled with the PCM (simplified)

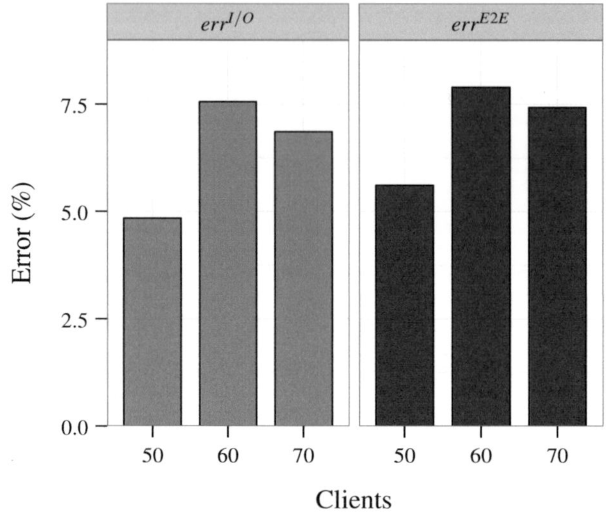

Clients	50	60	70
$err^{I/O}$	4.84 %	7.56 %	6.86 %
err^{E2E}	5.62 %	7.90 %	7.43 %

Figure 9.17.: Prediction Error in Case Study I

9.5.3. Case Study II: Mail Server on Sun Fire

In our second case study, we use another application and model the mail server in the Sun Fire environment. We adapt the PCM model shown in the previous case study to fit to the description of the mail server application. Similar to the previous case study, we calibrate the PCM model of the mail server with a number of clients below the default value with 10 clients and calibrate the operations using the CPU and Delay resources as well as the memory length for the I/O analysis model and the passed parameters. We increase the number of clients in steps of 10 and evaluate both the mean I/O response time prediction as well as the end-to-end response time prediction.

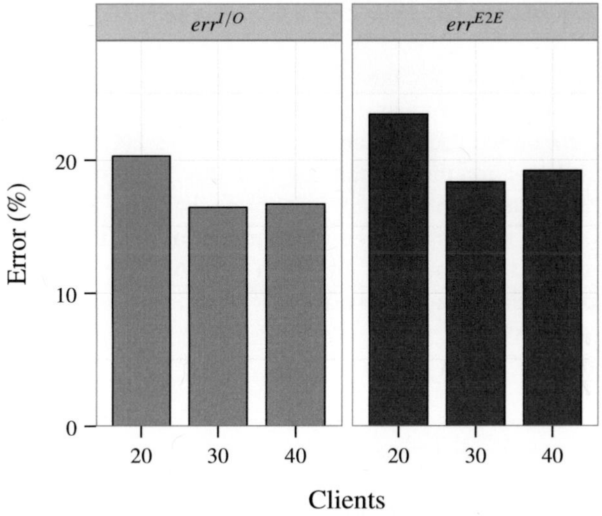

Clients	20	30	40
$err^{I/O}$	20.31 %	16.43 %	16.68 %
err^{E2E}	23.44 %	18.36 %	19.21 %

Figure 9.18.: Prediction Error in Case Study II

When we increase the number of clients up to 40, we observe that the end-to-end response time measurements increase from 24.98 ms (10 clients) to 56.40 ms (40 clients). Figure 9.18 illustrates the prediction error with the PCM model. Compared to our previous case study, the prediction error is higher, however, we also increased the workload intensity from calibration to prediction by up to 300 % for this application. Still, the accuracy with an I/O prediction error between 16 % and 20 % and an end-to-end prediction error between 18 % and 23 % is well within acceptable ranges.

9.5.4. Case Study III: File Server on System z

In this case study, we use another system environment and model the file server application considered in our first case study in the IBM System z environment. Since we use the same application as before, we can reuse the structural information that is modeled with the PCM. We merely have to exchange the I/O analysis model and recalibrate the PCM model. Similar to the first case study, we calibrate the PCM model of the file server with 40 clients and increase the number of clients in steps of 10 to evaluate both the mean I/O response time prediction error $err^{I/O}$ and the end-to-end response time prediction error err^{E2E}.

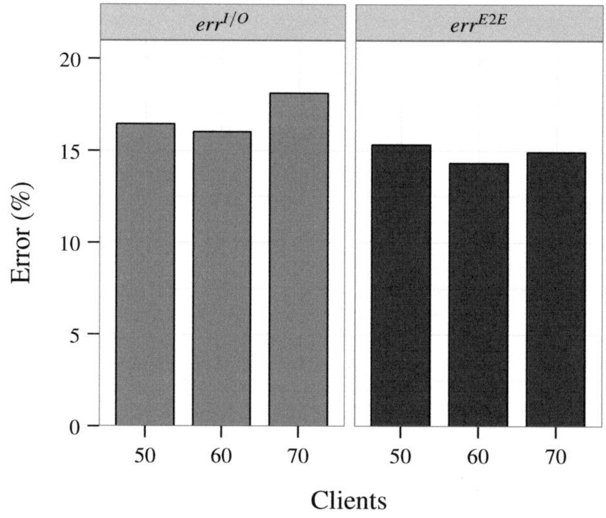

Clients	50	60	70
$err^{I/O}$	16.45 %	16.02 %	18.12 %
err^{E2E}	15.33 %	14.34 %	14.93 %

Figure 9.19.: Prediction Error in Case Study III

Increasing the number of clients up to 70, we observe that the end-to-end response time measurements increase from 38.66 ms (40 clients) to 68.55 ms (70 clients). Figure 9.19 shows the prediction error with the PCM model for the configurations. The prediction error in this case study is encouraging with a prediction error between 16 % and 18 % for the I/O response time and a prediction error of approximately 15 % for the end-to-end response time. Compared to the first case study employing the Sun Fire environment, we observe higher prediction errors in this case study. This is due to the high processing speed of the storage system resulting in a software bottleneck in the Filebench application during the response time measurements, which we first had to mitigate manually to obtain acceptable results.

9.5.5. Case Study IV: File and Mail Server on System z

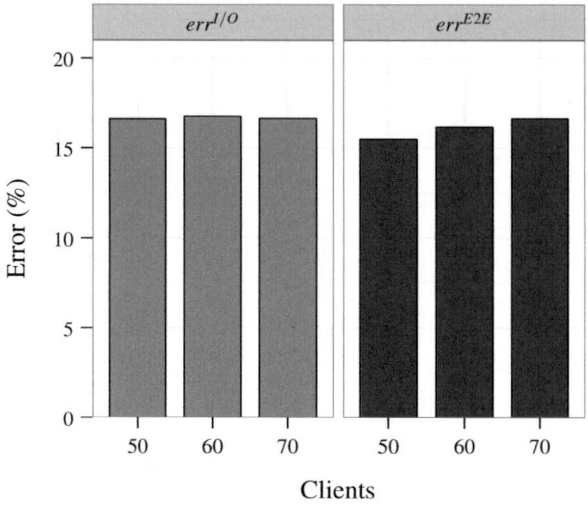

Clients	50	60	70
$err^{I/O}$	16.62 %	16.77 %	16.64 %
err^{E2E}	15.49 %	16.17 %	16.64 %

Figure 9.20.: Prediction Error in Case Study IV – File Server

In our final case study, we use the System z environment and extend the application setup modeling the file server as well as the mail server application, where each application runs in a separate VM. We measure the file and the mail server with 40 and 10 clients, respectively, and increase the number of clients for both applications simultaneously in steps of 10 to predict the mean I/O response time prediction error $err^{I/O}$ and the end-to-end response time prediction error err^{E2E}.

For the applications, we observe that the end-to-end response time measurements are between 52.67 ms (40 clients) and 106.87 ms (70 clients) for the file server and between 37.03 ms (10 clients) and 65.25 ms (40 clients) for the mail server. To predict the I/O performance, we still use a single regression model integrated into the PCM to capture the I/O performance of the consolidated applications. The prediction errors are summarized in Figure 9.20 and Figure 9.21 for the file and the mail server, respectively. For the file server, the model exhibits a constant prediction accuracy across the scenarios with approximately 16 % mean I/O response time prediction error as well as end-to-end response time prediction error. For the mail server, the prediction error is again higher than the file server application as the workload intensity is again increased from calibration to prediction by up to 300 %. Still, the prediction error is acceptable with approximately between 18 % and 25 % mean I/O response time prediction error and between 18 % and 28 % end-to-end response time prediction error.

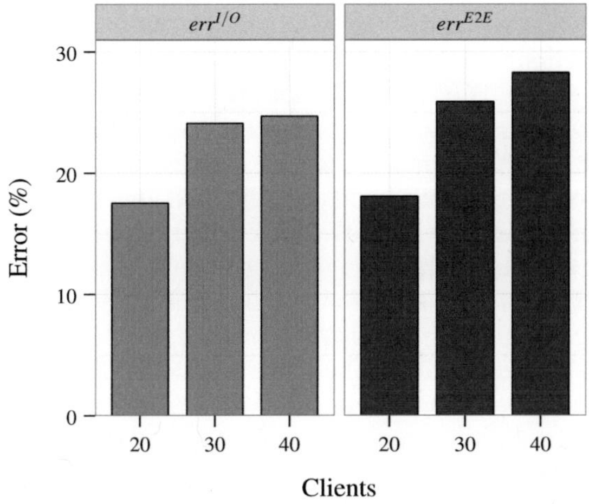

Clients	20	30	40
$err^{I/O}$	17.54 %	24.09 %	24.68 %
err^{E2E}	18.10 %	25.91 %	28.29 %

Figure 9.21.: Prediction Error in Case Study IV – Mail Server

9.5.6. Summary and Discussion

In this section, we presented four case studies modeling a file server and a mail server application at the software architecture level running in two representative virtualized environments, whose I/O performance is not easily modeled manually (cf. Chapter 7). To capture the I/O performance of the system environments, we employed our regression analysis-based modeling approach in an automated process to obtain an I/O analysis model with reduced manual effort. We integrated the regression models into the software architecture model of the PCM and demonstrated that the combination approach can be used to predict the performance of the considered I/O-intensive applications. We evaluated the prediction accuracy for capacity planning scenarios when the number of users increases and obtained an average end-to-end prediction error across the prediction scenarios of 6.98 %, 20.34 %, 14.87 %, and 20.39 % in the four case studies. Overall, this addresses our first evaluation goal and shows that the combined model can be used to predict the performance with sufficient accuracy. Furthermore, the case studies showed relevant results regarding our second evaluation goal and the modeling overhead and transferability. As the regression models were created in an automated process, the modeling overhead of the storage infrastructure was minimal. This is especially beneficial to capture both the I/O performance as well as the mutual performance influences of parallel workloads at the storage resources as shown in our final case study, where two parallel applications running in separate VMs share the storage resources. Also, the structural and behavioral model of the applications captured with the PCM could be reused when the system environment changed, which increases the transferability of the architecture model. Only the regression model capturing the I/O performance needed to be exchanged and the resource demands in the PCM needed to be re-calibrated.

Realizing the case studies also revealed some considerations beyond the prediction results. A first observation is that the prediction accuracy of the combined model might also depend on the calibration of the I/O analysis model parameterization. For instance, the overall I/O load produced on the storage system in our IBM System z environment was reduced as mentioned above because of a software bottleneck in the Filebench applications during the response time measurements as a result of very fast I/O request processing by the storage system, which resulted in overestimations of the I/O delays by the combined model. To address this issue, we had to manually identify the bottleneck in Filebench and mitigate its effect. Furthermore, in our final case study we reduced the calculated *concurrent request* parameter by 25 % when passed to the I/O analysis model during simulation. In general, further tailoring of the calibration might increase the prediction accuracy, however, we limited the calibration process in the case studies to a practically reasonable amount to obtain sufficiently accurate performance predictions. A further consideration is that the regression models employed in the case studies to capture the I/O performance are created at a certain abstraction level with the goal to predict mean response times, thus the models abstract the distributions of the response times and have an inherent potential for inaccuracies. To extend the approach to provide response time distributions, the simulation could use further regression models that model and predict response time quantiles. However, this also increases the modeling overhead. Finally, a significant observation in the case studies is that to obtain a regression model for the I/O performance, a large number of measurements is needed in general to cover all configuration combinations. In the case studies, we reduced the number of required measurements for the regression models by first testing the parameter ranges produced by the application workload. The regions around those ranges were then explored with measurements to create the regression model. An alternative approach would be to use our queueing theory-based modeling approach to predict the I/O response times, however, creating the model requires more manual effort in general.

9.6. Discussion of the Approach

Overall, the case studies in the previous sections showed that we are able to obtain reasonable I/O performance predictions in non-trivial virtualized environments. After the presentation of the prediction results along the previous case studies, this section highlights the scope of our work by discussing the applicability and the evaluation criteria as well as the assumptions of the approach. In the following sections, we elaborate on these considerations grouping the discussion along multiple aspects: i) Automation, ii) modeling abstraction, iii) complementary formalisms, iv) predicting the performance without our approach, v) discussion of the evaluation criteria, and vi) assumptions and limitations. Overall, aspects i) and ii) are important aspects that allow to employ our approach by non-performance engineering experts. These aspects as well as aspect iii) are significant for an increased applicability of our work.

9.6.1. Automation

One of the key factors for the applicability and reproducibility of the approach presented in this thesis is its high degree of automation and tool support (cf. Section 5.4, Noorshams et al. 2015). More specifically, all measurements, monitoring, and I/O performance model creations presented in the case studies of this chapter are fully automated. Merely the software architecture-level model in the PCM was created manually in our case studies, however, existing approaches showed how to create PCM models from running applications (e.g., Brosig et al., 2011; Brosig et al., 2009) and from source code (e.g., Krogmann, 2010), which was not the focus of our work. As a result, this supports the applicability and the reproducibility of the approach through the reduced manual effort and limited vulnerability to manual errors during the performance evaluation, which in turn increases the efficiency of the work. Furthermore, this reduces the required expertise for performance model creation as well as required depth of analysis of the system environment.

9.6.2. Modeling Abstraction

Our overall approach is targeted at obtaining practical performance models including the modeling and prediction at the software architecture level. As part of our approach, the storage-level I/O analysis models were generally developed to provide easily parameterizable abstractions. The regression analysis-based models introduced in Chapter 6 merely require observations in form of measurements, which were obtained in our case studies using different I/O benchmarks. Similarly, the queueing theory-based models presented in Chapter 7 are calibrated with response time measurements only and do not require in-depth monitoring data. While the modeling formalisms and elements of the storage-level I/O analysis models are at a lower abstraction level, as detailed in Chapter 8 we employ the I/O analysis models and integrate them into the software architecture-level modeling approach of the PCM, which is generally characterized by a high modeling abstraction level and comprised of largely intuitive modeling constructs. The combined models in our extension of the PCM as evaluated in Section 9.5 are key for the I/O performance models at the high abstraction level. Simply the structure and the behavior of an application need to be specified as indicated in Figure 8.3 and Figure 8.4 as well as Figure 9.16.

Addressing the relevance of this extension of the PCM, Chapter 7 presented how the modeling of I/O performance can be done explicitly with the use of modeling formalisms for request scheduling. Modeling such a request scheduling in the PCM is not intended and it is therefore not natively supported. Without our extension, it is required to extend the PCM by an explicit scheduler (e.g., realized by a simulator) to enforce the request scheduling as needed and identified by example in Chapter 7. This scheduler extension, however, has to be realized manually, which is not only demanding expertise and system understanding, but also a significant amount of time. From a practical point of view, the benefit of our approach combining storage-level models with software architecture-level models is that it abstracts the complexity and modeling overhead and hides them into tools and automated processes, since the target group of the PCM is comprised of software developers that are not necessarily performance engineering experts. As shown in Chapter 8, the modeler only provides estimations for the I/O requests without their resource demands or scheduling behavior at the storage level. All the request information from the application level to the storage level is mapped in the PCM during a simulation-based model solving and our storage scheduler in the simulation is able to estimate the actual I/O request delays.

9.6.3. Complementary Formalisms

For our I/O performance analysis, we have used and tailored multiple, complementary formalisms to increase the applicability of our work. We used both an implicit and an explicit modeling approach to create the storage-level I/O analysis models. The implicit, regression analysis-based modeling approach is fully automated. The caveat of this approach is, however, that the required number of measurements grows exponentially with the number of modeled factors. Still, a possible use case for such an approach is to create the regression models automatically by the system manufacturer when deploying the system environment. In general, newly developed systems are usually evaluated with benchmarks and extending the process by an automated model creation step can provide a benefit and support the customers to use the resources efficiently. If the required measurements need to be reduced, the explicit, queueing theory-based modeling approach can be used by a performance expert to create the performance model initially. As the measurements for calibration can be automated as done in our work, the model can be calibrated automatically if a similar system environment is to be modeled. Finally, we use and integrate our I/O analysis models into a software architecture-level modeling approach developing a high-level modeling approach that is simple to employ. Overall, these modeling approaches can be used to find the best fitting system environment for given applications by estimating the applications' performance and the required resources to guarantee a certain level of application responsiveness.

9.6.4. Predicting the Performance without our Approach

The multiple case studies of this chapter showed that our approach is able to predict the I/O performance in virtualized environments with a high degree of automation. By extending the PCM, we developed an approach to predict the I/O performance at the software architecture level, since we claimed that the existing software architecture-level modeling approaches do not sufficiently consider the performance-influencing factors. At this point, however, the questions arise: What is the prediction accuracy of the PCM without our extension? Are the additional modeling artifacts of our extension justified? To support our claim that our approach is key to obtain accurate predictions, we find an example showing that the PCM without our extension struggles to predict the I/O performance in virtualized environments with sufficient accuracy.

For this example, we exploit our knowledge gained in Chapter 7. There, we analyzed the effects of different types of I/O requests on the performance of the respective requests. More specifically, we observed in our reference environment that read and write requests are processed depending on the ratio of the request types. In the PCM without our extension (in the following denoted *PCM Standard*), I/O requests are abstracted and represented by their demand. In the PCM with our extension (in the following denoted *PCM Extended*), we are able to explicitly distinguish between read and write requests and their I/O delay is determined by our I/O analysis model. Consequently, our hypothesis is that if we change the ratio of read and write requests of an application deployed in our reference environment, we find an example where the prediction accuracy of PCM Extended excels the prediction accuracy of PCM Standard.

To this end, we modify the setup of one of our previous case studies. Similar to the third case study shown in Section 9.5, we model the file server application in the IBM System z environment (cf. Section 9.2). For both PCM Extended and PCM Standard, we calibrate the PCM model of the file server application with a given number of clients. Then, we predict the effect when the number of read operations in the file server application is increased by a factor of five, i.e., we predict the effect of five reads instead of one in the sequence of the application. The performance predictions of this scenario are given in Figure 9.22, where we have indicated the target prediction accuracy of up to 30 % prediction error (cf. Menascé et al., 2000). We evaluated the mean I/O response time prediction error $err^{I/O}$ and the end-to-end response time prediction error err^{E2E} as defined in Equation (9.3) and Equation (9.4), respectively. We calibrated the PCM models with 50 clients (default value) as well as with 60 clients and predicted the performance in each case when the read proportion increases. As shown in Figure 9.22, PCM Extended exhibits a good prediction accuracy with approximately 20 % mean I/O response time prediction error and approximately 12 % end-to-end response time prediction error. By contrast, the prediction error is significantly higher with PCM Standard exceeding the prediction error threshold. We purposefully triggered the high prediction errors of PCM Standard of more than 50 % in these scenarios. Overall, this confirms our hypothesis showing that our approach is required and allows for accurate I/O performance predictions in virtualized environments at the software architecture level.

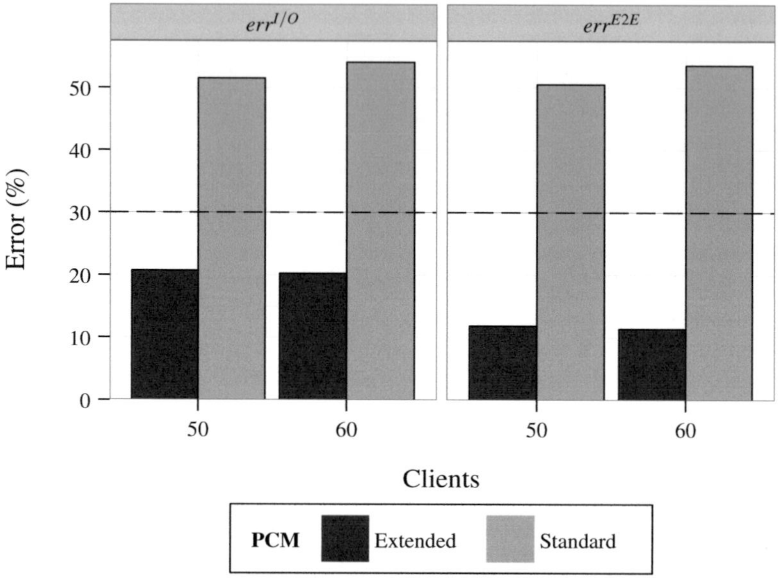

(a) PCM Extended

Clients	50	60
$err^{I/O}$	20.72 %	20.25 %
err^{E2E}	11.90 %	11.44 %

(b) PCM Standard

Clients	50	60
$err^{I/O}$	51.49 %	54.05 %
err^{E2E}	50.52 %	53.58 %

Figure 9.22.: Prediction Error of the Standard PCM and the PCM with our Extension

9.6.5. Discussion of the Evaluation Criteria

In the introduction of this work in the first chapter, we highlighted the five evaluation criteria our approach aims to fulfill, we aim i) to provide an *abstraction* of the system environment, ii) to *accurately* predict the performance, iii) to create the models *efficiently*, iv) to *scale* and model realistic environments, and v) to provide *automation* and tool-support:

1. Abstraction: Overall, we can summarize that we abstracted two real-world, realistic environments with manageable performance models. Our regression analysis-based approach derives the relationship between the performance-influencing factors and the I/O performance statistically and in an automated process. Our queueing theory-based approach requires an analysis by an expert, but allows for simplified reuse by only requiring to calibrate a few queueing stations and model parameters as described in Chapter 7. By allowing to use our I/O performance modeling approach at the software architecture level, we enable to model and predict the I/O performance at a high abstraction level without demanding deep knowledge of the system details.
2. Accuracy: Across the multiple case studies, we successfully predicted the I/O performance in different environments and in many scenarios with the required accuracy of less than 30 % prediction error. As described in the final case studies, our approach does not only provide accurate prediction, but also showed to successfully capture the I/O performance and hide the complexity of virtualized environments at the software architecture level.
3. Efficiency: In our I/O performance modeling approach, we increase the model building efficiency by providing a high degree of automation and clear processes throughout the different aspects. In regard to the software architecture-level modeling approach, we were even able to reduce the model parameterization effort while at the same time increasing the prediction accuracy as demonstrated in the final case studies and the previous section. More specifically, while it was previously necessary to manually estimate the resource demands of I/O requests, our approach merely requires to specify parameters of the requests, such as the request type and size, which can be specified from the workload description or easily estimated because of the tangible nature of the

parameters. Furthermore, using the fully automated regression analysis-based modeling approach reduces the required expertise and analysis of the system environment allowing to capture the I/O performance effects with reduced manual effort. If the number of measurements needs to be reduced, our queueing theory-based modeling approach can be applied, where only calibration measurements are required after the structure of the model is identified.

4. Scalability: Across the case studies, we evaluated our approach in two realistic, state-of-the-art system environments based on IBM System z and Sun Fire server hardware. The two systems are not only representative, non-trivial environments, but also heterogeneous in both virtualization architecture and hardware infrastructure. This allows to draw the conclusion that our approach can scale to further environments and in real-world scenarios.

5. Automation: As dedicatedly discussed above, we automated our modeling approach to a high extent to simplify the applicability and efficiency of our approach and reduce the risk for manual errors. More specifically, all measurements and monitoring data collections as well as the I/O performance model creations as part of our approach that are demonstrated in the case studies of this chapter are automated and tool-supported.

9.6.6. Assumptions and Limitations

A central challenge of this thesis is to provide I/O performance predictions with a reasonable trade-off between modeling applicability and prediction accuracy. For the presented case studies, we have demonstrated that we are able to obtain sufficiently accurate performance predictions. In general, however, our modeling approach has assumptions and limitations.

Since the storage-level I/O analysis models are measurement-based, the probably most apparent assumption for the I/O performance models is that the regarded system environment needs to be available to obtain measurements at the time of the model creation. This has implications for performance evaluations at software design time and requires that at least the target system or a comparable one can be used to create the I/O analysis models. Estimations may help as well, but are probably less effective. Once such a system environment is available, the benefit of our approach is that the storage-level performance model is represented by the workload characterization in a generic manner, such that the model can be created once and can be used for different applications and workload profiles for performance predictions at the software architecture level.

Regarding the application, our modeling approach was designed to model stable workload as opposed to, e.g., bursty and fluctuating workload. Although we have not demonstrated this, we reason that we are able to at least obtain a reasonable pessimistic performance estimation of bursty and fluctuating workload. If the application is modeled at the time of the highest load, an estimation for the worst case performance of the system is still helpful to plan the system capacity accordingly. For example, an application may have usually 20 users and 50 users during peak hours. Our approach can be used to predict the performance for 20 users first, and then for 50 users afterwards, such that the system environment can be optimized for both situations individually.

In the models, we abstracted the workload factors and used mean values for the dimensions of the workload characterization throughout the modeling process. Similarly, the I/O performance predictions aim to predict the mean response times and throughputs and are not intended to predict the performance distributions per se. Usually, the average performance is a reasonable indicator for the overall system performance and a metric that is easy to understand and interpret. In general, however, SLAs may include worst case performance guarantees in terms of the maximum response time or the 95th percentile of the response time, for example. For such cases, our approach needs to be extended to consider distributions for the workload factors as well as for the modeling formalisms, for example by using multiple regression analysis models capturing the relevant performance quantiles or approximating the distributions of the performance in the queueing models more closely.

In the case studies on our software architecture-level modeling approach, the applications modeled with the PCM were straightforward to capture at the architecture level. This is because the focus of our work was not to evaluate if the PCM can capture a complex application, but to analyze how the I/O performance in complex environments can be predicted by providing only the architecture-level application information and using this information in a combined model solving approach to obtain the results. At this point, more complex applications with bursty and varying behavior, for example, might require to extend the models employed within our approach as discussed above by using response time distributions and possibly refining the performance-influencing factors. Still, the considered applications are representative, typical I/O-intensive applications and sufficient as a proof-of-concept of our approach.

In our performance modeling process, we analyzed the different modeling approaches assuming to have enough time for the model creation, calibration, and validation, which is a reasonable assumption at software design time. During software runtime, further constraints typically arise, such as limited amount of time and data available for the modeling process. While we were focused on efficiently creating the performance models, it needs to be investigated if and how our approach needs to be extended to account for online performance prediction scenarios. For example, our automated workload characterization approach can be used to first extract the workload characteristics of a running application, and then our regression analysis-based modeling approach specifically focusing on an efficient model creation can be applied to obtain a performance model. This model created under online conditions can then be evaluated for its applicability and prediction accuracy.

Considering the modeled resource, the focus of our work was exclusively I/O performance of storage resources. While we abstracted some file system operations as CPU operations, a combined consideration of CPU, memory, and network resources with the storage resources including mutual performance effects is not addressed in our work. Generally, there can be mutual performance influences and bottlenecks that can be investigated in modeling approaches analyzing such effects. Still, our work is beneficial for I/O performance analysis when the storage resource is the bottleneck and provides a basis for extension to account for combined effects with other resources. Such a combined consideration is useful in heterogeneous environments that serve different applications that are not necessarily all I/O-intensive as well as in cases where the bottleneck shifts from resource to resource depending on the workload profile. For example, light data workload may be served from memory, thus putting the burden on the CPU and memory resources, whereas heavy data workload may not be buffered by the memory sufficiently, thus shifting the bottleneck to the storage resource.

In the context of storage resources, the focus of our work is block-based storage as described in Chapter 2. Other storage paradigms, such as file-based and object-based storage, were not analyzed as part of our work and may reveal other abstractions and opportunities for performance modeling approaches. These approaches could in turn be tailored to efficiently obtain performance results in scenarios that were not in the focus of this work, for instance, when employing object storage in Cloud environments.

Finally with regard to our system setup, our work was applied to up to three VMs accessing and sharing a storage system. Typical productive environments are comprised of many VMs and storage systems and it needs to be investigated if our work can be applied in such scenarios and possibly how it needs to be extended to capture larger setups efficiently. Still, the case studies of our work in the non-trivial environments encourage the applicability of our work in further, complex scenarios.

In summary, we have shown that our approach is able to predict the performance of I/O-intensive applications in sufficiently complex environments with generally acceptable accuracy. In our approach, we were focused on modeling mean performance characteristics of block-based storage in cases where the storage resource is the bottleneck. Given the required time and data, our modeling approach provides tailored techniques for virtualized environment using different modeling formalisms to model and predict the performance depending on the available expertise. For a further applicability, our approach can serve as a basis for different extensions and investigations along multiple dimensions as highlighted in this section revealing paths for future research.

Part III.

Related Work and Conclusion

10. Related Work

There are multiple fields concerned with performance evaluation and modeling that are related to the work presented in this thesis. The focus of this chapter is to systematically analyze existing approaches and address their relationship to our work. To this end, in the following we broadly survey related work grouped into multiple areas. We begin with a brief overview of the related areas in Section 10.1. We then in Section 10.2 discuss related approaches that analyze and model I/O performance in virtualized environments. Section 10.3 summarizes approaches concerned with analyzing and modeling of I/O performance interference. As part of our work, we integrated our I/O performance models into software architecture modeling approaches and we focus on similar approaches in Section 10.4. We further expand the discussion to more broadly related work. We introduce selected, established approaches for modeling disk and disk array performance in Section 10.5 and in Section 10.6, we elaborate on general system performance evaluation and modeling approaches. To conclude, Section 10.7 summarizes this chapter and highlights the main distinguishing aspects of this thesis.

10.1. Overview

To give an overview of the performance evaluation and modeling approaches presented in this chapter, in this section we briefly introduce the areas of related work. The general areas are illustrated in Figure 10.1, where we color-coded the areas w.r.t. their relation to our work. The areas are i) I/O performance analysis and modeling in virtualized environments, ii) I/O performance interference analysis and modeling in virtualized environments, iii) software architecture-level I/O performance modeling, iv) disk-based I/O performance modeling in native environments, and v) general systems performance evaluation and modeling in virtualized environments. Among these areas, our work fits into the areas i) – iii) and is highlighted in their intersection in Figure 10.1.

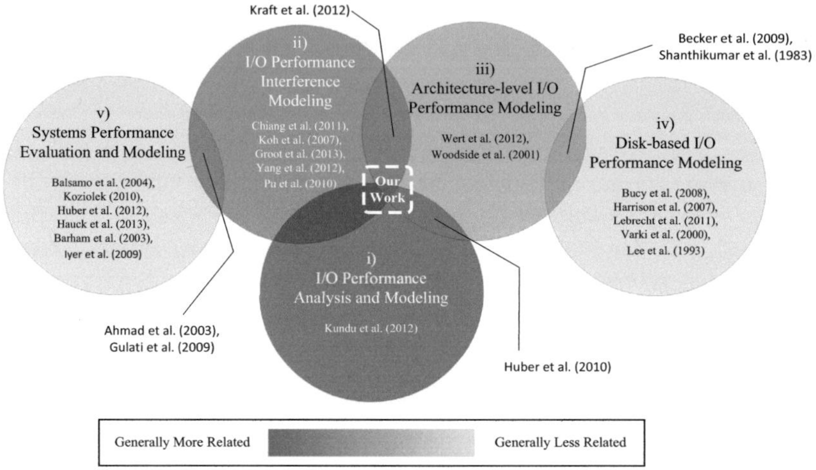

Figure 10.1.: Areas of Related Work with the Center *I/O Performance Analysis and Modeling in Virtualized Environments*

The areas and the related approaches can be roughly classified along the following three dimensions:

- *Modeling in Virtualized Environments – Modeling in Native Environments*

  Approaches modeling performance in virtualized environment are in the areas i), ii), the intersecting parts of area iii) with areas i) and ii), and area v). The remaining parts are addressing performance in native environments.

- *Modeling of I/O Performance – Modeling of System Performance*

  Areas addressing and analyzing I/O performance are areas i) – iv) and the intersecting part of area v) with area i).

- *Modeling at the Architecture Level – Modeling at the Storage Level*

  Evaluation approaches at the architecture level are in area iii) and its intersecting parts with areas i), ii), and iv). The rest is focusing on a more lower, storage level.

In the following sections, we will discuss the related work within the five areas. For the sake of clarity, a compact overview of the related work can be found in Appendix A.

10.2. I/O Performance Analysis and Modeling

The first area of related work is focused on analyzing and modeling storage I/O performance in virtualized environments. The approaches in this area are closely related to the I/O analysis models of our work, however, the approaches are primarily focused on capturing the I/O performance-influencing factors at a low abstraction level and it is not straightforward to include such models into software architecture models, since the required information between the two modeling abstraction levels needs to be synchronized.

Closest to our work among the approaches in this area, Kraft et al. (2012) present two queueing theory-based approaches to model and predict the I/O performance in virtualized environments. They focus on scenarios when consolidating multiple VMs that run I/O-intensive applications. In their first approach, they develop a simulation model for consolidated homogeneous workloads. They model the storage resource in the virtualized environment as a single multi-server queue whose service times are fitted to a Markovian Arrival Process (MAP) with measurements. They extend their work in a second approach, where they model and predict the I/O performance when consolidating heterogeneous workloads. They develop a closed queueing model where the storage resource is also abstracted as a single queue whose service times are fitted to a MAP. In both of their approaches, the authors employ monitored measurements on the block layer abstracting the application and file layer. Moreover, in contrast to our work the approaches are focused on I/O performance prediction of VM consolidation scenarios and do not evaluate, e.g., performance and interference effects due to changes in the workload intensity in the VMs.

To evaluate the I/O performance of VMware's ESX Server virtualization, Ahmad et al. (2003) run I/O benchmarks in multiple environments whose storage subsystem is comprised of a direct-attached disk, a RAID array, and a SAN built with a Fibre Channel-attached RAID array, respectively. Their goal is to evaluate the virtualization overhead and compare the virtual to the native I/O performance using benchmarks. In one of their case studies, they emulate a mail server workload with a disk benchmark, which can be compared to our workload characterization approach. The authors, however, do not compare the performance of the emulated workload with the original one. They further derive mathematical models to estimate the virtualization overhead and use it to predict the resulting I/O performance deterioration.

By applying different machine learning techniques, Kundu et al. (2012) use artificial neural networks and support vector machines to model the performance of applications deployed in virtualized environments. The applications are obtained from two different benchmarks, whose throughputs are collected. They predict the performance of the application as a function of the resources allocated to the host VM. In their models, they use CPU, memory, and I/O allocation as independent variables and application performance as dependent variable. The models are then used for capacity planning and VM sizing scenarios in terms of CPU and memory allocation for a given I/O latency.

In a further work, Gulati et al. (2009) present a study on storage workload characterization in virtualized environments. The authors analyze four workloads generated from both applications and benchmarks. The workloads are characterized with storage metrics, e.g., seek distances, request sizes, and burstiness. They also analyze consolidated workloads in separate VMs, but they do not develop any performance models.

10.3. I/O Performance Interference Modeling

The second area of related work analyzes and models I/O performance interference effects in virtualized environments. This area is primarily focused on evaluating how co-located workloads sharing the physical storage resources are affecting the performance of one another. This area is also closely related to the first area and similarly analyzes I/O performance-influencing factors at a low abstraction level. To further highlight the difference of our work to the approaches presented next, none of these approaches uses queueing theory-based or architecture-level modeling approaches to capture the I/O performance interference effects. Furthermore, some of the approaches use vendor-specific monitoring tools (e.g., *xen-top*) to obtain internal information of the global system environment, which is not necessarily always feasible in every environment.

Closest to our work among the approaches in this area, Chiang et al. (2011) use linear and second degree polynomials to create models of I/O performance interference. As independent variables, they use read and write request arrival rates as well as local and global CPU utilization. In contrast to our work, however, they do not distinguish between, e.g., request sizes and access patterns. Our measurements have shown that such factors have a significant impact on the I/O performance. Furthermore, we observed a logarithmic effect on the I/O performance for some of the factors we consider (cf. Chapter 7), which cannot be captured accurately by linear and second degree polynomials. The models created in their work are used for scheduling algorithms to manage task assignments in virtualized data centers. Their approach is evaluated using simulation results.

Koh et al. (2007) analyze performance interference across multiple resources including storage resources in a Xen-based virtualized environment. They use benchmarks and applications, such as *gzip*, running in two VMs – the physical hardware environment is not detailed. They develop two types of linear models to predict the performance of an application in consolidation, which is normalized w.r.t. the application performance in isolation. The first type is based on principal component analysis. The second type is a linear regression model using low-level monitoring data across the resources as independent variables, for example, CPU time, cache hits, VM switches per second, numbers of read and write requests issued, and time spent for I/O requests. Similar to the previous approaches, they do not consider, e.g., the access pattern of the I/O requests.

Addressing I/O performance interference for a certain domain, Groot et al. (2013) model and predict the I/O performance when running multiple processes of MapReduce applications simultaneously on the same host. For their model, they split the tasks of a MapReduce application into multiple phases, which issue certain read and write requests, and for each phase, the authors develop mathematical models to use for prediction. Overall, while the approach addresses I/O performance interference among workloads, it differs from our work primarily in two aspects. First, the focus of their work is modeling

MapReduce applications. Second, they model the I/O performance interference among MapReduce processes rather that among workloads running in co-located VMs.

In more remotely related work, Yang et al. (2012) present a framework that uses a set of I/O operations to identify and reveal I/O scheduling characteristics of the hypervisor. They experiment in Xen-based and in VMware-based virtualized environments as well as in a public Cloud environment. They show how the scheduling information can be exploited to slow down the I/O performance of co-located virtual machines.

Further, Pu et al. (2010) present an experimental study to analyze and evaluate CPU and network I/O performance interference in a Xen-based virtualized environment with two VMs. They evaluate different workload combinations using workloads that access different sized files. They conclude that the least performance deterioration occurs for the consolidation of workloads with different resource demands, i.e., CPU-bound and network I/O-bound demand in the case of mixing small with large file requests.

10.4. Architecture-level I/O Performance Modeling

As a unique distinguishing factor, we are to the best of our knowledge the first work to address capacity planning questions using performance models of I/O-intensive applications deployed in virtualized environments at the software architecture level. We realized our approach by combining architecture-level with storage-level performance models. In this section, we highlight both aspects and discuss approaches for architecture-level performance modeling as well as approaches for combining different types of performance models.

As a basis of our work, we use the PCM as presented by Becker et al. (2009). As discussed before, storage resources in the PCM are represented as a single queue with a given scheduling strategy and I/O requests are represented by one parameter, which is the request demand. While this is a reasonable abstraction for traditional environments, our analysis revealed that the model of I/O requests needed to be extended to accurately capture the I/O performance in virtualized environments.

Using the PCM, Huber et al. (2010) present an industrial case study on design alternatives for storage virtualization. The authors evaluate in the case study synchronous and asynchronous I/O request handling in the virtualization layer of a system environment based on an IBM System z server. As emphasized in their work, the goal of the study is to evaluate whether the PCM can be applied in industry rather than, in contrast to the goal of our approach, aiming to generally predict the performance of I/O-intensive applications in virtualized environments.

The remaining approaches in this section address how low-level performance models for resources can be used in higher-level performance models. Closest to our work among those approaches, Wert et al. (2012) develop a concept for combining statistical, measurement-based performance models with software architecture-level models. Their goal is to support performance predictions for systems that include parts whose internal structure is unknown, e.g., external services and legacy systems. The work outlines the general, domain-independent concept and technical realization to achieve their goal. Furthermore, they present an example of a statistical model for a MySQL database to illustrate such a measurement-based performance model, however, they do not show the result when the model is integrated into the software architecture model. Moreover, the difference to our work is that we propose a specific approach for integrating I/O performance models into software architecture models including a concrete design of relevant parameters that need to be specified both at the software architecture level and at the storage level. Thus, we specifically analyzed what information is required for I/O performance prediction at the architecture level and how it can be realized.

The previous work uses an automated approach to obtain a statistical performance model. A similar approach is presented by Woodside et al. (2001) for abstracting resources. In this work, the authors present an environment comprised of a measurement harness, a statistical modeling module, and a model repository. The goal of their approach is to develop statistical models for resource demands of software components and subsystems. The authors indicate that the resource demand models could be used in a performance model of the software environment, however without going into specific details how this could be realized.

In a further work that is related to our work methodologically, Shanthikumar et al. (1983) present a general classification scheme for hybrid modeling using analytical and simulation models. In their work, the authors present several case studies and include ones abstracting simple disks as queues. This is the typical abstraction level for traditional disks and considered in, e.g., the PCM before. Our approach extends the I/O performance modeling concepts allowing to predict the performance in more complex, virtualized system environments.

10.5. Disk-based I/O Performance Modeling

There are a number of classical performance modeling approaches for disks and disk arrays in native environments. The major distinguishing factor in comparison to our approach is that the disk models typically rely on low-level instrumentation and monitoring data, such as allocation of data to disk sectors, disk seek times, disk rotation time, and single disk utilization. In typical virtualized environments, such information is hardly available for storage users, if available at all, hampering the practicability and reliable parameterization of these models. Among the disk-based I/O performance models, the most prominent approaches are briefly summarized next.

Bucy et al. (2008) have developed DiskSim, a very detailed and accurate simulator of disk systems. DiskSim particularly simulates fine-grained disk system components, such as the devices, buses, device drivers, and request schedulers, for example, to obtain the performance behavior in a high level of detail. Harrison et al. (2007) use queueing models to capture the performance behavior of RAID arrays focusing on RAID-01 and RAID-5 systems. They model the disks analytically, where the disk response time is comprised of the waiting time in the disk queue, the seek time, the rotational latency, and the transfer time. Lebrecht et al. (2011) extend the work to RAID arrays with zoned disks that have more disk sectors on the outer tracks than in the inner tracks. They also consider key disk characteristics, such as the seek time, the rotational latency, and the data transfer time, to model the disk response times. Comparable work has been proposed by Varki et al. (2000) and Lee et al. (1993) developing analytical, closed queueing models for disk arrays. Varki et al. (2000) use a network and model the disks as queues similar to the previous approaches. In their approach, the performance of a request is derived from single disk response times. Lee et al. (1993) create analytical functions to first estimate the utilization of the disks in the array, which is then used to derive the response time and the throughput.

10.6. Systems Performance Evaluation and Modeling

The final area of related work deals with general system performance evaluation and modeling in virtualized environments that are not specifically addressing I/O performance. The selected approaches presented in this section are related from a methodological point of view how the performance is analyzed for different resources and purposes. As the approaches are more distantly related to the work presented in this thesis, we only briefly summarize the concepts in this section. A more detailed and general overview is presented, for example, by Balsamo et al. (2004) and Koziolek (2010), who broadly survey approaches for performance evaluation and modeling of software systems without explicitly focusing on I/O performance as in our work.

Among the approaches in this area, Huber et al. (2012) present an approach for quantitative evaluation of performance-influencing factors in virtualized environments. They employ their approach to evaluate the performance overhead in VMware-based and in Xen-based virtualized environments. Furthermore, they create linear regression models for the scalability of virtualized CPU and memory performance. Comparable to this approach, Hauck et al. (2013) present an automated approach for goal-oriented measurements to evaluate performance-relevant infrastructure properties. The measurements are defined in their approach as experiments with certain workload patterns. In their work, the authors analyze OS scheduler properties as well as CPU and disk I/O virtualization overheads. In an earlier work, Barham et al. (2003) have developed the Xen hypervisor. The authors evaluate the hypervisor and compare its performance to a native system as well as to other virtualization technologies. For their evaluation, they use a variety of benchmarks, e.g., a file system benchmark and a web server benchmark, to stress the system throughout the resources and analyze key performance indicators, such as the hypervisor overhead and scalability. Finally in a further work, Iyer et al. (2009) analyze resource contention and performance interference when sharing resources in virtualized environments. The authors analyze and evaluate primarily core, cache, and memory effects in a multi-core environment.

10.7. Summary

In short, there are generally different approaches concerned with I/O performance analysis in virtualized environments. In contrast to our work, however, the existing approaches capture the I/O performance-influencing factors at a low abstraction level as well as with focus on specific scenarios only or with validation limited to basic environments. Moreover, we are to the best of our knowledge the first work to propose a performance modeling approach of I/O-intensive applications in virtualized environments at the software architecture level. Finally, we provide multiple tailored approaches using different modeling formalisms to practically and reasonably abstract real-world system environments and capture their I/O performance.

Overall, we surveyed related work and grouped the approaches into five areas. The approaches in the first and second areas analyze and model I/O performance as well as I/O performance interference effects in virtualized environments. Approaches in these areas are typically modeling at a low abstraction level and are not intended for their applicability within higher-level modeling approaches. Moreover, the approaches focus on specific modeling formalisms, which are subject to inherent limitations regarding their applicability. The third area addresses I/O performance modeling at the software architecture level as well as combining low-level models with software architecture models, where in this thesis we propose a novel approach for I/O performance modeling in virtualized environments. The final two areas comprise approaches dealing with disk-based I/O performance analysis and modeling in native environments, which require low-level instrumentation and monitoring data for parameterization, and approaches for systems performance evaluation and modeling in virtualized environments not specifically focusing on I/O performance, which consequently do not address the specific challenges of I/O performance modeling.

11. Conclusion

In the final chapter, we conclude the thesis summarizing the results. Further, we discuss the limits of our work highlighting paths for future research.

11.1. Summary

In this thesis, we presented a novel approach for performance analysis and modeling of I/O-intensive applications in virtualized environments using multiple, complementary formalisms and combined them with modeling approaches at the software architecture level. For the practical use, we identified the required modeling parameters at a reasonable abstraction level and automated the modeling process to a high degree. We evaluated the thesis' contributions in multiple case studies using real-world, representative system environments based on IBM System z and Sun Fire server hardware demonstrating that we are able to successfully predict the performance of I/O-intensive applications in sufficiently complex system environments.

For our approach, we extended the model-based performance prediction process by first analyzing important performance-influencing factors. We then used those factors to create I/O performance models using multiple formalisms. We finally used these models in software architecture models, which were extended with the performance-influencing factors and solved in a simulation combined with the I/O performance models to obtain prediction results. To realize our approach, we identified major performance-influencing factors that we have grouped into workload-relevant and system-relevant factors. Based on these factors, we derived a workload characterization, which can be obtained from running applications automatically, and used it in the I/O performance modeling approaches. Here, we created implicit and explicit performance models based on regression analysis and queueing theory, respectively. Regression analysis-based models learn the I/O behavior implicitly by generalizing from measurements without modeling the causes for the performance behavior. To use such models, we have developed an automated regression technique parameterization and selection approach. As the number of measurements required for the regression analysis-based models grows exponentially with the number of modeled factors, we developed a tailored process based on queueing theory to model the I/O performance explicitly. Compared to creating regression analysis-based models, this process requires more manual effort and expertise for the model creation initially. However, the resulting models can be reused more easily by recalibrating the model parameters if the system is changed or a similar system is used. To use the I/O performance models at the software architecture level, we used and extended the Palladio Component Model, a model-based performance prediction approach for component-based software architectures. We identified the required parameters at the software architecture level that can be used during the simulation of the application's architecture model to map the parameters on the required parameters of the I/O performance models. The I/O performance models are then solved to capture the storage resource contention and to estimate the I/O request delays of the modeled application.

The evaluation of our approach showed very good results in terms of prediction accuracy across the different case studies. In general, we were able to successfully predict the I/O performance with close conformance to measurements on the real systems in various scenarios using both our regression analysis-based and queueing-theory-based approaches. Furthermore, to the best of our knowledge, we were the first work to predict the performance of I/O-intensive applications in virtualized environments at the software architecture level. In the case studies of our software architecture-level modeling approach, we modeled a file server and a mail server application in the two environments based on Sun Fire and IBM System z servers. For the prediction of the applications, we evaluated the mean I/O response time prediction error and the end-to-end response time prediction error when predicting the application performance in typical capacity planning scenarios if the number of users increases. We used the applications in isolation as well as in consolidation and were able to predict the response times with the required accuracy and less than 30 % mean prediction error.

Overall, we were able to fulfill our five evaluation criteria. First, we developed I/O performance models that were able to abstract the complexity of representative, sophisticated virtualized infrastructures into practical performance models. Second, as highlighted above, we were able to successfully capture and predict the I/O performance behavior with sufficient accuracy as demonstrated across our case studies. Third, we defined clear processes and automated approaches to increase the efficiency of our approach especially reducing the effort for software architects to model and predict the performance at the software architecture level. Further, we demonstrated our approaches throughout our work in representative, state-of-the-art environments to show the scalability of our work and its applicability to real-world systems. Finally, we automated the processes and modeling steps to a high extent providing tool-support where applicable.

In short, the main results of our work for modeling and predicting I/O performance and interference effects can be summarized as follows. i) We developed a workload characterization that can be obtained from running applications in an automated manner and that can be used to describe the I/O behavior of typical I/O-intensive applications. ii) We developed a fully automated regression analysis-based modeling approach that can optimally parameterize and choose from a set of regression techniques. iii) We developed a tailored process for queueing theory-based modeling to capture the hardware as well as request scheduling and optimization aspects of representative storage systems. We demonstrated our process creating a queueing model, where we used only few queueing stations and calibrated the model with observations in form of end-to-end response time measurements only. iv) We combined our I/O performance models with the Palladio Component Model bridging the gap between low-level I/O performance models and high-level software architecture models. v) In various case studies, we successfully predicted the performance of I/O-intensive applications deployed in sufficiently complex storage environments with reduced manual effort due to the high degree of automation throughout our approach.

Our approach is intended for multiple use cases and application scenarios. Data center operators can use the I/O performance models for an analysis and evaluation of capacity planning decisions and for system sizing. Furthermore, they can evaluate the scalability of their infrastructures and the impact of workload and VM consolidation. Software developers and architects can predict the performance at the architecture level to evaluate components that result in bottlenecks or disturb co-located components or applications. Finally, they can use the models to optimize the system configurations and to evaluate resource allocation decisions. In general, our approach supports tailoring resource allocations as needed as well as evaluating workload deployment and consolidation decisions and their trade-offs.

11.2. Limitations and Outlook on Future Research

The approach presented in this thesis was evaluated specifically in realistic environments with the goal to develop practical prediction models for typical environments. The prediction results presented throughout the case studies showed to be promising and accurate such that we can conclude that the models can be applied in similar contexts. For the approach in general, there are limits to the applicability as discussed in the validation of the approach. Thus, we identify multiple options for future research:

- *Bursty and Fluctuating Workload*

  In our work, we focused on steady, non-varying workload. To account for bursty workloads and workloads fluctuating over time in our approach, it is first required to find an appropriate metric, which can be a more sophisticated metric (cf. Mi et al., 2008; M. Wang et al., 2002) or a rather pragmatic one, e.g., the number of users issuing requests. Since for our approach the metric is used in our measurements as input to create the models, this metric needs to be fairly simple enough such that it can be emulated, i.e., that it can be reasonably reproduced with measurements. Finally, the models need to be extended to be able to include such varying workloads.

- *Horizontal Scaling of Workloads, VMs, and Storage Systems*

  While we applied our approach in representative and realistic environments, our approach is evaluated with up to three virtual machines running up to two workloads each. Data centers operate many more applications per storage system and many of them as well. It is an open question how our approach can scale to such large numbers or how it needs to be adapted such that it can be applied efficiently.

- *Online Regression Analysis-based Modeling*
  Our regression analysis-based approach assumes that the I/O performance model is created having sufficient time, e.g., by the system manufacturer when the storage system is deployed. While this is a reasonable assumption at software design time, it is interesting to investigate online approaches to collect the required data and measurements during operation to increase the applicability of the approach pursued in this thesis. Here, it is unclear how to monitor the system environment and what data to collect to efficiently create such prediction models.

- *File-based and Object-based Storage Services*
  The focus of our work was block-based storage. There are interesting storage paradigms, such as file-based and object-based storage. The latter is also often used in Cloud environments, for instance, to store static data produced by backups and archives. Evaluating the possibilities to extend our work in these directions can be interesting to provide more insights and tailored approaches in these areas. To account for these two paradigms, an additional abstraction layer can be defined atop our performance models, for instance. Another possibility can be to develop a tailored workload characterization and then adapt our I/O performance modeling approaches and processes.

- *Virtualization of Memory and Storage Resources*
  In our work, we specifically modeled I/O performance considering storage virtualization. In general, the storage scheduling and the memory management of both the operating system and the hypervisor can have mutual effects that were not subject of our analysis. For example, overcommitted or insufficient memory usually leads to frequent memory swapping and, thus, to intensive storage accesses.

- *Network Performance Effects in Network Virtualization and Storage Area Networks*
  The assumption in our work is that the storage resource is the bottleneck. Usually, network virtualization as evaluated by Rygielski et al. (2014), for instance, or network effects in storage area networks can impact the I/O performance as well, especially in highly distributed environments.

- *Big Data and Storage Virtualization*
  In recent years, the term Big Data for handling massive volumes of data emerged and its importance motivated new programming models,

such as MapReduce. In this domain, important aspects are storage performance as well as efficient storage and network usage in virtualized environments for Big Data applications that distribute and analyze the data. Future research can analyze the performance of such Big Data applications that are based on virtualized resources to improve their performance and resource efficiency.

- *Coupled Simulation of Application and I/O Performance Models*

  In our work, we integrated solving the I/O performance model into the software architecture model's simulation, which in this work is the SimuCom simulator for PCM models (Becker et al., 2009). In general, there are several strategies for coupled simulations as discussed by Shanthikumar et al. (1983) that can be followed to evaluate their effect.

- *Self-aware Computing Systems*

  The long-term vision by Kounev et al. (2010a) is to develop self-aware computing systems that are able to optimally allocate resources in an autonomic manner. Elements of their vision are approaches for online performance prediction (Brosig, 2014) as well as approaches for autonomic resource management (Huber, 2014). Such approaches are developed to manage all resources in a data center and can be combined with the analysis of storage resources and I/O performance as presented in this work to develop a holistic self-aware system environment.

11.3. Concluding Remarks

I/O performance in virtualized environments is critical for today's data centers. It can cause application performance penalties in several orders of magnitude if the storage resources turn out to become a bottleneck. This risk is typically addressed by highly overprovisioning the expensive storage resources. The goal of this work was to develop practical performance engineering approaches that can be employed to address the I/O performance issues in virtualized environments. Our vision is that the approach of this thesis can provide a basis for further research as well as for performance analysis and efficient resource management in productive environments in the future.

A. Related Work at a Glance

In the following, Tables A.1 – A.5 give a compact overview summarizing the approaches related to the approach presented in this thesis. For a quick assessment, we summarize how related the approaches are to our work, for a more detailed discussion please refer to Chapter 10. The approaches are grouped by the presented areas of related work illustrated in Figure 10.1 and ordered by their appearance in Chapter 10, which was usually in descending order of their relation to our work.

I/O Performance Analysis and Modeling		
Approach	Related to Our Work	Summary and Main Difference
Kraft et al. (2012)	★★★★★	I/O queueing models with focus on VM consolidation scenarios.
Ahmad et al. (2003)	★★★☆☆	Evaluate the I/O performance of VMware ESX Server virtualization and model the virtualization overhead.
Kundu et al. (2012)	★★★☆☆	Use machine learning approaches to model the performance of applications in virtualized environments depending on the allocated resources.
Gulati et al. (2009)	★★☆☆☆	Workload characterization in terms of key storage metrics for I/O workload, but without performance modeling.

Table A.1.: Summary of Related Work in Area i)

I/O Performance Interference Modeling		
Approach	Related to Our Work	Summary and Main Difference
Chiang et al. (2011)	★★★★☆	Use polynomial models with request arrival rates and CPU utilizations as independent variables.
Koh et al. (2007)	★★★★☆	Use linear models to predict normalized performance in consolidation across different resources.
Groot et al. (2013)	★★★☆☆	Model I/O performance interference between processes of MapReduce applications.
Yang et al. (2012)	★★☆☆☆	Develop a framework to identify characteristics of the hypervisor I/O scheduler.
Pu et al. (2010)	★☆☆☆☆	Present an experimental study to analyze CPU and network I/O performance interference.

Table A.2.: Summary of Related Work in Area ii)

Architecture-level I/O Performance Modeling		
Approach	Related to Our Work	Summary and Main Difference
Becker et al. (2009)	★★★☆☆	Develop the PCM, which is a basis for our work. Storage resources are abstracted as a single queue.
Huber et al. (2010)	★★★☆☆	Present an industrial case study on design alternatives for storage virtualization to evaluate the applicability of the PCM in industry.
Wert et al. (2012)	★★★★☆	General concept, which is not specific to a certain domain, for combining measurement-based with software architecture-level performance models.
Woodside et al. (2001)	★★☆☆☆	Present an environment to develop statistical models for resource demands of software components and subsystems.
Shanthikumar et al. (1983)	★★☆☆☆	Present a general classification scheme for hybrid models that are comprised of analytical and simulation models.

Table A.3.: Summary of Related Work in Area iii)

Disk-based I/O Performance Modeling		
Approach	Related to Our Work	Summary and Main Difference
Bucy et al. (2008)	★☆☆☆☆	Very detailed and fine-grained disk system simulator.
Harrison et al. (2007)	★☆☆☆☆	Analytical RAID model including low-level disk information.
Lebrecht et al. (2011)	★☆☆☆☆	Analytical RAID model with zoned disks including low-level disk information.
Varki et al. (2000)	★☆☆☆☆	Analytical RAID model including single disk response times.
Lee et al. (1993)	★☆☆☆☆	Analytical disk array model calculating utilizations of disks in the array.

Table A.4.: Summary of Related Work in Area iv)

Systems Performance Evaluation and Modeling		
Approach	Related to Our Work	Summary and Main Difference
Balsamo et al. (2004)	★☆☆☆☆	Survey for performance evaluation and modeling of software systems.
Koziolek (2010)	★☆☆☆☆	Survey for performance evaluation and modeling of software systems.
Huber et al. (2012)	★★☆☆☆	Present an approach to evaluate performance-influencing factors in virtualized environments and create linear models for virtualized CPU and memory scalability.
Hauck et al. (2013)	★★☆☆☆	Approach for goal-oriented measurements to quantify performance-relevant infrastructure properties.
Barham et al. (2003)	★☆☆☆☆	Introduce the Xen hypervisor and evaluate its performance across resources.
Iyer et al. (2009)	★☆☆☆☆	Analyze core, cache, and memory resource contention in a multi-core virtualized environment.

Table A.5.: Summary of Related Work in Area v)

Glossary

Analysis Model	performance model that can be analytically solved or simulated to obtain performance results
Dom0	Domain 0; privileged VM in Xen-based environments
I/O	data access; storage access
I/O Analysis Model	performance model that can be analytically solved or simulated to obtain results of I/O performance
LPAR	Logical PARtition; a virtual machine on System z
PR/SM	Processor Resource and System Manager; System z hypervisor
Storage	one of the main resources of a computer system: processing, memory, communication, and storage
z/Linux	Linux distribution for System z
z/OS	classical System z operating system

Acronyms

FCP	Fibre Channel Protocol
HDD	Hard Disk Drive
ICT	Information and Communications Technology
IT	Information Technology
NAS	Network Attached Storage
NVC	Non-Volatile Cache
PCM	Palladio Component Model
PE	Performance Engineering
QN	Queueing Network
QPN	Queueing Petri Net
RDSEFF	Resource Demanding Service EFFect specification
SAN	Storage Area Network
SCSI	Small Computer System Interface
SPE	Software Performance Engineering
SSD	Solid State Disk
VC	Volatile Cache
VM	Virtual Machine
VMM	Virtual Machine Monitor

Bibliography

Ahmad, I., Anderson, J., Holler, A., Kambo, R., and Makhija, V. (2003). „An analysis of disk performance in VMware ESX server virtual machines." In: *IEEE International Workshop on Workload Characterization, 2003. WWC-6*. Pp. 65–76 (cit. on pp. 5, 241, 256).

Balsamo, S., Di Marco, A., Inverardi, P., and Simeoni, M. (2004). „Model-Based Performance Prediction in Software Development: A Survey." In: *IEEE TSE* 30.5, pp. 295–310 (cit. on pp. 6, 247, 260).

Barham, P., Dragovic, B., Fraser, K., Hand, S., Harris, T., Ho, A., Neugebauer, R., Pratt, I., and Warfield, A. (2003). „Xen and the Art of Virtualization." In: *SIGOPS Oper. Syst. Rev.* 37 (5), pp. 164–177 (cit. on pp. 6, 54, 247, 260).

Baun, C., Kunze, M., Nimis, J., and Tai, S. (2011). *Cloud computing: Web-based dynamic IT services*. Springer (cit. on pp. 17, 18).

Bause, F. (1993). „Queueing Petri Nets - A formalism for the combined qualitative and quantitative analysis of systems." In: *Proceedings of the 5th International Workshop on Petri Nets and Performance Models* (cit. on p. 35).

Bause, F. and Kritzinger, F. (2002). *Stochastic Petri Nets - An Introduction to the Theory*. Second. Vieweg Verlag (cit. on p. 35).

Becker, S. (2008). „Coupled model transformations for QoS enabled component-based software design." PhD thesis. Universität Oldenburg (cit. on pp. 7, 37, 38, 43, 163, 172).

Becker, S., Koziolek, H., and Reussner, R. (2009). „The Palladio component model for model-driven performance prediction." In: *Journal of Systems and Software* 82.1, pp. 3–22 (cit. on pp. 5, 36, 38, 43, 163, 244, 254, 258).

Bolch, G., Greiner, S., Meer, H. de, and Trivedi, K. (2006). *Queueing Networks and Markov Chains: Modeling and Performance Evaluation with Computer Science Applications*. Wiley-Interscience publication. Wiley (cit. on pp. 33, 35, 106).

Boutcher, D. and Chandra, A. (2010). „Does virtualization make disk scheduling passe." In: *SIGOPS Oper. Syst. Rev.* 44.1, pp. 20–24 (cit. on p. 110).

Breiman, L., Friedman, J., Stone, C. J., and Olshen, R. (1984). *Classification and Regression Trees*. The Wadsworth and Brooks-Cole statistics-probability series. Chapman & Hall (cit. on p. 83).

Brosig, F. (2014). „Architecture-Level Software Performance Models for Online Performance Prediction." PhD thesis. Karlsruhe Institute of Technology (KIT) (cit. on pp. 6, 254).

Brosig, F., Huber, N., and Kounev, S. (2011). „Automated Extraction of Architecture-Level Performance Models of Distributed Component-Based Systems." In: *26th IEEE/ACM International Conference On Automated Software Engineering (ASE 2011)*. Oread, Lawrence, Kansas (cit. on p. 226).

Brosig, F., Kounev, S., and Krogmann, K. (2009). „Automated Extraction of Palladio Component Models from Running Enterprise Java Applications." In: *Proceedings of the 1st International Workshop on Run-time mOdels for Self-managing Systems and Applications (ROSSA 2009). In conjunction with Fourth International Conference on Performance Evaluation Methodologies and Tools (VALUETOOLS 2009), Pisa, Italy, October 19, 2009.* ACM, New York, NY, USA (cit. on p. 226).

Bruhn, D. (2012). „Modeling and Experimental Analysis of Virtualized Storage Performance using IBM System z as Example." Master's Thesis (Diplomarbeit). Karlsruhe Institute of Technology (KIT) (cit. on pp. 70, 179).

Bucy, J. S., Schindler, J., Schlosser, S. W., Ganger, G. R., and Contributors (2008). *The DiskSim Simulation Environment - Version 4.0 Reference Manual*. Carnegie Mellon University, Pittsburgh, PA (cit. on pp. 6, 246, 259).

Busch, A. (2013). „Workload Characterization for I/O Performance Analysis on IBM System z." Master's Thesis. Karlsruhe Institute of Technology (KIT) (cit. on pp. 50, 179).

Busch, A., Noorshams, Q., Kounev, S., Koziolek, A., Reussner, R., and Amrehn, E. (2015). „Automated Workload Characterization for I/O Performance Analysis in Virtualized Environments." In: *Proceedings of the ACM/SPEC International Conference on Performance Engineering*. ICPE '15. Austin, Texas, USA: ACM (cit. on pp. 9, 50, 58, 59, 179).

Chiang, R. C. and Huang, H. H. (2011). „TRACON: Interference-aware Scheduling for Data-intensive Applications in Virtualized Environments." In: *Proceedings of 2011 International Conference for High Performance*

Computing, Networking, Storage and Analysis. SC '11. Seattle, Washington: ACM, 47:1–47:12 (cit. on pp. 5, 243, 257).

Clark, T. (2005). *Storage virtualization: technologies for simplifying data storage and management*. Addison-Wesley Professional (cit. on p. 20).

Czarnecki, K. (1998). „Generative Programming: Principles and Techniques of Software Engineering Based on Automated Configuration and Fragment-Based Component Models." PhD thesis. Technical University of Ilmenau (cit. on p. 52).

Dean, J. and Ghemawat, S. (2008). „MapReduce: Simplified Data Processing on Large Clusters." In: *Communications of the ACM* 51.1, pp. 107–113 (cit. on p. 24).

Dufrasne, B., Bauer, W., Careaga, B., Myyrrylainen, J., Rainero, A., and Usong, P. (2010). *IBM System Storage DS8700 Architecture and Implementation*. `http://www.redbooks.ibm.com/abstracts/sg248786.html` (cit. on pp. 45, 55, 186).

Elish, M. and Elish, K. (2009). „Application of TreeNet in Predicting Object-Oriented Software Maintainability: A Comparative Study." In: *13th European Conference on Software Maintenance and Reengineering, 2009. CSMR '09*. Pp. 69–78 (cit. on p. 69).

Filebench. `https://github.com/Filebench-Revise/Filebench-Revise` (version with fixes of `http://sourceforge.net/apps/mediawiki/filebench/`). [Online; last accessed: Dec 2014] (cit. on p. 183).

Flexible File System Benchmark (FFSB). `http://github.com/FFSB-prime` (version with fixes and extensions of `http://ffsb.sf.net`). [Online; last accessed: Dec 2014] (cit. on pp. 109, 182).

Friedman, J. H. (1991). „Multivariate Adaptive Regression Splines." In: *Annals of Statistics* 19.1, pp. 1–141 (cit. on p. 82).

Gantz, J. and Reinsel (IDC), D. (2012). *THE DIGITAL UNIVERSE IN 2020: Big Data, Bigger Digital Shadows, and Biggest Growth in the Far East*. `http://www.emc.com/collateral/analyst-reports/idc-the-digital-universe-in-2020.pdf`. [Online; last accessed: Dec 2014] (cit. on p. 2).

Goldberg, R. P. (1974). „Survey of Virtual Machine Research." In: *Computer* 7.9, pp. 34–45 (cit. on p. 17).

Gregg, B. (2005). *DTrace Tools: iopattern*. `http://www.dtracebook.com/index.php/Disk_IO:iopattern`. [Online; last accessed: Dec 2014] (cit. on p. 58).

Groot, S., Goda, K., Yokoyama, D., Nakano, M., and Kitsuregawa, M. (2013). „Modeling I/O Interference for Data Intensive Distributed Applications." In:

Proceedings of the 28th Annual ACM Symposium on Applied Computing. SAC '13. Coimbra, Portugal: ACM, pp. 343–350 (cit. on pp. 5, 243, 257).

Gulati, A., Kumar, C., and Ahmad, I. (2009). „Storage workload characterization and consolidation in virtualized environments." In: *2nd International Workshop on Virtualization Performance: Analysis, Characterization, and Tools (VPACT)* (cit. on pp. 5, 242, 256).

Guo, J., Czarnecki, K., Apel, S., Siegmund, N., and Wasowski, A. (2013). „Variability-Aware Performance Prediction: A Statistical Learning Approach." In: *28th IEEE/ACM International Conference on Automated Software Engineering (ASE)*. Silicon Valley, California, USA: IEEE (cit. on p. 69).

Harrison, P. and Zertal, S. (2007). „Queueing models of RAID systems with maxima of waiting times." In: *Performance Evaluation* 64 (7-8), pp. 664–689 (cit. on pp. 6, 246, 259).

Hastie, T., Tibshirani, R., and Friedman, J. (2008). *The Elements of Statistical Learning: Data Mining, Inference and Prediction*. 2nd ed. Springer (cit. on pp. 30–32, 81, 83, 95).

Hauck, M. (2013). „Automated Experiments for Deriving Performance-relevant Properties of Software Execution Environments." PhD thesis. Karlsruhe Institute of Technology (KIT) (cit. on p. 17).

Hauck, M., Kuperberg, M., Huber, N., and Reussner, R. (2013). „Deriving performance-relevant infrastructure properties through model-based experiments with Ginpex." In: *Springer Journal of Software and Systems Modeling*, pp. 1–21 (cit. on pp. 6, 247, 260).

Hauck, M., Kuperberg, M., Krogmann, K., and Reussner, R. (2009). „Modelling Layered Component Execution Environments for Performance Prediction." In: *Proceedings of the 12th International Symposium on Component Based Software Engineering (CBSE 2009)*. LNCS 5582. Springer, pp. 191–208 (cit. on pp. 43, 163, 167).

Huber, N. (2014). „Autonomic Performance-Aware Resource Management in Dynamic IT Service Infrastructures." PhD thesis. Karlsruhe Institute of Technology (KIT) (cit. on p. 254).

Huber, N., Becker, S., Rathfelder, C., Schweflinghaus, J., and Reussner, R. (2010). „Performance Modeling in Industry: A Case Study on Storage Virtualization." In: *ACM/IEEE 32nd International Conference on Software Engineering (ICSE 2010), Software Engineering in Practice Track*. Cape Town, South Africa: ACM, pp. 1–10 (cit. on pp. 5, 43, 163, 245, 258).

Huber, N., Quast, M. von, Brosig, F., Hauck, M., and Kounev, S. (2012). „A Method for Experimental Analysis and Modeling of Virtualization Performance Overhead.“ In: *Cloud Computing and Services Science*. Ed. by I. Ivanov, M. van Sinderen, and B. Shishkov. Service Science: Research and Innovations in the Service Economy. New York: Springer, pp. 353–370 (cit. on pp. 6, 247, 260).

InformationAge (2011). *The year of virtual storage*. `http://www.information-age.com/channels/the-cloud-and-virtualization/perspectives-and-trends/1596523/the-year-of-virtual-storage.thtml`. [Online; last accessed: Dec 2014] (cit. on p. 2).

Iyer, R., Illikkal, R., Tickoo, O., Zhao, L., Apparao, P., and Newell, D. (2009). „VM3: Measuring, modeling and managing VM shared resources.“ In: *Computer Networks* 53 (17), pp. 2873–2887 (cit. on pp. 6, 247, 260).

Izenman, A. J. (2009). *Modern Multivariate Statistical Techniques: Regression, Classification, and Manifold Learning*. New York, NY: Springer (cit. on pp. 30–32, 72).

Jensen, K. (1981). „Coloured Petri Nets and the Invariant Method.“ In: Mathematical Foundations on Computer Science, LNCS 118:327-338 (cit. on p. 35).

Kaplan, J. M., Forrest, W., and Kindler, N. (2008). *Revolutionizing Data Center Energy Efficiency*. Tech. rep. McKinsey & Company (cit. on p. 1).

Kapova, L. and Goldschmidt, T. (2009). „Automated feature model-based generation of refinement transformations.“ In: *Software Engineering and Advanced Applications, 2009. SEAA'09. 35th Euromicro Conference on*. IEEE, pp. 141–148 (cit. on p. 165).

Koh, Y., Knauerhase, R., Brett, P., Bowman, M., Wen, Z., and Pu, C. (2007). „An Analysis of Performance Interference Effects in Virtual Environments.“ In: *IEEE International Symposium on Performance Analysis of Systems Software, 2007. ISPASS-2007*. Pp. 200–209 (cit. on pp. 5, 243, 257).

Kounev, S. (2006). „Performance Modeling and Evaluation of Distributed Component-Based Systems using Queueing Petri Nets.“ In: *IEEE TSE* 32.7 (cit. on pp. 35, 106, 109).

Kounev, S., Brosig, F., Huber, N., and Reussner, R. (2010a). „Towards self-aware performance and resource management in modern service-oriented systems.“ In: *Proceedings of the 7th IEEE International Conference on Services Computing (SCC 2010), July 5-10, Miami, Florida, USA*. Miami, Florida, USA: IEEE Computer Society (cit. on p. 254).

Kounev, S., Spinner, S., and Meier, P. (2010b). „QPME 2.0-A Tool for Stochastic Modeling and Analysis Using Queueing Petri Nets.“ In: *From active data management to event-based systems and more*. Springer, pp. 293–311 (cit. on pp. 35, 36).

Koziolek, H. (2010). „Performance Evaluation of Component-based Software Systems: A Survey.“ In: *Performance Evaluation* 67.8, pp. 634–658 (cit. on pp. 6, 247, 260).

Kraft, S., Casale, G., Krishnamurthy, D., Greer, D., and Kilpatrick, P. (2012). „Performance Models of Storage Contention in Cloud Environments.“ In: *Springer Journal of Software and Systems Modeling* (cit. on pp. 5, 241, 256).

Krogmann, K. (2010). „Reconstruction of Software Component Architectures and Behaviour Models using Static and Dynamic Analysis.“ PhD thesis. Karlsruhe Institute of Technology (KIT) (cit. on pp. 43, 163, 226).

Kuhn, M. and Johnson, K. (2013). *Applied Predictive Modeling*. Springer (cit. on pp. 29–33, 73, 98).

Kuhn, M., Witson, S., Keefer, C., and Coulter, N. (2012). *Cubist Models for Regression*. `http://cran.r-project.org/web/packages/Cubist/vignettes/cubist.pdf`. [Online; last accessed: Dec 2014] (cit. on p. 85).

Kundu, S., Rangaswami, R., Gulati, A., Zhao, M., and Dutta, K. (2012). „Modeling Virtualized Applications using Machine Learning Techniques.“ In: *Proceedings of the 8th ACM SIGPLAN/ SIGOPS conference on Virtual Execution Environments*. VEE '12. London, England, UK: ACM, pp. 3–14 (cit. on pp. 5, 242, 256).

Kuperberg, M., Krogmann, K., and Reussner, R. (2008). „Performance Prediction for Black-Box Components using Reengineered Parametric Behaviour Models.“ In: *Proceedings of the 11th International Symposium on Component Based Software Engineering (CBSE 2008), Karlsruhe, Germany, 14th-17th October 2008*. Vol. 5282. Lecture Notes in Computer Science. Springer-Verlag Berlin Heidelberg, pp. 48–63 (cit. on pp. 43, 163).

Lebrecht, A. S., Dingle, N. J., and Knottenbelt, W. J. (2011). „Analytical and Simulation Modelling of Zoned RAID Systems.“ In: *The Computer Journal* 54 (5), pp. 691–707 (cit. on pp. 6, 246, 259).

Lee, E. K. and Katz, R. H. (1993). „An analytic performance model of disk arrays.“ In: *SIGMETRICS Perform. Eval. Rev.* 21.1 (cit. on pp. 6, 246, 259).

Ling, X., Ibrahim, S., Jin, H., Wu, S., and Songqiao, T. (2013). „Exploiting Spatial Locality to Improve Disk Efficiency in Virtualized Environments.“ In: *Proceedings of the IEEE 21st International Symposium on Modeling,*

Analysis and Simulation of Computer and Telecommunication Systems (MASCOTS 2013). San Francisco, USA (cit. on pp. 54, 110, 185).

Massiglia, P. and Bunn, F. (2003). *Virtual Storage Redefined: Technologies and Applications for Storage Virtualization*. VERITAS Software Corporation (cit. on pp. 20, 21).

Menascé, D. and Almeida, V. (2000). *Scaling for E-Business: Technologies, Models, Performance, and Capacity Planning*. Prentice Hall (cit. on pp. 6, 106, 109, 229).

Menascé, D., Almeida, V., and Dowdy, L. (1994). *Capacity Planning and Performance Modeling: From Mainframes to Client-Server Systems*. New Jersey: Prentice-Hall (cit. on p. 105).

Menascé, D., Almeida, V., Dowdy, L. W., and Dowdy, L. (2004). *Performance by Design: Computer Capacity Planning by Example*. Prentice Hall science explorer. Prentice Hall (cit. on pp. 33, 35, 106, 109).

Mesnier, M., Ganger, G. R., and Riedel, E. (2003). „Object-based storage." In: *IEEE Communications Magazine* 41.8, pp. 84–90 (cit. on p. 24).

Mi, N., Casale, G., Cherkasova, L., and Smirni, E. (2008). „Burstiness in multi-tier applications: symptoms, causes, and new models." In: *Proceedings of the 9th ACM/IFIP/USENIX International Conference on Middleware*. Middleware '08. Leuven, Belgium: Springer-Verlag New York, Inc., pp. 265–286 (cit. on p. 252).

Mills, M. P. (2013). *The Cloud Begins with Coal – Big Data, Big Networks, Big Infrastructure, and Big Power – An Overview of the Electricity used by the Global Digital Ecosystem*. http://www.tech-pundit.com/wp-content/uploads/2013/07/Cloud_Begins_With_Coal.pdf?c761ac. [Online; last accessed: Dec 2014] (cit. on p. 1).

Noorshams, Q., Bruhn, D., Kounev, S., and Reussner, R. (2013a). „Predictive Performance Modeling of Virtualized Storage Systems using Optimized Statistical Regression Techniques." In: *Proceedings of the ACM/SPEC International Conference on Performance Engineering*. ICPE '13. Prague, Czech Republic: ACM, pp. 283–294 (cit. on pp. 10, 70, 179).

Noorshams, Q., Busch, A., Kounev, S., and Reussner, R. (2015). „The Storage Performance Analyzer: Measuring, Monitoring, and Modeling of I/O Performance in Virtualized Environments." In: *Proceedings of the 6th ACM/SPEC International Conference on Performance Engineering*. ICPE '15. (Invited Demo Paper). Austin, Texas, USA (cit. on pp. 9, 50, 62, 182, 226).

Noorshams, Q., Busch, A., Rentschler, A., Bruhn, D., Kounev, S., Tůma, P., and Reussner, R. (2014a). „Automated Modeling of I/O Performance and Interference Effects in Virtualized Storage Systems." In: *34th IEEE International Conference on Distributed Computing Systems Workshops (ICDCS 2014 Workshops). 4th International Workshop on Data Center Performance, DCPerf '14*. Madrid, Spain, pp. 88–93 (cit. on pp. 10, 70, 179).

Noorshams, Q., Kounev, S., and Reussner, R. (2013b). „Experimental Evaluation of the Performance-Influencing Factors of Virtualized Storage Systems." In: *Computer Performance Engineering. 9th European Workshop, EPEW 2012, Munich, Germany, July 30, 2012, and 28th UK Workshop, UKPEW 2012, Edinburgh, UK, July 2, 2012, Revised Selected Papers*. Ed. by M. Tribastone and S. Gilmore. Vol. 7587. Lecture Notes in Computer Science. Springer Berlin Heidelberg, pp. 63–79 (cit. on pp. 9, 44, 50, 52, 65).

Noorshams, Q., Reeb, R., Rentschler, A., Kounev, S., and Reussner, R. (2014b). „Enriching Software Architecture Models with Statistical Models for Performance Prediction in Modern Storage Environments." In: *Proceedings of the 17th International ACM Sigsoft Symposium on Component-Based Software Engineering*. CBSE '14. Marcq-en-Bareul, France: ACM, pp. 45–54 (cit. on pp. 11, 38, 42, 160, 179).

Noorshams, Q., Rentschler, A., Kounev, S., and Reussner, R. (2013c). „A Generic Approach for Architecture-level Performance Modeling and Prediction of Virtualized Storage Systems." In: *Proceedings of the ACM/SPEC International Conference on Performance Engineering*. ICPE '13. Prague, Czech Republic: ACM, pp. 339–342 (cit. on pp. 11, 42, 160).

Noorshams, Q., Rostami, K., Kounev, S., and Reussner, R. (2014c). „Modeling of I/O Performance Interference in Virtualized Environments with Queueing Petri Nets." In: *Proceedings of the IEEE 22nd International Symposium on Modeling, Analysis and Simulation of Computer and Telecommunication Systems*. MASCOTS '14. France, Paris (cit. on pp. 10, 104).

Noorshams, Q., Rostami, K., Kounev, S., Tůma, P., and Reussner, R. (2013d). „I/O Performance Modeling of Virtualized Storage Systems." In: *Proceedings of the IEEE 21st International Symposium on Modeling, Analysis and Simulation of Computer and Telecommunication Systems*. MASCOTS '13. San Francisco, USA, pp. 121–130 (cit. on pp. 10, 104).

Object Management Group (OMG). *Unified Modeling Language (UML)*. http://schema.omg.org/spec/UML/index.htm. [Online; last accessed: Dec 2014] (cit. on p. 36).

Oliveira, S. F., Furlinger, K., and Kranzlmüller, D. (2012). „Trends in Computation, Communication and Storage and the Consequences for Data-intensive Science.“ In: *Proceedings of the 2012 IEEE 14th International Conference on High Performance Computing and Communication & 2012 IEEE 9th International Conference on Embedded Software and Systems*. IEEE Computer Society, pp. 572–579 (cit. on p. 1).

open – Linux man page. http://linux.die.net/man/2/open. [Online; last accessed: Dec 2014] (cit. on pp. 109, 182).

Open Stack Object Storage (Swift). http://www.openstack.org/software/openstack-storage/, http://docs.openstack.org/developer/swift/overview_architecture.html. [Online; last accessed: Dec 2014] (cit. on p. 24).

Pu, X., Liu, L., Mei, Y., Sivathanu, S., Koh, Y., and Pu, C. (2010). „Understanding Performance Interference of I/O Workload in Virtualized Cloud Environments.“ In: *IEEE 3rd International Conference on Cloud Computing (CLOUD)*, pp. 51–58 (cit. on pp. 5, 244, 257).

Quinlan, J. R. (1992). „Learning with Continuous Classes.“ In: *Proceedings of the 5th Australian joint Conference on Artificial Intelligence*. World Scientific, pp. 343–348 (cit. on p. 84).

– (1993). „Combining Instance-Based and Model-Based Learning.“ In: *ICML '93*, pp. 236–243 (cit. on p. 85).

R Core Team (2013). *R: A Language and Environment for Statistical Computing*. R Foundation for Statistical Computing. Vienna, Austria (cit. on p. 86).

Rathfelder, C. (2012). „Modelling Event-Based Interactions in Component-Based Architectures for Quantitative System Evaluations.“ PhD thesis. Karlsruhe Institute of Technology (KIT) (cit. on p. 6).

Reeb, R. (2014). „Modellierung von virtualisierten Speicher-Systemen mit dem Palladio Component Model.“ Bachelor's Thesis. Karlsruhe Institute of Technology (KIT) (cit. on pp. 160, 179).

Reussner, R., Becker, S., Burger, E., Happe, J., Hauck, M., Koziolek, A., Koziolek, H., Krogmann, K., and Kuperberg, M. (2011). *The Palladio Component Model*. Tech. rep. Karlsruhe Institute of Technology (KIT). Karlsruhe Reports in Informatics 2011, 14 (cit. on pp. 36, 38).

Rostami, K. (2012). „Workload Characterization for I/O Performance Analysis on IBM System z.“ Bachelor's Thesis (Studienarbeit). Karlsruhe Institute of Technology (KIT) (cit. on p. 104).

– (2014). „Modellierung von Performanzinterferenz datenintensiver Anwendungen in virtualisierten Umgebungen am Beispiel IBM System z.“ Master's Thesis (Diplomarbeit). Karlsruhe Institute of Technology (KIT) (cit. on pp. 104, 130, 133, 139).

RuleQuest Research Pty Ltd (2012). *Data Mining with Cubist*. `http://rulequest.com/cubist-info.html`. [Online; last accessed: Dec 2014] (cit. on p. 85).

Rygielski, P. and Kounev, S. (2014). „Data Center Network Throughput Analysis using Queueing Petri Nets.“ In: *34th IEEE International Conference on Distributed Computing Systems Workshops (ICDCS 2014 Workshops). 4th International Workshop on Data Center Performance, (DCPerf 2014)*. Madrid, Spain, pp. 100–105 (cit. on p. 253).

Shanthikumar, J. G. and Sargent, R. G. (1983). „A Unifying View of Hybrid Simulation/Analytic Models and Modeling.“ In: *Operations Research* 31.6, (cit. on pp. 5, 245, 254, 258).

Smith, C. U. (1990). *Performance engineering of software systems*. Addison-Wesley Longman Publishing Co., Inc. (cit. on p. 27).

SNIA Shared Storage Model. `http://www.snia.org/education/storage_networking_primer/shared_storage_model`. [Online; last accessed: Dec 2014] (cit. on pp. 20, 23).

Snyman, J. (2005). *Practical Mathematical Optimization: An Introduction to Basic Optimization Theory and Classical and New Gradient-Based Algorithms*. Vol. 97. Springer (cit. on p. 73).

Spinner, S., Casale, G., Zhu, X., and Kounev, S. (2014). „LibReDE: A Library for Resource Demand Estimation.“ In: *Proceedings of the 5th ACM/SPEC International Conference on Performance Engineering*. ICPE '14. Dublin, Ireland: ACM, pp. 227–228 (cit. on p. 176).

TechNavio (2013). *Global Server Virtualization Market 2012-2016*. `http://www.technavio.com/content/global-server-virtualization-market-2012-2016`. [Online; last accessed: Dec 2014] (cit. on p. 1).

Troppens, U., Erkens, R., Müller-Friedt, W., Wolafka, R., and Haustein, N. (2009). *Storage Networks Explained: Basics and Application of Fibre Channel SAN, NAS, ISCSI, InfiniBand and FCoE*. John Wiley & Sons (cit. on pp. 20–23).

Varki, E. and Wang, S. X. (2000). „A Performance Model of Disk Array Storage Systems.“ In: *Int. CMG Conference*, pp. 635–644 (cit. on pp. 6, 246, 259).

Vaupel, R. (2013). *High Availability and Scalability of Mainframe Environments using System z and z/OS as example*. KIT Scientific Publishing (cit. on p. 17).

Walpole, R. E., Myers, R. H., Myers, S. L., and Ye, K. (2007). *Probability and statistics for engineers and scientists*. Upper Saddle River, NJ: Pearson Prentice Hall (cit. on p. 30).

Wang, M., Ailamaki, A., and Faloutsos, C. (2002). „Capturing the Spatio-Temporal Behavior of Real Traffic Data.“ In: *IFIP WG 7.3 Symposium on Computer Performance*, pp. 23–27 (cit. on p. 252).

Wang, W. and Casale, G. (2013). „Bayesian Service Demand Estimation Using Gibbs Sampling.“ In: *Proceedings of the 2013 IEEE 21st International Symposium on Modelling, Analysis and Simulation of Computer and Telecommunication Systems*. MASCOTS '13. Washington, DC, USA: IEEE Computer Society, pp. 567–576 (cit. on p. 113).

Wert, A., Happe, J., and Westermann, D. (2012). „Integrating Software Performance Curves with the Palladio Component Model.“ In: *Proceedings of the 3rd ACM/SPEC International Conference on Performance Engineering*. ICPE '12. Boston, Massachusetts, USA: ACM, pp. 283–286 (cit. on pp. 5, 245, 258).

Westermann, D. (2014). „Deriving Goal-oriented Performance Models by Systematic Experimentation.“ PhD thesis. Karlsruhe Institute of Technology (KIT) (cit. on p. 99).

Wolf, C. and Halter, E. M. (2005). *Virtualization: From the Desktop to the Enterprise*. Apress (cit. on p. 17).

Woodside, M., Petriu, D., and Siddiqui, K. (2002). „Performance-related completions for software specifications.“ In: *Proceedings of the 24rd International Conference on Software Engineering, 2002* (cit. on p. 165).

Woodside, M., Vetland, V., Courtois, M., and Bayarov, S. (2001). „Resource Function Capture for Performance Aspects of Software Components and Sub-systems.“ In: *Performance Engineering, State of the Art and Current Trends*. Ed. by R. Dumke, C. Rautenstrauch, A. Scholz, and A. Schmietendorf. Vol. 2047. Lecture Notes in Computer Science. Springer Berlin Heidelberg, pp. 239–256 (cit. on pp. 5, 245, 258).

Woodside, M., Franks, G., and Petriu, D. C. (2007). „The Future of Software Performance Engineering.“ In: *Future of Software Engineering, 2007. FOSE'07*. IEEE, pp. 171–187 (cit. on p. 27).

Yang, Z., Fang, H., Wu, Y., Li, C., Zhao, B., and Huang, H. (2012). „Understanding the Effects of Hypervisor I/O Scheduling for Virtual Machine Performance Interference.“ In: *IEEE 4th International Conference on Cloud Computing Technology and Science (CloudCom)*, pp. 34–41 (cit. on pp. 5, 244, 257).

Yigitbasi, N., Willke, T., Liao, G., and Epema, D. (2013). „Towards Machine Learning-Based Auto-tuning of MapReduce.“ In: *IEEE 21st International Symposium on Modeling, Analysis Simulation of Computer and Telecommunication Systems (MASCOTS)*, pp. 11–20 (cit. on p. 69).

The Karlsruhe Series on Software Design and Quality

Edited by Prof. Dr. Ralf Reussner // ISSN 1867-0067

Band 1 **Steffen Becker**
Coupled Model Transformations for QoS Enabled Component-Based Software Design. 2008
ISBN 978-3-86644-271-9

Band 2 **Heiko Koziolek**
Parameter Dependencies for Reusable Performance Specifications of Software Components. 2008
ISBN 978-3-86644-272-6

Band 3 **Jens Happe**
Predicting Software Performance in Symmetric Multi-core and Multiprocessor Environments. 2009
ISBN 978-3-86644-381-5

Band 4 **Klaus Krogmann**
Reconstruction of Software Component Architectures and Behaviour Models using Static and Dynamic Analysis. 2012
ISBN 978-3-86644-804-9

Band 5 **Michael Kuperberg**
Quantifying and Predicting the Influence of Execution Platform on Software Component Performance. 2010
ISBN 978-3-86644-741-7

Band 6 **Thomas Goldschmidt**
View-Based Textual Modelling. 2011
ISBN 978-3-86644-642-7

The Karlsruhe Series on Software Design and Quality

Edited by Prof. Dr. Ralf Reussner // ISSN 1867-0067

Band 7 **Anne Koziolek**
Automated Improvement of Software Architecture Models for Performance and Other Quality Attributes. 2013
ISBN 978-3-86644-973-2

Band 8 **Lucia Happe**
Configurable Software Performance Completions through Higher-Order Model Transformations. 2013
ISBN 978-3-86644-990-9

Band 9 **Franz Brosch**
Integrated Software Architecture-Based Reliability Prediction for IT Systems. 2012
ISBN 978-3-86644-859-9

Band 10 **Christoph Rathfelder**
Modelling Event-Based Interactions in Component-Based Architectures for Quantitative System Evaluation. 2013
ISBN 978-3-86644-969-5

Band 11 **Henning Groenda**
Certifying Software Component Performance Specifications. 2013
ISBN 978-3-7315-0080-3

Band 12 **Dennis Westermann**
Deriving Goal-oriented Performance Models by Systematic Experimentation. 2014
ISBN 978-3-7315-0165-7

Die Bände sind unter www.ksp.kit.edu als PDF frei verfügbar oder als Druckausgabe bestellbar.

The Karlsruhe Series on Software Design and Quality

Edited by Prof. Dr. Ralf Reussner // ISSN 1867-0067

Band 13 **Michael Hauck**
Automated Experiments for Deriving Performance-relevant Properties of Software Execution Environments. 2014
ISBN 978-3-7315-0138-1

Band 14 **Zoya Durdik**
Architectural Design Decision Documentation through Reuse of Design Patterns. 2016
ISBN 978-3-7315-0292-0

Band 15 **Erik Burger**
Flexible Views for View-based Model-driven Development. 2014
ISBN 978-3-7315-0276-0

Band 16 **Benjamin Klatt**
Consolidation of Customized Product Copies into Software Product Lines. 2016
ISBN 978-3-7315-0368-2

Band 17 **Andreas Rentschler**
Model Transformation Languages with Modular Information Hiding. 2015
ISBN 978-3-7315-0346-0

Band 18 **Omar-Qais Noorshams**
Modeling and Prediction of I/O Performance in Virtualized Environments. 2017
ISBN 978-3-7315-0359-0

Die Bände sind unter www.ksp.kit.edu als PDF frei verfügbar oder als Druckausgabe bestellbar.